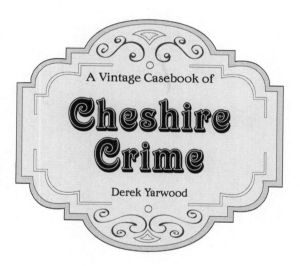

A Vintage Casebook of

Cheshire Crime

Derek Yarwood

A Vintage Casebook of

Cheshire Crime

Derek Yarwood

DB PUBLISHING

First published in Great Britain in 2012 by The Derby Books Publishing Company Limited, 3 The Parker Centre, Derby, DE21 4SZ.

Copyright © Derek Yarwood, 2012

ISBN 978-1-78091-065-9

Also by the same author: *Cheshire's Execution Files*

Contents

Preface

The origins of this book go back to the start of the 1980s, when I was working as a feature-writer for the *Warrington Guardian* group of newspapers. It all began after I learned that the Warrington Reference Library possessed some interesting 18th-century accounts of post-boys being held up as they rode about the country on horseback delivering the mails and that, in Warrington Museum, there was on display an amazing iron 'suit' in which the body of an executed highwayman had been hung on a gibbet on the outskirts of the town following one such local robbery.

It seemed a lively topic for a feature, or even a series; then I discovered that the library's extensive archives also contained printed case histories relating to other types of crime in 18th and 19th century Cheshire. It soon became apparent that some official corroboration was required to do the subject justice, as it were. But that would have meant some fairly lengthy study of the assize court files preserved in what was then the Public Record Office in London (now the National Archives). As the source material I had begun to turn up extended beyond not only my brief but also the confines of the group's circulation area, that was an expensive undertaking that my employers, understandably, were not too enthusiastic about financing.

So I submitted my highway robbery feature for the paper, determined to continue the broader research – and eventually write a book on the subject – in my own time.

It was a long, at times frustrating, but ultimately hugely rewarding experience and I am as proud of the result today as I was when, in 1991, my book was finally published. Others, too, seem to have found it a stimulating read – not least those fellow authors who have drawn on it (sometimes with due acknowledgement, sometimes not) in the intervening years.

Now, I am delighted that it is in print once again, this time in an updated and expanded version.

For that I am grateful to Mr Steve Caron and his colleagues at Derby Books Publishing. I also wish to thank the following for their assistance in compiling this new edition: Richard Clark (of Capital Punishment UK), Paul Leyland (www.historyofwallasey.co.uk), Mark Bevan (Cheshire Country Publishing), Jane Parr (The Manchester Room and County Record Office), Jo Unsworth (Warrington Library), Michelle Hill and Janice Hayes (Warrington Museum & Art Gallery), Andrew Parry (Gloucestershire Archives), Margaret Spate of the Crewe Group of the Family History Society of Cheshire, and my wife Christine for her vauluable assistance with proof-reading. Any mistakes that remain are entirely of my own making.

Derek Yarwood
Barnton, Autumn 2012.

Introduction

The crimes and criminal themes recalled in this book span four centuries. For most of that time there was nothing we would recognise nowadays as a police force. Towards the end of the period there was; but it bore only scant resemblance to the organised, mobile, highly efficient and high-tech specialist law enforcement agency we have in this country today.

Following an Act of 1361, responsibility for law and order was for nearly 500 years largely in the hands of Crown-appointed Justices of the Peace, county High Constables and, at the sharp end, the parish or petty constables. They were augmented in some of the larger urban areas by beadles and watchmen. The parish constables were unpaid, though once they had been 'volunteered' for the job by the local magistrates' bench their duties were compulsory.

By the same principle, all citizens were expected to take an active part in community discipline, while the repressive legal code, which prescribed hanging or banishment for all but the most trivial offences, was designed to take care of the more intractable elements in society. And, should civil disorder threaten, the authorities could always call out the militia.

It was a system (or, rather, the lack of one) that was particularly stretched during the 16th century and at other times of sharply increasing crime. The creation, by Henry Fielding, of the Bow Street Runners in 1753 was the first major attempt to counter the inadequacies of old-style 'policing' in London. But the concept of a countrywide network of police forces was not realised until the middle of the 19th century, when the social problems caused by the nation's burgeoning population and its increased urbanisation and industrialisation finally exerted sufficient pressure for reform.

Legislation passed in 1856 required each county to establish its own constabulary, a measure which had followed, albeit slowly, the pioneering work of Sir Robert Peel, who had founded the Metropolitan Police to tackle the special problems of the capital as early as 1829. That same year, Cheshire became the first county to respond to Peel's promptings by appointing nine stipendiary Deputy High Constables to supervise a force of paid petty constables. The experimental project was eventually superseded by the new county force, which came into operation under Cheshire's first Chief Constable, Captain Thomas Johnnes Smith, in 1857.

Some boroughs, like Chester and Warrington, had established their own local forces before then, empowered by the 1835 Municipal Corporations Act. But, by the end of our period, the police were still a long way from being the high-speed cops they are now. The Cheshire force acquired its first motor car (for the Chief Constable's personal use) in 1908. But regulation issue transport for a superintendent was still a horse-and-cart.

And lower ranks were expected to travel on foot or by bicycle to avoid the expense of rail fares.

This, then, was the political background to the case histories and trials in this true-crime anthology, the details of which I have validated wherever possible by reference to original sources. During extensive research at the National Archives in London (formerly the Public Record Office), I scoured assize court and Home Office files, reports of coroners' inquisitions, judges' private communications and other official documents, to try to separate fact from fiction and to present the most complete and fully authenticated account of the events recounted here.

As a former journalist I was also keen to see how the newspapers of the day reported the crimes and trials featured in my casebook. We tend to regard sensational journalism as a modern phenomenon; but in the past, and notably during the 19th century – when newspapers were inhibited by few publishing restrictions – crime reports contained the kind of detail that even the racier tabloids would baulk at today. It was often sensational stuff, and all highly quotable, and I have drawn extensively on this rich fountainhead to lend my narrative colour and to flesh out the dry bones of official documentation.

In the middle of the 19th century, 'Outrages – fatal & other' (the phrase that inspired the original title of this book) was a standing headline in the *Warrington Guardian*. It capped a column of closely-printed paragraphs which, alongside such other regular features as 'Rural Notes' and 'Ecclesiastical Intelligence', recorded all the week's murders and other assorted mayhem from around the country...in pretty much the same casually routine manner. Succinct, perfectly accurate and nicely understated, the headline was an apt, if possibly unintentional, commentary on the inevitability of crime; its unchanging presence week by week a reflection of the public's abiding eagerness to 'read all about it'. It survived up until the 1890s, when it was replaced by the more prosaic 'Crimes

Of Violence'. But the style and content remained the same...and 'outrage' continued to be a much over-worked word.

That 'inspiring' *Warrington Guardian* headline.

Along the way, I have also tried to reveal as much as is now discernible of the characters of the principle actors in the various dramas, of the times and social conditions in which they lived and the evolving legal framework within which their deeds were judged. The result is not a who-dunnit; it is more concerned with the when, the where, the how and the why. Nor does it set out to re-examine the evidence in any crusading effort to challenge the official verdicts; that would, I feel, be a dangerous presumption, considering how long ago some of these events occurred, that much of the evidence has been lost and that, because of the strong prosecution bias that existed within the legal system for most of the period, sworn testimony from the defendants themselves was not so much unrecorded as unlawful.

I wish to offer my sincerest thanks to everyone who helped in the production of the original version of this book, however small the contribution.

1

An Adventurer of the First Rank

On Saturday was brought to our Castle, in a Post-Chaise and Four, by Mr Hucklebridge, the Keeper of Newgate in Bristol, a Person of a very extraordinary Character, who has lived for near Two years past at French-Hay, near Bristol. He called himself Edward Hickson, but since he has been apprehended, he says his real name is Higgins. At French-Hay he appeared and lived like a Gentleman...but a few Days ago he was apprehended at Bristol, by the Vigilance and Activity of Mr Hucklebridge, upon Suspicion of returning from transportation...and other capital Offences...

Gloucester Journal, 16 February 1767

A BOOK of horoscopes helped seal the fate of one of the 18th century's most notorious criminals.

The theft of the almanac, stolen in desperation during a burglary that went disastrously wrong, brought an unpredictable end to the remarkable career – and extraordinary double life – of Edward Higgins, the bogus country squire with an impressive line…in villainy.

Higgins – outwardly respectable, a man of apparently independent means, friend and confidant of some of the leading figures in county society – was, in reality, a cunning and compulsive thief. Behind the façade of rural gentility, he lived comfortably off the proceeds of house-breaking and highway robbery. He made a fortune from crime and may have resorted to murder in his determination to hold on to it.

Yet he was destined to lose everything for the sake of a 2s 6d copy of *The Universal Pocket Companion.*

The slim volume, of little worth in re-sale terms, was all that Higgins would later have to show for the robbery that closed the book on his otherwise hugely successful story.

Lady Luck finally deserted 'Gentleman' Higgins the night he raided a house near the small riverside town of Laugharne in Carmarthenshire in the summer of 1767. It was his second break-in in the area in the space of three days. And he bungled it badly, leaving behind a 'prize' – a piece of broken skeleton key that would eventually place him at the scene of the crime – far more valuable than the one he carried off.

And as he fled from this isolated corner of South Wales, under cover of a dark June morning – with the astrological guide tucked away in one of the pockets of his faded broadcloth coat – the stars shone unfavourably on Edward Higgins for a second time. The man who had outfoxed the law officers of half a dozen counties, and who was then on the run after jumping bail, was finally netted following a chance meeting with…a fisherman.

The seafaring Welshman had fallen in with the shadowy figure in the threadbare riding coat, leather breeches, cut brown wig and flap-brimmed hat on the dusty road to Carmarthen. And, his suspicions aroused, he seized his chance to tackle the mysterious stranger when a compatriot (a butcher of the town making his regular early-morning trip to Carmarthen market accompanied by his dog) appeared fortuitously on the scene.

In the scuffle that followed, Higgins, big and strong, had threatened to overpower his two would-be captors…until the dog decided to grab a bite of the action and sank his teeth into the struggling fugitive. Finally subdued, Higgins was dragged off to the home of a nearby magistrate…and the fisherman and his friend discovered just how big a catch they had landed.

Five months later, on 7 November 1767, aged about 41, Edward Higgins, con-man, burglar, highwayman, escaped convict and murder suspect, went to the gallows at Carmarthen with a posy in his buttonhole and protestations of innocence on his lips. It was the last defiant gesture of an outlaw who, through a hair-raising mixture of audacity and good fortune, had cheated the hangman for 15 years.

Today, though he was headline news throughout the country at the time, his name is barely remembered outside the pleasant Cheshire commuter town of Knutsford. For it was there that his amazing double-life began; where, for seven years, he assumed the guise of Edward Higgins Esquire, gentleman, landlord and family man, effectively concealing his clandestine activities, from friends and neighbours alike, under the trappings of rich respectability.

Yet the exploits of 'Highwayman Higgins', as he is characterised in local folklore, rival even those of Dick Turpin. In many ways the two stories, in terms of both fact and fiction, are remarkably similar. And in each case, the blurring effect of time and the more deliberate efforts of writers of historic romance have combined to portray the central figure as a handsome, swashbuckling adventurer, one of that colourful brotherhood euphemistically dubbed 'Gentlemen of the road' who, with a brace of pistols and a hearty 'Stand and deliver!', set about re-distributing the nation's wealth in 18th-century England.

So far as Higgins is concerned, the image could not be further from the truth. In what is believed to be the only recorded description of him, contained in a warning notice dated 27 June 1767, and printed in the *Gloucester Journal*, Higgins is depicted as fat and ugly, an incredible hulk of a man who had taken to wearing a pocket watch whose seal, appropriately enough, bore the crest of a bear.

The notice stated, in part, 'He…is about five feet ten inches high, has a very full eye, is pitted with the small-pox and is exceeding stout and well made.'

As with Turpin, a cowardly murderer who was executed at York in 1739 for horse-stealing, there are many other aspects of the Higgins tradition that are at odds with the evidence. But, conversely, careful study of all the available records reveals the reality to be even more fascinating than the legend.

The story begins Somewhere-in-the-Midlands. From the sketchy biographies published in the newspapers after his death, it would appear Higgins was born in Worcestershire – 'in the parish of Cradley near the city of Worcester', as it was most frequently stated. But there is strong historical and geographical evidence that points to the Cradley in neighbouring Herefordshire as the more likely place of his birth.

At that time only Cradley, Herefordshire, was officially designated a parish. The similarly named north Worcestershire township did not achieve parochial status until 1785. And of the two locations, the Herefordshire Cradley – right on the boundary of the two counties – is markedly nearer to the city of Worcester.

Research among the local church registers also tends to the conclusion that Higgins had his origins in Herefordshire: that he was, in fact, the same Edward Higgins who was baptised on 8 November 1726, at Suckley, one of the parishes adjoining Cradley, Herefordshire, but actually situated on the Worcestershire side of the border. If so, he was certainly not the 'natural son of a nobleman' he later claimed to be (hardly a credible notion in the circumstances); but was one of the 10 children of John and Anne Higgins, citizens of more modest standing in the community.

It may be more than coincidence, too, that all the Suckley parish register entries accord closely with what little is recorded about Higgins's early life…not least in relation to a previous blot on the family's escutcheon.

For Edward, the eldest of five surviving brothers, was not the only one to turn to crime. Or to swing for it. The middle brother, John, 26, was hanged at Worcester on 29 July 1763 after being found guilty at the county's summer assizes of returning from transportation before his seven-year sentence had expired. As shall emerge in due course, Edward Higgins was to stand in the same dock on the same charge four years later – but with less disastrous consequences.

Brother John, a labourer then living in the parish of St Swithin in Worcester, had received the sentence at the 1761 summer assizes after being convicted of stealing a silver half-pint cup worth £1 from Thomas Watkins, a local attorney.

Many such minor offences carried the death penalty. But, under one of the Parliamentary enactments that were making transportation an increasingly popular alternative punishment for certain crimes, he had 'prayed the benefit of the statute' and was spared the short trip to oblivion in favour of a longer journey and the more predictable purgatory of an American penal plantation. He was to be given no second chance to escape the rope, however, when he was discovered at large in Claines, on the northern outskirts of Worcester, only 21 months later.*

By comparison, brother Edward had something of a charmed criminal life. His first brush with the law resulted in his appearance at Worcester Assizes on 1 August 1752. At the time he was living with a woman, Hannah Groom, in a house in the parish of St Andrew in the city. He was indicted for 'feloniously stealing one weather (*sic*) sheep, 20s, goods of Giles Blower' in St Peter's parish just beyond the south-eastern city limits.

Sheep stealing had been a hanging matter since 1741; but, although a large quantity of mutton was found in Higgins's room, the jury believed his story that he had bought it off an itinerant butcher's stall in The Shambles at Worcester, and acquitted him.

Less than two years later he was brought before the same court on house-breaking charges. He was by then living in Birmingham, where he carried on the trade of 'huckster', a petty retailer, from a shop in Edgbaston Street (no doubt using the business to peddle some of his ill-gotten gains).

After his arrest he was imprisoned in Warwick Gaol to await transfer to Worcester and the start of the Lent assizes. And so it was that on Saturday 9 March 1754, he once again witnessed the unusual sight of the foreman placing the written outcome of the grand jury's preliminary deliberations into a long cleft rod and handing it down from the Shire Hall's high gallery to the Clerk of Assize seated in the well of the court below. Their verdict, a 'true bill' on each of two indictments, meant Higgins went for trial by common jury charged with breaking into the house of Mr Lawrence Jacob of Moseley and stealing seven guineas and a large quantity of plate and stealing a further sizeable amount of plate from the house of Mr Chambers at Yardley.

Burglary was another of the 200 or so capital offences that early in the next century would prompt legal reformer Sir Samuel Romiley to declare that the laws of England were 'written in blood'. But not all juries were prepared to follow blindly the harsh penal code of the day that could send a hapless wretch to the scaffold for nothing more than the theft of a handkerchief.

And Higgins's luck was in. The benevolent jury returned a 'partial verdict': instead of house-breaking – very definitely non-clergyable and usually dealt with severely – he was found guilty of the lesser, clergyable offence of grand larceny, technically the theft of goods worth more than 1s. And as it was his first conviction, he was sentenced to seven years' transportation.

The wholesale transportation of felons had begun early in the 18th century. Up to the outbreak of the War of Independence in 1775, they were sent to the American colonies, mainly Maryland and Virginia. One estimate puts the total figure at more than 30,000. The practice was resumed in 1787, though this time the convicts were shipped to Australia – a regular (one-way) trade in human cargo that was to continue, at the rate of about 2,000 a year, until 1867.

The British Government saw transportation, on the one hand, as a cheap deterrent; on the other, a means of ridding the country of those undesirables it failed to deter, simultaneously providing the criminals with a chance of reform through honest toil and the colonies with a steady supply of labour to aid their economic development. Daniel Defoe (1660–1731), in the robustly romantic style of his hero Robinson Crusoe, said he believed that a transported felon was 'a much happier man than the most prosperous untaken thief'.

As far as Edward Higgins was concerned, however, he had no intention of spending seven years as a transported felon, happy or otherwise. He much preferred the role of prosperous untaken thief. He had neither wish to reform, nor appetite for honest work. And the only economic advancement he was interested in was his own. He determined to make his sentence as short as possible...and succeeded spectacularly.

In the summer of 1754 Higgins was moved from the county gaol in Worcester, where he had been imprisoned since the end of his trial, and taken to Bristol, then the largest city in England outside London. There, in company with other convicts, he was put on board the *Frisby*, bound for Maryland. Ahead of them was a perilous two-to-three-month trans-Atlantic voyage that was even more daunting than the rigours to come on the plantations. Outside they faced the natural dangers of sea and weather; while inside, in their reeking hell-hole between decks, the shackled prisoners had to contend with overcrowding, inadequate rations and disease. Many of those who embarked on the journey died on the way. The previous year, of nearly 800 convicts who had set out on the hazardous crossing, an estimated one in six never made it to the other side.

Higgins survived – possibly because, unlike most of his fellow sufferers, he had the means to pay for what few creature comforts were available on the leaky transport. When he arrived aboard the *Frisby* he was said to have had with him at least £14 (a fair sum in the days when £1 could provide the weekly needs of the average family). With his 'cash float' – and there can be no doubt he possessed the resourcefulness to hang on to it even in such corrupt surroundings – and the assumed air of superiority that was to impress men of more discerning rank later, Higgins would have been well equipped to persuade the ship's master to make his experience as comfortable as conditions would allow.

The story of how he came by the money indicates that there was a third member of his family imbued with the Higgins streak of dishonesty. The events were recounted in an article that appeared in both *The London Magazine or Gentleman's Monthly Intelligencer* and *The Universal Museum and Complete Magazine*, two popular periodicals of the day. In what was described in the former as 'Some account of the life and conversation of the noted Higgins', published in November 1767, shortly after his death, an assiduous correspondent reported,

> The day before the transports were to be sent off from Worcester his sister came to him early in the morning, and desired to speak with him in a private room. This was refused. She then requested he might have permission to show her the dungeon; thither they went and stayed some time in close conference. She had not left the gaol more than half-an-hour when a farmer, who lived near Worcester, came in to enquire whether his [Higgins's] sister had been there, for, says he, 'I have been robbed of £14 and I have reason to suspect her, and that she has given the money to her brother.' The turnkey told him what had passed. Higgins was

searched, but nothing was then found. The farmer came with him from Worcester to Bristol, and when Higgins was stripped on board the transport, the farmer's money was found concealed in the lining of Higgins's hat; but, as it could not be taken from him, the farmer was obliged to be content with the loss of it.

According to the same source, Higgins, along with the other surviving transports, eventually landed at Annapolis. Whether he actually started work as an agricultural conscript, or jumped ship immediately upon his arrival, is not clear. But it was not long before he was grafting away at his old 'profession'. Within a month of disembarking, the journals recorded, he broke into a merchant's house in Boston and made off with 'a considerable sum'. With his new stake he booked passage on a ship sailing for England... and was back on home soil before the turn of the year.

Of his movements during the first months of his return, nothing is known. He lived for a short time, apparently, in Manchester. Then, in late 1755 or early 1756, he first became acquainted with Knutsford and, more intimately, a certain Katherine Bertles, spinster of that parish. The couple married, started raising a family (though not, as the records show, in that order) and, for better or worse, quaint and comfortable old Knutsford had not so much lost a favourite daughter as gained its most infamous adopted son.

Over the next seven years Edward Higgins established the legend that has become inextricably linked with the fashionable North Cheshire town and which is still commemorated today by one of the characters in the annual Royal May Day parade. By day he was the respectable country gentleman, hobnobbing with some of the county's most aristocratic families, enjoying their hospitality, joining them at the hunt, the races and the gambling table and generally pursuing all the usual society pleasures. But by night, this plausible con-man played a different game with his wealthy neighbours, breaking into their homes and stealing their gold and silver or relieving them of their money and jewellery along some deserted highway as they travelled the countryside in their fine carriages.

That dark and daring side of his schizophrenic lifestyle was not immediately in evidence, however, when the Knutsford chapter of the Higgins story opened. A check on the local parish registers reveals that in April 1757 he was preoccupied with affairs of a much more solemn and dutiful nature. The same records put a dent, too, in the traditional image of Higgins's bride as the coyly virginal daughter of prominent parents. And calendar a sequence of life and death events that made the couple's honeymoon week memorable, to say the least.

Katherine Bertles was 21 when she went down the aisle of the parish church of St John the Baptist. And already a mother. It was probable that she presented Higgins with his first child, a daughter called Nancy, uncomfortably close to the wedding, which took place by licence on 21 April. Whatever complications the approaching birth might have caused, however, the child's arrival was attended by more serious problems. She was hurriedly baptised on 23 April, but died shortly afterwards and was buried the following day.

As the weeks went by, however, life settled down into a more orderly pattern up at the big ivy-covered house overlooking Knutsford Heath. It had previously been the Cann Office, where weights and scales were tested; now it was the home of calculating Edward Higgins and his new bride.

Heath House, the home Edward Higgins shared with his wife Katherine and family from about 1756 to 1764. Now much altered, it still stands on the edge of Knutsford Heath. Photograph courtesy of Knutsford Heritage Centre.

The entry relating to Edward Higgins's marriage to Katherine Bertles in the Knutsford parish registers. His signature indicates an educated hand, but could he really have been 'the natural son of a nobleman' as he later claimed? Reproduced by permission of Knutsford Parochial Church Council.

Katherine's early history is as obscure as that of her husband. She was born in December 1735, the daughter of William Bertles, a wealthy mercer of Nether Knutsford, and his wife Mary; she was the seventh of 10 children, five of whom survived. Her mother died in 1746 at the age of 41 and her father two years later, aged 53. At that time Katherine would have been 13 and her two sisters and two brothers aged variously between 11 and 20.

What happened to the orphaned family Bertles in the intervening period is not known. It is likely, however, that Katherine would have been a beneficiary of her father's will, and her share of the estate – held in trust until her 21st birthday – would have made a reasonable dowry to present to her doubtless delighted husband upon their marriage four months later. A financial assessment that may be confirmed by the singular fact that virtually overnight Edward Higgins's marital status dramatically changed his social standing, too.

In the marriage entry in the church registers he was described as a 'yeoman', a modest land-owning member of the rural middle class. Yet only two days later, when the details of his daughter's baptism were recorded, he had been elevated to the rank of 'gentleman', a class distinction then more meticulously applied than today.

However sound his funds were when he settled in Knutsford, Higgins quickly found means of augmenting them. By his own account, some were quite legitimate. He was to tell the reporters who assembled at Carmarthen Castle Gaol to record his 'last dying speeches', that he bred 'some of the finest horses that appeared upon the turf' and also sold cheese and hops. These, he said, were the products of his land holdings, which adjoined the Tatton Park estate of Squire Samuel Egerton, head of one of Cheshire's most well-respected families, ancestor of the Lords of Tatton, Member of Parliament for the county and, Higgins claimed, a personal friend of his.

But it was in the business of robbery that Edward Higgins worked hardest to reap success – and to sustain a comfortable lifestyle for himself, his wife and his by now expanding family. Up to 1764, when the law finally began closing in on him and he was forced to flee the county, Higgins fathered six children, four boys and two girls. Three of them (John, Edward junior and Kitty) lived to endure the shame of their father's guilty secret. But it was not until the last months of Higgins's life that they and their mother learned the full extent of his duplicity.

Higgins maintained to the last the myth that he had a paternal estate in Worcestershire worth between £60 and £70 a year. And it was by the pretext of journeying to collect his rents there that he explained his regular absences from Heath House and hid his crooked alter ego from his family for so long. He was often away for weeks on end, occasionally returning in the small hours with his horse's hooves heavily muffled – a device, he said, to avoid awakening his own household and that of his neighbour, whose stables were in the same cobbled courtyard.

For a considerable time, too, Higgins escaped the notice of the law, despite living openly under a name that would have been familiar to the authorities in at least one not-too-far-distant county. But, while there is no official evidence of his skulduggery during this period, several revealing anecdotes are recounted with sufficient consistency in local histories to suggest they might have some basis in fact.

One such tale concerns the theft of a valuable snuff-box belonging to the head of another of Cheshire's famous old families, Mr Philip Egerton, of Oulton Hall. Built in 1715 to replace the original Tudor manor house, Oulton Hall was a massively-grand mansion set in the heart of the Cheshire countryside. It was destroyed by fire in 1926 and Cheshire's internationally-known Oulton Park motor race circuit now stands on the site. It was then the scene of a more select and sedate gathering. One of the house-guests at this upper-crust affair was Edward Higgins. During his overnight stay, so the story goes, he stole the highly-prized snuff-box that his host had been showing off at the card-table during the evening. When, next morning, the theft was discovered, Higgins impressed the whole company by the business-like manner in which he took charge of the investigation, at one point summoning all the servants into the main hall while their quarters were searched. All to no avail, of course. After pocketing the snuff-box, Higgins had hidden it in a safe place outside the house – to where he would return later to collect it.

Oulton Hall, where Higgins is reputed to have stolen the silver snuff-box of his host, Mr Philip Egerton, following a fashionable society gathering at the massively-grand country mansion. Reproduced from *Tarporley & Beeston Country* by R.M. Bevan.

Another reputed incident is said to have occurred during Christmas festivities in the county town of Chester. In the early hours of the morning following one particularly glittering gala event, Higgins prowled the old Roman walled city looking for a likely house to rob. He chanced upon it when, after descending from the famous Rows into Watergate Street, he turned into Stanley Street.

Workmen carrying out repairs to one of the imposing three-storey town houses had carelessly left a ladder propped up against their scaffolding. Climbing to the top, Higgins watched through a partially-curtained window as a young woman discarded her ball-gown and jewellery before dismissing her maid and retiring to bed. After waiting for some time, he entered the bed-chamber through the unfastened window and proceeded to rifle the woman's jewellery-box and chest of drawers as she drifted into sleep only a few feet away. As he did so one of the drawers creaked. The noise disturbed the room's occupant who, thinking it was her maid returned to tidy her clothes away, muttered drowsily, 'Mary, you know how tired I am. Can't you put the things straight in the morning?'

A rush-light still burned in the room and Higgins froze, his mind racing ahead to consider what he would do if she awoke and discovered him there. But after what must have seemed like an eternity, all was quiet again and he was able to leave the house as swiftly and silently as he had entered it and return to his city centre lodgings.

Higgins was said to have confessed later, 'If that girl had risen up in bed and seen me, I should have murdered her on the spot.' The comment, though apocryphal, nevertheless provides an interesting prelude to what is by far the most intriguing aspect of this absorbing story: did Edward Higgins eventually turn killer?

The circumstances that beg the question surround the murders of Mrs Frances Ruscombe and her maid, Mary Sweet, at her fashionable home on the west side of College Green, Bristol, close to the Cathedral, in the late morning of Thursday 27 September 1764. It was a particularly ferocious attack carried out in broad daylight as local people were passing by the house on their way to attend college prayers. The bodies were discovered shortly after noon by a female relative who was expecting to join Mrs Ruscombe for lunch. Instead, on entering the house, she was confronted by a scene of heart-stopping horror.

The *Bristol Journal* of 29 September reported the chilling details, 'On opening the door, she immediately saw Mrs Ruscombe dead on the stairs, with her throat cut, a wound on her mouth, one of her eyes beat out and a wound in her head so violent that the skull was beat into the brain.'

Mary Sweet had been just as brutally despatched. The *Journal* report went on, 'The maid was found in the back parlor with her head almost severed from her body, her jaw broke, a violent blow on her forehead, and her skull cleaved as with a wedge. The wounds appear as though they were given with a hammer.' The intruder had not long departed the bloody scene, either, for the newspaper revealed, 'When the murder was discovered the bodies were not cold.'

Almost £100 in cash was later found to have been stolen from a portmanteau trunk in the house. But, despite rewards totalling more than £300, no one was charged with the double killing; to this day, officially at least, it remains an unsolved case in Bristol's annals of crime.

Higgins, who was believed to have been in the area at the time on one of his periodic 'rent-collecting' trips, was strongly suspected of being the murderer. He may even have confessed to the crime; he was certainly pressed closely to do so while awaiting execution in Carmarthen Castle. But, according to several sources, including the aforementioned *Bristol Journal*, he claimed vehemently to be innocent.

The paper's man-in-the-condemned-cell wrote on the day Higgins died, 'He denied the murder…and declared he was 150 miles from Bristol, when it was perpetrated.'

Three pieces of 'evidence' have been cited to support the Higgins-the-murderer theory, two of which are hearsay and the third is of similarly questionable authenticity.

He was said to have attracted suspicion firstly by blabbing details of the Bristol murder and robbery to an acquaintance in Knutsford over a drink in a local inn – well before word of such distant events would normally have reached the town. Then, he began paying local tradesmen in Spanish dollars; this in itself was not that significant (the coins were acceptable tender at a time when English silver currency was scarce), but it was made so by the fact that Spanish dollars were supposed to have been among the treasure stolen from the Bristol murder house.

In fact, Mrs Ruscombe's two sisters, in a reward advertisement that appeared in the *Bristol Journal* on 1 October 1764, listed the missing money as 78 guineas and seven 36-shilling pieces – no reference to any dollars.

But what is claimed to be the single most damning exhibit in the posthumous murder trial of Edward Higgins is an alleged 'true coppy' (*sic*) of a letter he was observed to hand to the Sheriff of Carmarthenshire shortly before being (as the newspapers invariably put it) 'launched into eternity'.

I traced the document to Dr Robin Jamison of Bristol, great-grandson of the Reverend Henry Green, who first revealed its contents in his episodic account of Higgins's life in *Knutsford: Its Traditions and History*, published in 1859. Green, who was at that time Minister of Knutsford's Unitarian Chapel, dignified it with the sub-title 'Higgins' own confession'. But the statement, printed on a thin foolscap sheet and headed by three crude woodcut illustrations, does not stand up well to close scrutiny.

The phraseology smacks of the more colourful excesses of the contemporary Press; the various acknowledgements of guilt are irreconcilable with the strenuous denials Higgins was reported to have issued right up to the time of his execution; the consistently remorseful tone at variance with Higgins's rancorous behaviour on the way to the gallows. The letter also says that crown pieces were among the cash taken from the Ruscombe house; while, demonstrably more untrue, is the description of Mrs Ruscombe as a widow at the time of her death. She was not. Her sailmaker husband, James, was one of those who offered rewards for the apprehension of her killer. The date of Higgins's house-breaking trial in 1754 is also inaccurately given as 14 May.

But perhaps most bewildering of all is the way in which the so-called confession makes reference to Mrs Ruscombe's horrific murder. The relevant passage runs, '...from the time I left my Mother's house and went off with a neighbour's wife, I became guilty of all kinds of wickedness, murder excepted, which I never committed only once upon a widow Gentlewoman at Bristol...for which I am heartily sorrier than for all other villainies by me transacted...'

The most dreadful incident in his life reduced to an almost casual afterthought. And not a mention of the poor serving girl who was nearly decapitated in the horror attack.

The Higgins 'confession' is, in fact, no more than a typical example of the 'gallows literature' which, like the fairground booths and refreshment-sellers, was a commercial by-product of public executions in the 18th and 19th centuries. Sensationally recording the criminal history and dying words of the 'star' of the grim show, the broadsides and pamphlets converted the callous brute into a grovelling penitent and endowed even the most illiterate rogue with a near-poetic command of language. Like modern-day cheque-book journalism, it should be treated with caution. But, at a time when newspapers were not so readily available, gallows literature made popular reading; it satisfied the public's abiding appetite for the morbid and, like the crime reports in the papers, seemed at great pains to reassure the community's collective conscience of the guilt of the condemned and, therefore, the correctness of the law's ultimate sanction.

Thomas De Quincey (1785–1859), Manchester-born writer and self-confessed opium-eater, seemed hooked on the belief that Higgins murdered Mrs Ruscombe and her maid during an epic 300-mile ride to Bristol and back in the space of 48 hours – though, in his jokey treatise, *On Murder, Considered as One of the Fine Arts*, published in February 1827, the two days had become two weeks and the Cheshire highwayman transplanted in Lancashire.

On the strength of this alleged evidence – and bearing in mind the stark contrast between the savage killings and his usually more subtle style of operation – it would be unsafe, therefore, to brand Higgins as a double-murderer.

Of which there can be no doubt, however, is that by this time his comings and goings had begun to arouse suspicion not only among the 1,500 inhabitants of Knutsford but well beyond the borders of Cheshire, too. Shortly after the Bristol murders the house of a draper named Wilson was broken into at nearby Gloucester and a considerable sum of money was stolen. Higgins was implicated. And on 1 November 1764 Knutsford's parish constables, Abel Mossley and William Hill, paid an official visit to the big house on the heath.

The date marked the turning point in Higgins's life; the stage was now set for the final eventful act in the drama.

It began, paradoxically, with a quick exit – Higgins giving the constables the slip in typically impudent manner. Under the pretence of changing his clothes, he left the officers waiting downstairs while he made good his escape through a bedroom window. With his sudden departure, the cat, too, was out of the bag. And, like wildfire, the sensational details of his Jekyll and Hyde existence spread through the town and surrounding district. For Edward Higgins there was now no going back.

From Knutsford the scene switched to Liverpool, where Higgins was reportedly seen next. Then, in about June 1765, he settled in Frenchay, four miles from Bristol. After apparently sending instructions to his wife to sell off his property in Cheshire, he assumed the name of Edward Hickson, took up residence in a handsome house...and resumed the grand style of his former life in Knutsford.

As the *Gloucester Journal* reported later, '[He] kept a pack of hounds, and three or four of the finest hunters that have ever been seen in this part of the world, and was remarkable for his liberality in relieving the distress of his poor neighbours...By what we have heard of this Man, he seems to have been an Adventurer of the first rank. He appears to be very well bred and accomplished, and gives out that he is the natural Son of a nobleman.'

In this fashion, Higgins continued to avoid the clutches of the law for almost two years... until 6 February 1767, when a keen-eyed gaol-keeper named Hucklebridge spotted the by-now notorious outlaw near Lawford's Gate in Bristol and had him confined in the city's Newgate. A week later, on 14 February 1767, Mr Hucklebridge, the gaol's governor who was to be a constant companion of Higgins in his final days, took his charge by post-chaise and four to Gloucester Castle to stand trial for returning from transportation.

It was the start of an astonishing series of court appearances, in the course of which Higgins was to wriggle out of the hangman's noose twice more before he was finished.

At Gloucester Assizes at the end of March the case against Higgins, described in the indictment as 'gentleman', was thrown out of court even before the jury had had a chance to hear the evidence. The decision followed an opening exchange between the two opposing lawyers. Prosecuting counsel argued that as Higgins had not been seen at large in Gloucestershire, the court had no jurisdiction to try him. At once, the defence, showing the court did possess such jurisdiction, insisted on the prisoner's discharge for lack of prosecution evidence.

The legal wrangle continued for some time, before Higgins was finally bailed in the sum of £100 to answer the charge at the next assizes at Worcester, where he had been originally sentenced.

He was released from Gloucester gaol after seven weeks in custody and, with no thoughts of surrendering to his bail, he immediately went on the run. His freedom was short-lived, however. For on 24 June he crossed the border into Carmarthenshire on the ill-fated mission that was to lead to his capture...and eventual death.

It was a disastrous trip from the word go. On the face of it, he had chosen his targets well: remotely-situated, lavishly-furnished and (as he soon discovered) ill-secured, the fat mansion-house homes of two well-to-do and prominent local women promised rich pickings. But he found little in the way of plunder.

His first intended victim was Mrs Bridget Bevan of Laugharne, widow and noted patroness of a well-endowed educational foundation. But Higgins quickly learned that charity does not always begin at home. His pitiful haul comprised a few silver trinkets, two yards of lace and an enamel miniature...total value about 25s.

He fared no better when, two nights later, some careless tavern talk lured him to the home of Dame Elizabeth Maude at nearby Westmead. He had overheard that her Ladyship's steward had just been sent £300 in cash. But, as it turned out, he had left it too late; the agent had despatched the money to London that very evening. And Higgins was to have an even unluckier break (in more senses than one) after ransacking the house in his quest for the non-existent hoard. For, in his frustration, he left a vital clue amid the wreckage of a smashed-up trunk.

He had found the trunk in a first-floor parlour. It was locked; so, after an unsuccessful search of the rest of the premises, he returned to collect the chest, carrying it downstairs, out through the front door and on to a nearby bowling green, where he could work on it undisturbed. As he tried in vain to open it with a skeleton key, however, the end snapped off and jammed in the lock. Ironically, that crucial piece of evidence would later prove his own undoing when it was produced dramatically at his trial.

Higgins managed eventually to force his way into the trunk...only to discover it was mostly full of private papers. The little pocket almanac, the only item in the box vaguely worth stealing, was the paltry reward for his efforts – though before leaving the house Higgins had made sure he had something to savour from his disappointing night's work. With characteristic coolness he lit a candle, laid a cloth on the kitchen table and, as the household slept on unawares, helped himself to food and a full bottle of Lady Maude's finest Madeira.

If the latter ensured that Higgins left the Maude mansion in comparatively high spirits on that fateful morning of 27 June, however, he was about to come crashing down to earth... literally.

At around 2am, as he hastened to put the house and his latest misfortune behind him, he had that unexpected, and violent, encounter on the main road between Laugharne and Carmarthen. And two unsung heroes – with a little help from a trusty dog – finally brought the master criminal to heel.

During his subsequent interrogation by local JP John Ravenscroft, Higgins made another bid to escape and was only restrained after one of his captors set about him with a walking stick. So, according to the *Worcester Journal*, when he was finally lodged in Carmarthen Castle he was bound with 'some very heavy irons'.

The chain of events that was to lead Higgins to his date with the hangman had now been indestructibly forged. But there were still more twists to come in this extraordinary affair.

The next unpredictable turn came when he was sent back to Worcester to answer the charge of returning from transportation. The trial was fixed for Saturday evening, 8 August, but the press of people crowding into the courtroom to see 'the famous Mr Higgins' made the heat so intense that the judge, Sir Edward Clive, postponed the proceedings until 7 o'clock the following Monday morning.

The *Gloucester Journal*, reporting that the grand jury had found two bills of indictment against him, observed, 'Seven powerful witnesses appeared, who swear to him positively, and people in general are now of opinion that there is no room to doubt his conviction.'

Higgins, too, feared the worst. The same newspaper item said of him, 'When he first came to Worcester he affected great gaiety of heart, but on Saturday his countenance dropped, and he appeared to have no final apprehensions of the consequences of his trial.'

LAUGHARNE, Carmarthenshire, June 27.

A BURGLAR.

WHEREAS in the Night between the 24th and 25th Instant, the Manfion-Houfe of Mrs. Bevan, of this Town, was broke open, and robbed of feveral Effects; and laft Night the Manfion-Houfe of Lady Maude, at Weftmead, near this Town, was alfo broken open, and robbed of a Draught for Money, and other Things: And whereas, about Three o'Clock this Morning, a Man was apprehended in the Street in this Town on Sufpicion of the above Burglaries, and being immediately carried before a Magiftrate, was by him fearched, and fome of the Effects ftolen from both the Ladies were found on him, and the other Part he threw out of his Pocket during the Scuffle he made when he was apprehended, and which are fince found: And upon infpecting his Pocket-Book, he appears to be Edward Higgins, of French-Hay, near Briftol, (which he alfo confeffed to the Magiftrate) and that he is the fame Perfon who was confined in Glocefter Gaol for returning from Tranfportation, and was difcharged from that Gael laft Affize upon his Recognizance. And as it is apprehended he might lately have committed feveral other Felonies, it is thought proper to give this Information to the Public, and that he was this Day committed to the County Gaol of Carmarthen for the above Burglaries. He appears to be a Man about 40 Years of Age, is about five Feet ten Inches high, has a very full Eye, is pitted with the Small-Pox, and is exceeding ftout and well made. He has on a mixed Colour Broadcloth Coat and Waiftcoat a good deal faded, a Pair of Leather Breeches, a cut brown Wig, and a flapped Hat; and in his Pocket was a Pinchbeck Watch, No. 1441, Mr. REIREP, London, with a Steel Chain, and a Seal fet in Gold hanging to it, which is either red Glafs or a Compofition: The Creft on it is a Bear.

A notice in the *Gloucester Journal* informing the public of Edward Higgins's capture and arrest for two burglaries in Carmarthenshire. The depiction of him, as fat and ugly, gives the lie to the image of the handsome and swashbuckling adventurer he has acquired over the years. Illustration supplied by Gloucester Archives.

There was no dispute, either, about the evidence that Higgins had been seen in Yardley, near Birmingham, before his term had expired. Yet, amazingly, he got off on a technicality.

His lawyers pleaded that the prosecution had not formally produced any of the relevant documents – the court's order for transportation, the shipboard indenture or the plantation master's contract – to prove conclusively that Higgins had been sentenced to transportation in 1754.

The judge also considered the omission crucial. On his direction, the jury acquitted Higgins after a trial lasting three hours.

By now, however, the wily Higgins had but one more 'life' left. From the Worcester courtroom he went straight back into custody. And on the morning of Monday 31 August 1767, he was returned by writ of *habeas corpus* to Carmarthen where, on 11 September, he stood in the dock for the third time in six months.

The grand jury returned a true bill on both the Lady Maude and Madam Bevan burglary charges. But, after the trial jury had brought in a guilty verdict on the former – in keeping with the legal practice of the day – the second charge was not proceeded with.

The trial lasted six hours and ended late in the day. As a result Higgins was forced to spend an agonising night in the castle gaol before hearing the judge pass sentence of death early the next morning.

The formal indictment, which this time ranked him merely as 'yeoman', alleged that Higgins 'feloniously and burglariously' broke into and entered Lady Maude's and that, as well as the almanac, he stole a bill of exchange for £4 19s 6d. The bill, however, was never recovered, and there was only a passing reference to it at the trial. It was left to that seemingly worthless little book to speak volumes for Higgins's guilt.

Though circumstantial, the evidence that sent Edward Higgins to the gallows raised few doubts in the minds of the jury and the large crowd of onlookers packed into the Guildhall throughout the sitting. A witness testified to seeing him less than 100 yards from Lady Maude's house shortly before the robbery; the missing almanac was found on him when he was captured. But, more devastatingly, a locksmith confirmed that a broken key also in his possession at the time matched the snapped-off ward-end retrieved from the lock of Lady Maude's ransacked trunk.

As one damaging testimony followed another, Higgins's mood of arrogant unconcern gradually changed to one of tearful resignation, and he was reduced to ranting at the judge about an unfair trial and how he had been 'used very ill'. He was still protesting as he was led back to his verminous cell to await execution.

A week's incarceration did little to improve his humour. The *Gloucester Journal* reported on 21 September, 'He appears to labour under great dejection of spirits, and makes no answer to the questions proposed to him by numbers of people who, out of curiosity, flock to see him. He is heavy loaded with irons, and the gaoler watches him with great vigilance, to prevent his escape.'

The gaoler's caution was well justified. For Higgins, though lodged now in the condemned cell, was about to make a last, desperate bid to save his skin.

After an uncommonly long delay (caused, apparently, by the preparations for the funeral of King George's brother, the Duke of York, who had died of malignant fever in Monaco on 17 September), Higgins's death warrant, properly authorised by the royal signature, did not arrive at Carmarthen until 23 October. In the six weeks that had elapsed since his trial, Higgins had begun to entertain hopes that his sentence would be commuted to transportation. But, in the meantime, he was taking no chances.

In a letter smuggled from gaol, probably by his wife Katherine, he had sought the help of some well-connected friends on the outside. Thus, when he was told of the warrant's arrival and the date of his execution, he was able to boast to the Sheriff, 'I'll get a reprieve before then.' And sure enough, on 3 November an impressive-looking letter, date-lined Whitehall, 29 October, and addressed to 'The High Sheriff of the county of Carmarthen or his Deputy, the Gaoler or his Deputy', was delivered to the castle.

The letter purported to come from Lord Shelburne, MP and Government Minister, and stated, 'Sir, notwithstanding his majesty's royal mandate for that purpose, you are hereby required to postpone the execution of Edward Higgins, convicted at your last assizes for burglary, till further orders.'

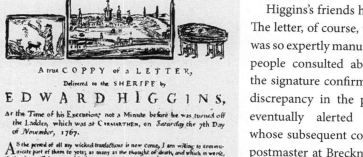

Higgins's friends had served him well. The letter, of course, was a forgery. But it was so expertly manufactured that several people consulted about the validity of the signature confirmed it as genuine. A discrepancy in the postmark, however, eventually alerted the under-sheriff, whose subsequent conversation with the postmaster at Brecknock convinced him the reprieve was indeed a fake. But it was not until the eve of Higgins's execution that the truth was established.

The so-called 'confession' of Edward Higgins: the overall tone of the letter, plus its many factual errors, leave little doubt that it was not the genuine article. Original supplied by the late Dr R.R. Jamison.

When the sheriff informed his prisoner of his decision to put the death warrant into effect, Higgins began a tirade of abuse that he and Mrs Higgins – who had taken lodgings in the town to be with her husband in his final hours – were to continue with increasing venom on the way to the scaffold the following day. But he was not so outspoken, it seems, when he was encouraged to make a confession.

Mr Hucklebridge, the Bristol gaoler with a particular interest in the College Green murders, was with him constantly in those last few days and tried repeatedly to prise an admission out of him – right up to the minute Higgins stepped on to the ladder at Pensarn, the little hill just across the River Towy from Carmarthen Castle, where the execution took place. It was reported, too, that 'some gentlemen of Bristol' had offered to give his wife 'a very considerable sum' in exchange for a full account of his crimes. But this Edward was no confessor. Higgins went to his death denying all charges ever laid against him and insisting he had 'never wronged any person of a shilling in his life'.

A week later the *Worcester Journal* was still hopeful that the Bristol murder riddle would at last be solved. On 12 November, the paper said of Higgins, 'Though he could not be prevailed upon to make any oral Confession, either publicly, or in private, he may perhaps have left one in writing with his Wife, as also in the letter he delivered to the Sheriff just before he was turn'd off; the Particulars of which, it is hoped, will soon be made known to the Publick, as they will serve either to confirm or undeceive many in their Opinion that he had been guilty of many atrocious Crimes; in particular, that he was no Stranger to the Murder of Mrs Ruscombe and her Servant-Maid, at Bristol. That he could be capable of so daring and horrid a Deed, is the rather to be believed (*sic*) from the harden'd, graceless Disposition he seemed to retain even to his last Moments.'

But both Press and 'Publick' were to be disappointed. That 'true coppy' notwithstanding, no such 'Particulars' appear to have been published. Edward Higgins, it seems, took most of his criminal secrets to the grave with him.

The events leading up to Higgins's execution shortly before 1pm on Saturday 7 November 1767, were vividly recalled in the following eye-witness account published in the *Worcester Journal*,

I am one who sat up with Mr. Higgins the night preceding his Execution. We went to him about Nine o'Clock, and found him carelessly turning over Jenks's Devotions, which, on our entering the Room, he laid aside, seeming to have not the least Relish for that, or for any Thing else that was serious. [The same correspondent had previously reported that local divinity students had composed a special prayer for Higgins's use but he returned it, telling them to 'wipe their Arses with it']. He was at first very sullen, reserved, and shy of entering into Conversation: But when he found that we came not to ask him any impertinent Questions, or to gratify a foolish Curiosity, but to give him serious Advice, and, as much as in us lay, to prepare him for his approaching Fate, he soon became as conversable as we could wish. He gave us (unasked) the History of his whole Life from Beginning to End, and cursorily mentioned all the Crimes that had been laid to his Charge from Time to Time; of all which, however, he solemnly affirmed that he was innocent. His parting, on Saturday Morning, with his Wife and Sister (who are yet in Town and inconsolable) was very affecting. His Wife made several rash Declarations against those who had a Hand in his Murder, as she termed it. When he set off for the Place of Execution he walked uncommonly fast; and I am sorry to say, that when he came there, he was very inattentive to the Prayers of the Clergyman who attended him. He was desired, by some Gentlemen present, to make a Confession; but he insolently answered, that he had no Confession to make, and that if he had, he would not so far gratify their Curiosity. He was impatient of Delays, and seemed eager to mount the Ladder, which he did with great Alertness, saying, as he was going up, that his Friends would take Care to bring those who were instrumental in his Death, to the very same Death that he was going to suffer. In his Way to the Gallows he cursed and swore most shockingly, calling the Under-Sheriff a Scoundrel for taking away his Life with a Reprieve in his Pocket. At the Gallows he delivered two Letters to his Wife, the Contents of which are not known. He mounted the Ladder boldly, and addressed the Spectators thus, 'Gentlemen, now is the Time, do as you please, you have my Reprieve in your Custody.'

He was observed to pray on the Ladder for some few Minutes, and then signified to the Sheriff that he was ready to be turned off.

According to custom, the body was left hanging some 40 minutes before being cut down and carried to the castle. Highwayman Higgins took his last ride – in a pine box on the back of a horse-drawn cart – later that evening when he was buried on the north side of nearby St Peter's Churchyard.

But if Higgins's final resting place was an unmarked plot in a Welsh graveyard, his most fitting memorial is the big house that still stands on the edge of Knutsford Heath, a small brass plate beside the front door recording the name of its most notable resident…a self-made gentleman of fortune who, if local legend is to be believed, still occasionally returns at dead of night riding a horse with woollen stockings and bulging saddle bags.

*Note

John Higgins had, in fact, claimed 'benefit of clergy'. The privilege, established as early as the 12th century, gave churchmen exemption from secular jurisdiction, the big advantage being that ecclesiastical courts had no power to impose the death penalty. Originally available to even the most minor clerks, the plea was later extended to virtually anyone who could demonstrate the ability to read; and by the 16th century had become a means by which Parliament was able to lessen the severity of the law, creating a category of so-called 'clergyable' offences for which the death penalty was imposed only on a second conviction. Though the privilege declined during the 16th century, larceny was added to the list as late as the 18th century. Benefit of clergy was finally abolished in 1827.

The Beast of Priesty Fields

At Chester Assizes ended Tuesday last, Samuel Thorley, for the murder of Ann Smith, near Congleton, was found guilty and sentenced to be hanged... and gibbeted on West-Heath, near Congleton. Accordingly on Thursday last he was executed at Boughton and on Friday, about one o'clock, his body was hung in chains, persuant to his sentence, to the general satisfaction of the inhabitants of Congleton and its neighbours. He...did not show the least remorse for the horrid and unparalleled crime which he had committed, and behaved, on the whole, with the greatest unconcern and indifference.

Chester Courant, 5 April 1777

LANDLADY Hannah Oakes did not like the look of the piece of 'pork' that her lodger Samuel Thorley brought home unexpectedly and insisted on boiling for his supper. And her misgivings seemed well-founded when, after swallowing a few mouthfuls only, her boarder was suddenly, and violently, ill.

It was four days, however, before the wary widow Oakes learned the awful truth about the discarded meal and the rest of the 'meat' lying untouched in her oven. Then it was her turn to feel decidedly queasy.

For the joint had come from no pig...it was human flesh. And Sam the butcher's man had done the carving himself.

The simple-minded Thorley had been attempting to eat what he imagined was the last remaining evidence of the hideous murder he had committed 24 hours earlier; all that was left of the young woman whose body he had hacked into more than a dozen pieces then flushed away, bit by bit, in a local brook.

The incomprehensible act of savagery that had its sickening sequel in the tiny back-kitchen of Hannah Oakes's timber-and-thatch cottage in the village of Astbury in east Cheshire occurred, probably in the failing light of the late afternoon or early evening of Wednesday 20 November 1776. Thorley, in his 50s and a rough and rootless labouring type who seems to have been most regularly employed as a butcher's 'follower' or assistant, was walking along a winding path connecting Astbury with the neighbouring town of Congleton. In a secluded valley known as Priesty Fields he met Ann Smith, aged 22 and described, charitably perhaps, as a 'strolling ballad singer'. Some time later, in a fit of uncontrollable rage, he attacked and killed the unfortunate woman with a knife. And there, in the wooded ravine through which the footpath runs – and within only a few minutes' walk of both communities – he stripped his victim and began the painstaking business of disposing of her body.

What happened next was straight out of the realms of nightmare: a study in sheer mind-numbing terror as the crazed Thorley, in a grotesque parody of an operation he had probably performed many times on animal carcases, systematically dismembered and mutilated the still warm corpse of Ann Smith.

He cleaved off the head, took the arms and legs off at the torso and disjointed the limbs at elbow and knee. He sliced off the breasts, opened up the trunk to remove the heart, lungs and bowels and cut out the woman's tongue. Then, after carving the leg portion he later carried back to his lodgings, he tossed the results of his exercise in carnage into the brook which also meanders through the little gorge, then swollen by the late autumn rains.

If Sam Thorley thought he had thereby washed his hands of murder, however, he was desperately mistaken. In the afternoon of the following Saturday, 23 November, a teenaged boy working in a field overlooking the valley of death fished a woman's cloak out of the murky waters of Howty Brook...and the full horror of the crime surfaced along with the first remnants of Ann Smith's mangled body.

Astbury village: though this is an early 19th-century engraving, the scene, dominated by the imposing Parish Church, would have been pretty much the same in Thorley's day.

Left: Howty Brook, Congleton, where 'The Beast of Priesty Fields' (Samuel Thorley) dismembered and disposed of his knife-attack victim Ann Smith. The brook was much swollen by heavy seasonal rain at the time.

Late the next day, Sunday, Thorley was arrested by a local constable at another house in which he occasionally lodged, in School Lane, Astbury. He spent the night locked up in Congleton Town Hall and was transferred next morning to Chester Castle Gaol to await his trial.

Ann Smith was buried the same day at St Peter's Church, Congleton, and one person at least was in no doubt about her killer. Whoever inscribed the entry in the church's burial register added, after the name of the deceased, 'A woman that was murdered by Sam'l Thorley.'

Suspicion had fallen on Thorley soon after the stunned townspeople heard the news of the murder. To begin with, the way in which the body was cut up immediately suggested a butcher's hand had been at work. Then, as the *Chester Courant* pointed out on 27 November, there was the matter of his 'well-known disposition'.

The *Courant* explained, 'He was, in general, looked upon as a man of very furious temper and dangerous to affront or banter.' The report added, 'It is well known the prisoner was not in necessitous circumstances, nor does it appear, from his own account, that the woman had by any means provoked him.'

Also, Thorley appeared to become particularly irritable at the mention of the crime which, understandably, was the one constant topic of conversation in the immediate aftermath of Saturday afternoon's grisly discoveries in Priesty Fields. And it seemed to some observers that he protested his innocence just a little too much... But the clincher came when old Hannah Oakes remembered the half-eaten piece of 'pork' in her oven. Despite the disagreeable effect it had had on her lodger, she had not, fortunately, thrown the rest of it away; instead, with that waste-not-want-not attitude of frugality common among the poorer country classes, she had decided to boil it up to make cooking fat of it. It did not take long for medical opinion to conclude that it was part of a woman's calf.

The official confirmation was given at the inquest on Ann Smith, held at Congleton in the afternoon of Sunday 24 November. It was one of several startling testimonies taken by the Coroner, Mr John Hollins of Knutsford, and which were to be repeated five months later when Samuel Thorley was indicted for murder.

As these written depositions are all that now survives of the evidence presented at Thorley's trial, they are referred to here at some length. Though the statements comprise the only factual record of the case, the dry, detached 'official' language in which the Coroner's clerk set them down does nothing to dispel the vague sense of unreality surrounding some of the events being described.

Newman Garside, a ribbon-weaver of Congleton, told of finding the chopped-up corpse of the murdered woman. He said that at about noon on Saturday 23 November, he turned out his cows to pasture in a field of his called the Shaw Field, which ran down to the edge of Howty Brook. The latter formed the boundary between his land and Priesty Fields. When he went to inspect the fence bordering the brook he saw in the water below what appeared to be a woman's blue cloak.

Having two young lads with him, he sent one of them, William Barratt, aged 13, scrambling down to the brook to check it out. The boy retrieved the garment and reported that there was 'something bloody' underneath.

Garside, 'suspecting something was amiss', crossed the little wooden bridge to the opposite side of the brook and saw it was a woman's gown. The statement went on, 'He observed some blood upon the lining…and, seeing one Humphrey Newton and John Beswick in a field above, he called to them to come to him, and on their coming to him the brook was searched, and an old gown, a petticoat, a cap, and a black ribbon and a pocket [small bag] were found.'

The next discoveries were to turn a ripple of apprehension into a wave of revulsion for the three searchers and the two boys watching intently from the bank…though it would hardly seem so from the tone of Newton Garside's deposition.

It stated, matter-of-factly, 'On looking further into the brook a woman's right arm was found and a leg, and it appeared upon examination that the arm was cut off at the elbow and the leg at the knee joint, and on their searching further into the brook another arm and a leg were found severed off in the above manner. A woman's breast was also found and afterwards the bowels of some person.'

In the meantime, someone – probably one of the two young cowhands – had been despatched to fetch a constable. One of the parish officers, John Martin, was quickly on the scene. But it seems to have been John Beswick who took charge of the situation.

Several other people, on hearing the commotion 'in the fields', had also arrived to join in the grim search when the murdered woman's head was recovered from the brook. Newman Garside deposed, 'There appeared to be two knife cuts on each jaw or cheek-bone.'

John Beswick described how, after responding to Garside's call, he had first examined the clothing floating in the brook. Grabbing hold of the woman's gown, he said he observed on its inside 'about a handful of jelleyed blood'. Next he pulled out of the water 'a petticoat and some pockets and an old apron'. In one of the pockets were a half-eaten threepenny brown loaf, an old tobacco box, a pair of scissors, a thimble, two ballads and a 'hussiff' (housewife: a case for needles, thread etc).

When the various parts of the murder victim's body started turning up, Beswick said he lifted out the right arm and leg. 'Then he found the head and afterwards some thigh bones', his deposition continued. 'When the water cleared they found the tongue, then the left arm and left leg and, nearby, the entrails and breast.'

Gradually, the pathetic human jigsaw that had once been Ann Smith was re-assembled on the brookside. At nightfall, when the hunt was called off for the day and the remains were given a temporary resting place in a local stable, one particular piece was still unaccounted for. No one appears to have realised the absence of the missing calf-section, much less its significance. But after the terrible scenes that had been witnessed on this day, it would have been hard for anyone to imagine there could be further horrors to come.

Thomas Cordwell, a weaver, also of Congleton, was another member of the Howty Brook search party. And, like Beswick, he took an active interest in the subsequent investigations. Crucially, he appears to have been the first to speculate that Thorley might be capable not only of murder but of cannibalism, too…and thus made the connection between the hacked-up body in the brook and the left-over contents of Hannah Oakes's oven.

He had joined the constable, Martin, on his way to Howty Brook after being told that 'a woman was murdered in the fields'. He watched as the first traces of the body were taken out of the water. At one point, according to Cordwell's deposition, he went down to the water's edge to 'look more diligently' and he 'saw the entrails or lights and heart of a person and brought them up to John Beswick'.

But it was on the following day, Sunday, that Thomas Cordwell began the real detective work. In the morning he went again to the brook but found 'only a ribband'. On his way home, however, he saw Sam Thorley talking to two other men and as he approached he heard Thorley proclaiming that he had known nothing of the murder until the previous evening. 'And', stated Cordwell, 'he repeated the words several times over.' Earlier, Thorley had also taken part in the murder hunt and expressed his disgust at the killing.

Cordwell said that when he got home his wife told him 'someone had reported Samuel Thorley had murdered the woman'. The statement continued, 'Then a jealousy [suspicion] struck into this deponent's mind and from what he had heard Samuel Thorley say he thought it might be true'. So, 'being uneasy', he made it his business to find out.

He first decided to seek the help of John Brittain. His friend, however, was not in; but at his home he found Charles Butterworth, another local man, and he told him of his suspicions and how he would like to examine Thorley 'to see if any blood could be found on him'. The two men then went looking for Thorley but could not find him.

Later Cordwell called on another neighbour, Thomas Elkin. Elkin recounted how the previous afternoon, while combing the countryside around the murder spot, he had found some blood on a stile across the path that led from Priesty Fields to Hannah Oakes's cottage.

When Cordwell went to the stile to see for himself, the bloodstains were still visible. And it was there that he made a seemingly amazing deduction.

'He determined to have all the barns searched for the remains of the flesh,' his deposition said, 'for he thought Samuel Thorley had taken it in order to eat it.'

It was a conclusion based, it seems, on the fact that Thorley was occasionally known to sleep rough in barns and had a penchant for raw meat…though there had been nothing to suggest that it might extend to cannibalism. Nothing, that is, until Thomas Cordwell went to visit the widow Oakes. What she had to tell him, and show him, meant there would be no need to look any further for the missing evidence.

Asked whether Thorley had been at the cottage recently, the old woman said he had turned up there at about 8 o'clock the previous Wednesday evening 'wet on his feet'. He explained that he had been walking through Priesty Fields when he had slipped and 'had been nigh tumbling into the brook'. To prevent himself falling full length into the brook he had jumped and landed safely on his feet in the water.

Hannah Oakes then related the story of Thorley's unfortunate experience with the boiled 'meat'. When Cordwell inquired about the left-over portion, she said it was 'in the back place'.

The Cordwell statement went on, 'In the back kitchen he laid his hand upon a piece of flesh that he took to be the calf of a woman's leg and he stroked his hand over it and found it was smooth and soft. He said he was positive it was woman's flesh.'

'God forbid!' exclaimed Hannah Oakes. 'He told me it was pork.'

Surgeon Charles Reade later provided professional corroboration of Thomas Cordwell's kitchen-table diagnosis.

A more detailed account of Thorley's Wednesday night visit, of the following evening's flesh-eating incident and of Thorley's general behaviour after the murder, was given by the widow Oakes in her statement to the coroner. She said she knew it had been Wednesday that Thorley had called as there had been a high wind blowing that night and she had had to untie the door to let him in.

'He seemed to have his apron full of meat and he threw the same down on the table', she said in her deposition. In view of his butchering connections Thorley's appearance would not have attracted undue suspicion; his bloodstained apron was a familiar sight around Congleton town.

'What has thou there?' Hannah asked him. Thorley said it was pork. Asked how he came by it, he said that a man had been driving a pig through Congleton when the animal 'drop't down as if he would dye'.

Thorley said someone pointed to him and joked to the pig's owner, 'Here is a butcher. He will stick him for you!' And Thorley said he had killed the pig and, as a reward, had been given some of the pork 'to live on'.

Hannah was curious to know whether the animal had 'bled well'. Thorley said it had and, rejecting the old woman's view that it was 'not fit to eat', he commented, 'It is very good and fat and will be very good [in] pyes.'

The deposition added, 'He would have some boiled but she would not suffer him. She said her daughter told him the dogs would run away with it. She bid him put the flesh into the oven cold.'

This he did, and the following night he returned to the cottage. 'And [he] took the flesh out of the oven and would have some of it boiled and cut some pieces and put them in a kettle on the fire. And he did eat some part and was sick and said they might give it to the dogs; he would have no more.'

The rest of the flesh, said Hannah, remained in the oven until Sunday when she put some of it into a pot over the fire to 'boil it for grease'. Later she took some of it out, 'not thinking that it was but swine's grease'.

The same morning, at about 9 o'clock, Sam Thorley called again and, 'on discoursing over the former subject' (the murder of Ann Smith), she said, 'Sam, this must be done that windy night when thou came here. Didst thou hear no noise or see anything?'

Thorley replied, 'No.' But, said Hannah, he seemed to 'take at her words'. She tried to placate him, 'I did not think it was thee, Sam.' To which Thorley responded, 'I would not have done it for £10 or £20. Nay, nor for a thousand.'

He departed soon afterwards but returned about noon to put on a clean shirt. On the 'belly' of the dirty one, Hannah Oakes said she 'thought she observed a spot of blood'.

Thorley left her house for the last time, still somewhat agitated, and with the parting comment, 'I am going to my masters at Astbury to get my wage and go to Leek as they are laying the charge of murder on me!'

There are two further witnesses' statements in the official file on the murder; both relate only to the formal evidence of identification heard at the coroner's inquisition, but they do tell us a little about the wandering lifestyle of poor Ann Smith.

Spinster Mary Amson deposed that, shortly after lunch on the day of the murder, a 'low broadset woman' of about 23 came into her shop in Newbold Astbury and purchased a ha'porth of 'shagged' tobacco and a penny loaf. The young woman, a stranger to her, was 'poorly dressed' in a blue cloak and a little black cap. The Mistress Amson said it was the same woman whose remains were found in Howty Brook and which she was later invited to identify.

Mary Fendale, described as 'wife of Joseph, brickmaker, of Congleton', stated that a woman who called herself Ann Smith had lodged with her until about a fortnight ago. She had left saying she would return on the Wednesday or Thursday before 'Congleton Fayre' (the annual Lammas Fair on 22 November) 'if it pleased God she lived'. The next she heard was that 'Ann the ballad singer' had been killed; so she went to see if it was true.

Her deposition added solemnly, 'She went to look upon her [remains] and John Beswick lifted up the head of the deceased and she verily believes it to be the head of Ann Smith.'

After the inquest jury had returned a verdict of wilful murder against Samuel Thorley, Coroner Hollins would have sent the complete file on the case to the assizes. At that time coroners played a more prominent role in the initial investigation of homicides than they do today. They conducted the initial interviews with suspects and committed them to prison where necessary; they bound over witnesses to appear at future court hearings and generally prepared much of the ground for the trial proceedings.

Thus, the six statements taken at the inquest into Ann Smith's death would have formed the basis of the prosecution's evidence when, at Chester Assizes beginning on Thursday 3 April 1777, Samuel Thorley was tried for murder.

Until 1790, when the Chester Castle complex was extensively re-constructed and the building was demolished, the sessions were held in the Great Hall, also called Hugh Lupus' Hall after the first of the Norman Earls of Chester, for whom the Castle was both

Chester Castle by Moses Griffiths (1747-1819). On the left is the Great Hall in which Samuel Thorley was tried for murder in 1777. The square turreted tower (Agricola's Tower), the lower half of the Flag Tower, the Half Moon Tower and a small section of the curtain wall of the inner bailey still remain of the Norman fortifications.

military base and administrative centre. Located on the east side of the lower ward, it was a large open-raftered building with massive, carved beams and dated back to the 13th century. In more recent times, the new county gaol had been conveniently re-sited alongside it.

Of Thorley's trial documentation, however, nothing survives beyond the formal indictment (which makes the nice distinction that the murder weapon was a knife 'to the value of two pence'). And contemporary newspaper reports made surprisingly brief mention of the case which, even amid the 18th century's passing parade of gallows fodder, must have been of more-than-usual interest.

The process of establishing his guilt seems to have been a fairly speedy formality. With characteristic stolidity, Thorley does not appear to have volunteered much in his own defence, after emerging from 128 days in the pig-sty squalor of the Castle cells into a courtroom atmosphere at that time notoriously hostile to the accused. He would have been prevented by law from making a sworn statement; not until as late as 1898 were defendants allowed into the witness box.

And if he did manage to articulate his version of events – and, critically, what occurred beside the rushing Howty Brook that Autumn day to transform a blockish butchering man into the Beast of Priesty Fields – there is now no official record of it. The most important piece of the puzzle, therefore, is missing.

The reports of Thorley's execution and the stories about the murder that appeared afterwards offer an explanation of sorts to account for the vital lost moments before the slaying and Thorley's subsequent actions. But they are all peculiarly unsatisfying…and many tantalising questions remain unanswered.

The *Manchester Mercury*, struggling to find a convincing solution to the riddle, said on 15 April, 'On being questioned what could induce him to commit so horrid a crime, he answered that, having frequently heard that human flesh resembled young pig in taste, curiosity prompted him to try, if it was true…'

The memorial obelisk overlooking the River Dee at Boughton, on the outskirts of Chester, marks the spot where, for centuries, the condemned criminals of Cheshire were executed. The gallows was moved to the other side of the road in 1791. The 'killing ground' was finally abandoned 10 years later.

Thorley was hanged on Thursday 10 April 1777, at Boughton on the eastern outskirts of Chester. This was Cheshire's Tyburn, the place, close to modern Barrel Well Hill, where for centuries the city sheriffs observed their solemn duty to execute condemned criminals from throughout the county palatine. It was here, in the same month of 1555, that the protestant martyr, the Reverend George Marsh, was burned at the stake. A monument recording the fact now marks the spot alongside the busy A556.

Unlike Edward Higgins (see Chapter One), the Congleton murderer was not 'turned off' – a method of execution in which the condemned person, the noose tightened around his neck, was made to mount a ladder propped up against the scaffold ('the fatal tree' of popular account). The ladder was then given a sharp twist and the victim went spinning to a less-than-instantaneous death. The mode of despatch at this time in vogue involved the use of a horse-drawn cart, open at the back, which was positioned beneath the crossbeam of the gallows and driven swiftly out from under the prisoner at the appropriate moment.

The *Mercury* report observed, 'He...behaved with great apparent indifference in his way to, and at the gallows; where he only asked the executioner if he intended to strip him after his death; and, on being answered in the negative, seemed to feel some satisfaction.'

And the paper added, equally mysteriously, 'The witnesses averred that the prisoner had never shown any marks of insanity, and appeared persuaded that extreme avarice was his principle inducement to the commission of this shocking crime.'

John Poole incorporated a similar account of the execution in a detailed review of the case in *The History of Cheshire* (Volume Two), published in 1778. And he painted this portrait of the murderer, 'Thorley...was known to be a vagabond-man, of an avaricious and ferocious disposition, frequently lying, to save the expense of lodging, in barns, and eating raw meat at butchers' stalls.'

His reason for dismembering his victim, it was surmised, was 'very probably a persuasion that the small parts would be speedily carried by the flood' into the River Dane, into which Howty Brook discharges at a point just upstream of Mill Bridge, a short distance away.

Poole, founding publisher-editor (in 1775) of the *Chester Chronicle*, stated that 'it appeared in proof that the prisoner met the deceased on a footway near Congleton and prevailed on her to accompany him to a hollow place a small distance from the road'. Here the writer declined to elaborate further, but was clearly hinting at some sexual motive. Ann Smith, we are told, was back in town ready to follow the crowds flocking to the Lammas Fair, anticipating a ready-made audience and, no doubt, generous appreciation of her vocal talents. But had Thorley more intimate overtures in mind? Was 'ballad singer', after the fashion of many of those modern professional ladies who style themselves 'model' or 'exotic dancer', a thin disguise for a much older occupation? And did the impoverished Miss Smith, who had recently been reduced to gathering rags in the neighbourhood to supplement her precarious living, go willingly with her killer in hopes of earning the price of her next meal and lodgings? Unfortunately, Poole's otherwise competent commentary is sufficiently lacking in this area to frustrate any such conclusions.

It was left to another newspaper pioneer, Robert Head, to provide the most explicit – and confident – exposition of the Priesty Fields tragedy. Its one major weakness, however, is that it was written 120 years after the event. In the intervening period it is clear that historic fact and local custom had become interwoven in the fabric of the story...and from this distance in time it is not always possible to pick out the unembroidered thread of truth.

Head, printer and first editor of the *Congleton Chronicle* (established 1893), in his *Almanack and Guide for 1897*, introduced his narrative thus, 'A few facts about Sam Thorley, the eccentric Congleton murderer, may not be without interest: the crime for which he suffered and the following incidents exhibiting so strange a mixture of the grotesque with the horrible as to account for the story being still frequently told, with all sorts of embellishments, in the locality. The inhabitants, who claim that this is the only Congleton murder on record for a hundred years, may be satisfied with it as a transaction quite sufficient for any single century at least.'

Thorley, said Head, was 'a half-thick', born in Leek but brought up in Astbury, adding, 'He got his living as a sort of helper or odd-man-about, and so carried on a stupid and bewildered but honest and laborious life to the occasion of its miserable ending at the age of about 50.'

Congleton in the 1770s was a prosperous town of around 500 houses. In most of them some form of cottage industry was going on, including the spinning and weaving of textiles and the manufacture of gloves and shoes – though the industrial revolution had already begun to change the traditional emphasis on home-based crafts here as elsewhere.

The foundations of Congleton's development as a major silk town had been laid in 1755 with the opening of the first mill; now it employed over 600 people. Three or four other silk mills were in production by this time, too. And local people also worked in corn-milling and copper-smelting and the manufacture of bricks, rope and agricultural implements.

Sam Thorley's limited capacity equipped him for none but the most basic labour, however. In his periodic employment in the butchery business, according to Head, he merely 'jobbed about in slaughter houses…doing some of the rougher work of that trade at busy times'. But it was during these spells that he acquired his crude handiwork with a knife as well as his taste for raw meat. It may not be without significance, too, that sharp instruments figured largely in the working life of the dull-witted Thorley. Apart from butchering, he also did occasional stints as a woodcutter and a grave-digger.

According to Head's *Almanack*, he had been returning from his fairly frequent duties as a grave-digger at Astbury Church when he encountered Ann Smith, 'the well-known tramping ballad-singer', in Priesty Fields. The area was so called because it was the route regularly used by the parish priests of Astbury on their way to conduct services at the daughter church of St Peter's, Congleton. In 1867 the latter became a parish in its own right; but Priesty Fields and the old footpath by the brook, tucked away in a little hollow on the rural fringe of the town, have changed little in two centuries.

In 1887, in his self-published *Congleton Past and Present*, Head had made this apt comment on the murder scene, 'The brook Howtie [*sic*] has its rise among the hills at Newport, and, winding by the outskirts of Astbury and Priesty Fields, flows through Congleton…on its way to join the river Dane. After incessant rains this little stream has been known to swell into disastrous floods, causing much destruction of property.'

Though in his *Almanack* account he did not say what the condition of Howty Brook was at the time of the murder, it was clearly not swollen enough to sweep away the evidence of Ann Smith's destruction. After a scholarly rendering of the murder details, Head set down what, by then, had obviously become the accepted – indeed, the only – explanation for the appalling crime.

He wrote, 'It will never be known what led to the horrible fate of Ann Smith. Thorley himself, in some interval of the stolid indifference with which he behaved after the event, let fall a sort of account of the matter to the effect that the woman met him and borrowed his pocket-knife…in order to cut some bread and cheese which she was carrying for her dinner [it will be remembered that a half-eaten brown loaf was found in one of the deceased's pockets], and that having got it she laughed at him and ran away with it. He followed her to the brook, and took the knife from her, and in a rage cut her throat, after which, in his fury, he committed the rest of the frightful excesses.'

Even in the context of a murder as inexplicable as this, it seems a barely believable motive; Head himself was not entirely content with it. But as his article concluded, 'There may be some truth in this, the poor wretch having been always reckoned dangerous if provoked, while quiet enough when let alone.'

Thus, history has branded Samuel Thorley a madman; and, after considering the evidence, few would disagree with that verdict. In the absence of Thorley's own explanation to provide a clue to his state of mind at the exact moment of murder, however, it is impossible now to judge whether, in a later and more enlightened age, he would have been certified as legally insane and, therefore, unfit to plead or whether, tested against the yardstick of the McNaghten Rules, he would have been allowed to plead guilty to the lesser charge of manslaughter on the grounds of 'diminished responsibility'.

The story goes that, in consequence of certain pre-trial doubts about his mental condition, Thorley was set to count out a score of hobnails. And when he succeeded in his task he was passed a fit candidate for the court...and the gallows.

It was, probably, one of the many myths with which, as Robert Head pointed out, the story of the Priesty Fields murder has become embellished over the years. Perhaps the most famous is the saying Thorley is supposed to have introduced into the local vernacular. When he fled his Astbury lodgings he is said to have announced he was 'going to Leek out of the noise'. And, although it may have been appropriate to Thorley's situation, Head seemed to think the expression, still in common use towards the end of the 19th century among older residents, had been around long before Thorley was born. What is certain is that, if he did indeed intend to return to his Staffordshire home town to lay low for a while, he never got there.

There is also the tale of a number of other people made ill by Thorley's 'gift of pork', several cuts of which he is supposed to have hawked around the pubs of Congleton.

And, maintaining the seemingly universal predilection for attaching prophetic significance to the recalled ramblings of simpletons, another remark of his has become a popular quotation from the Thorley story-book. He is said to have expressed the view that, although he had dug the graves of many people, no one would dig a grave for him. Mr Justice Moreton, the judge who presided over Thorley's trial, ensured that particular 'prediction' came true when he ordered that, after execution, the prisoner's body should be denied the absolution of burial and condemned to the further public indignity of being hung in chains by the roadside.

The 'chains' in this case were, in fact, a framework of hoop-iron which was riveted together around the body and then suspended from a gibbet at some strategic location close to the scene of the crime. The corpse, disembowelled and wrapped in a calico sheet soaked in pitch, was thus exhibited as a stark warning to the public at large...a black-shrouded bogeyman set to scare off other would-be law-breakers. Gibbeting was introduced during the 17th century; in 1752, in 'An Act for Better Preventing the Horrid Crime of Murder', it was reaffirmed as a key component of Parliament's repressive penal machinery, the so-called 'Bloody Code'.

Thorley's after-death sentence was put into effect the following day, Friday 11 April 1777, at West Heath, the most prominent place nearest to the murder spot and now an area long since covered over by private housing development alongside the A54 Congleton-Holmes Chapel Road. The event was greeted by no little rejoicing in the locality, and took place, as was the custom on these occasions, apparently, in an almost carnival atmosphere.

The Reverend Jonathan Wilson, headmaster of Congleton Grammar School, recorded in his diary that day, 'At school, after dinner, gave the boys leave to go and see Sam. Thorley drawn upon the gibbet.'

Thorley's second 'hanging' also added to the store of anecdotes relating to the Congleton murder. For it is told that the carter entrusted with bringing the body from Chester to the gibbeting stopped off at an inn on the road through Delamere Forest and, having, consumed more than was good for him, failed to notice when, shortly after resuming his journey, the coffin was jolted off the cart on to the bumpy highway. As soon as he realised what had happened, he went back to pick up his missing 'passenger' lying beside the road. But it meant that Thorley was late for his noon appearance at 'Congleton Town End' and the crowd gathered around the scaffold to witness the spectacle was kept waiting for over an hour.

How long the 'caged' Beast of Priesty Fields stayed in this suspended state is another unknown in a *cause célèbre* as mystifying as it was barbaric. It is a fact, though, that Sam Thorley, a man used to mopping up in the bloody wake of slaughter-house activity, left a stain on Congleton's past that nothing could erase.

And more than 230 years later, the *horrid* crime he committed remains *unparalleled* in the town's history.

A Most Melancholy Circumstance

It is with great concern we inform our readers that the post-boy carrying the mail, on horseback, from Warrington to Manchester, was robbed and murdered, a mile from Warrington, about five o'clock on Thursday morning...Two men were seen to leave the place...in a precipitate manner, and go towards Warrington...The reward for apprehending these villains is, by law, forty pounds, and the usual reward from the post-office is two hundred pounds. We hope this, added to the enormity of their crime, will be the means of their speedy apprehension...

Manchester Chronicle, 17 September 1791

PHANTOM horsemen, their faces masked and pistols primed, no longer haunt the place where, more than 200 years ago, real-life highwaymen staged a bloody hold-up.

The mounted bandits lurking by the roadside in more recent times were mere figments of the imagination: fanciful illustrations on the inn-sign that used to hang outside The Highwayman pub in the Warrington suburb of Woolston. But on 15 September 1791, the piece of land on which the pub was built was the scene of what started as a robbery...and ended in murder.

There it was, shortly after dawn, that James Hogworth, a post-'boy' (he was actually 24 years old) was ambushed by armed riders and relieved of his mail bags. Then, as he lay tied up and defenceless on the ground, he was callously knifed to death.

The former Highwayman pub in Woolston, Warrington, and (inset) the inn sign with its colourful illustrations. The events that occurred on this spot in 1791 were of a rather darker character.

When it was built in the mid-1960s, the pub took its dubious 'inspiration' from the terrible events of that blustery autumn morning and in the process became an unlikely monument to Edward Miles, the highwayman who was subsequently executed for his part in the crime. The hostelry closed a couple of years ago, though the property still stands at the junction of the A57 Manchester Road and the A50 (it is now a neighbourhood supermarket).

The little brook into which the post-boy Hogworth's belaboured body was dumped also remains, running along the rear boundary of the premises. And, a fact that can be confirmed from the property deeds, the pub was built on the very site – anciently called 'The Twystes' – where they erected the gibbet on which Miles's body was afterwards hung in chains.

In the local history books, Miles's name alone is linked with James Hogworth's death. But it was never proved who the murderer was. Or, for that matter, how many were concerned in the crime.

The Post Office, which prosecuted attacks on the mails with some vigour (and no little reward money), appeared to believe at least four were involved; certainly, four men were, at different times, charged with both robbing and killing the post-boy. Ultimately, only Miles was tried in connection with the crime; and while he was found guilty solely of robbery, under the savage rule of 18th century law that was enough to send him to the gallows.

By then two years had passed since the discovery of a murder that, even in those lawless times, shocked the nation. A report in the London-based *Star* newspaper of 21 September 1791, with uncharacteristic understatement, described it as 'a most melancholy circumstance'. The victim who, the paper recorded, 'bore a most excellent character', had been 'most inhumanly murdered' about a mile from Warrington on the turnpike road to Manchester.

A doubly cruel tailpiece to the story emerged, too, when the papers delved into Hogworth's background. The same *Star* edition reported, 'He has unfortunately left an unhappy widow, far advanced in pregnancy, to lament his loss.'

And three days later, the *Manchester Chronicle* revealed, 'It is remarkable that he felt great reluctance in going the journey which, had he survived, was to have been his last, as he was beginning another employment.'

The *Chester Chronicle* of 23 September was moved to comment, 'Murder, in its best of shapes is loathsome to the eye of humanity; but this from the description given of it, appears to wear peculiar marks of savage barbarity; the mangled carcase speaking to the heart of sensibility, in the dumb but loud eloquence of gaping wounds.'

Disdaining to reveal the extent of the post-boy's injuries – details it judged to be 'both unpleasing and unnecessary' – the paper concluded, 'Suffice it, that the *bloody business* was executed by the hand of a *master!*'

The *Liverpool Advertiser* was not so squeamish. 'It is,' wrote the paper's correspondent on 19 September, 'a most shocking murder, attended with the greatest cruelty imaginable.'

And, to demonstrate the bloody truth of its claim, the *Advertiser* catalogued Dr Pemberton's post mortem findings, '…a stab with a sharp instrument in the throat near the left jugular artery, two inches deep and near one inch wide, another stab something higher, near the middle of the throat about half an inch wide, but not penetrating the wind pipe, a violent bruise over the left eye-brow, the skin and flesh divided to the bone in three places…another bruise on the right side of the head near the crown, the skin and flesh divided down to the bone.'

James Hogworth had set off on his final journey at around 4.30 on a morning already made memorable by the rare appearance of a lunar rainbow. Emerging from a little lane off Market Place, in which Warrington's post office was then located, he skirted the big enclosed square which, until late the previous evening, had been the boisterous scene of the town's popular weekly market – at that time famous for its lampreys but which also did brisk business in a variety of fish, meat, cattle, corn and potatoes.

Into Horsemarket Street, he turned right towards Market Gate, busy hub of the town's road network; ahead of him, Bridge Street. It was all quiet now, but soon the southern entrance to the town – described in the following year's *Universal Directory of Trade and Manufacture* as 'narrow, long and ill-built' – would be alive with the clatter of carts and the general bustle of early-morning activity as men and women went to their jobs in pin, file or tool-making, brewing, copper smelting, the manufacture of fustian, huckaback and sailcloth and all the other commercial enterprises of a fast-growing trading town of around 8,500 people.

At the crossroads, however, the post-boy swung left into Buttermarket Street and continued on along Church Street, passing first the grey, unprepossessing slab of the town's workhouse then, a little further on, the more comforting sight of the ancient parish church of St Elphin, massively impressive but not yet crowned by the 281ft high spire added in 1860 and which still dominates the skyline today. Then, as the last straggling vestiges of thatch-roofed habitation gave way to the wilder vistas of the open countryside, he joined the great road to Manchester.

The turnpike, built under the expanding construction programme then beginning to replace the glorified cart-tracks that had previously passed for a national road network, cut through the mossland flanking the north bank of the Mersey. Not as polluted then as it is now, the river teemed with a variety of fish and shellfish, including cockles that were reputed to be 'the best and largest in England' and mussels 'in such abundance that they serve to manure the ground'. It was at a point where the road ran closest to the meandering watercourse, at around 5am, that the mail-robbers struck.

An hour later James Hogworth's horse was found unattended in an adjoining field. But it was not until late evening that the fact was communicated to officials at Warrington Post Office and a search was mounted for the missing post-boy.

His body was eventually found at 6 o'clock the following morning – more than 24 hours after the fatal incident – in Bruche Brook, important in medieval times as the western

boundary of the ancient manor of Bruche. It was lying face down in the water and it looked at first as if the young man had drowned after being bundled unconscious into the brook. But medical examination, the results of which would later be given in evidence at Edward Miles's trial, showed the post-boy had died from stab wounds in the neck. His horn was also recovered from the brook; nearby a leather portmanteau and four mail bags lay empty. The horse's saddle and the mail pillion had been discarded a short distance away beside a ditch.

Bruche Brook, into which the mail robbers dumped the lifeless body of post-boy James Hogworth and, in the background, the rear of the former Highwayman pub, now a supermarket.

William Orrett, the Warrington Postmaster, immediately had hand-bills and advertisements printed offering rewards totalling £240 for information leading to the capture of the gang. And, from the initial public response, the Post Office put out descriptions of several men wanted for questioning in connection with the crime. Some proved to have been based on mistaken reports and were withdrawn.

An announcement from the Postmaster-General's office in London, dated 20 September, cleared up one early misunderstanding. It stated, 'It is believed that the two Persons, appearing by their accent to be Irishmen, described in an Advertisement from this office of Yesterday's date, are not the Persons who committed this Robbery and Murder.'

The authorities were by that time concentrating on tracing 'two lusty men on horseback' who, the notice said, had been seen to follow the post-boy out of Warrington at full gallop and then return half an hour later with their boots dirty – 'as if they had dismounted in a miry place, such as where the Body of the deceased was found'.

At about 8am these two had breakfasted at an inn at Farnworth, about five miles west of Warrington and close to the main turnpike road to Liverpool. From the start the pair seem to have been bent on attracting attention to themselves: they ate in their great-coats, the pockets of which bulged suspiciously; and, although they were prepared to wait while a farrier fixed some loose shoes on their horses, they appeared impatient to be on their way, inquiring of the landlord when the next packet was due to sail from Liverpool to Dublin.

By the end of the month, the Post Office was starting to put names to its list of suspects. And a case was being built up against two men in particular: Edward Miles, aged 36, and Thomas Fleming, 31.

A hand-bill issued by Postmaster Orrett on 30 September described Miles as being 'about five feet six inches high, rather slender, thin visaged, of a pale complexion, very little (if anything) marked with the small-pox; has brown hair, short and lank, but is entirely bald on the crown of his head'. And the notice proclaimed, 'This man it is morally certain is one of the Mail Robbers.'

Irishman Fleming, described as 'five feet nine inches high, lusty but not corpulent, of a dark complexion, with dark or black hair tied', was one of three other named men who were believed to have negotiated, or offered, several of the bills of exchange stolen from the mail bags carried by Hogworth.

Fleming, a labourer then living in Manchester, was already in custody. He had been confined in Lancaster Castle Gaol for his alleged involvement in the robbery of Mr James Hall, a Liverpool wine merchant, on the highway near Prescot a month earlier. By the time he was brought to trial on that charge, however, he was also accused of the robbery and murder of the Warrington post-boy, after further inquiries established a link between the two crimes. As things turned out, though, the new evidence was to prove even more incriminating to Miles.

It was supplied by Mr Robert Jones, a Liverpool jeweller and silversmith, and his shop-assistant Mr John Fleetwood. They recalled that on 19 September, four days after the post-boy was attacked, a man visited their business premises in Castle Street with a letter requesting that 12 parcels of Spanish silver dollars worth £126 be handed to the bearer. The enclosed payment was made up of five bills of exchange totalling £121 12s 2d and the balance in cash.

The letter was sent by Miles. He had been purchasing dollars off Jones at regular intervals for almost a year. In that time at least £225 had exchanged hands in the transactions. But this was the first occasion on which bills of exchange had been presented in payment.

Noticing that none of the bills bore the necessary endorsement, the shopman Fleetwood became suspicious. And when the messenger declined to sign his name to the bills, Fleetwood refused to do business with the man...and alerted the authorities.

A check quickly established that one of the bills, for £60, had been stolen in the attack on Mr Hall in August and two others had been in James Hogworth's mail bags when he left Warrington in the early hours of 15 September.

The hunt for Miles began immediately. But he was not to be found at the Manchester address from which he had conducted the dollar deals with Jones or at the home of his mother and sister in Norfolk Street in the Park Lane district of Liverpool. And he was missing from his usual haunts in other parts of the two cities. In fact, despite what one Manchester newspaper described as a 'strict and active search' for him, he was to be on the run for nearly two years.

In the meantime, the dossier on Miles was slowly pieced together. He was born in Garston, Liverpool, where at one time he kept the Red Lion public house. He later moved into the city and lived near St James's Church, but for the past year he had resided in the Knott Mill area of Manchester. There he had been in the haulage business, keeping a cart and team for hire.

But it was in another line of work that he 'made' his money – in both senses of the word. For Miles was a member of a gang specialising in counterfeiting coins. With the funds the gang acquired from highway robbery and other illicit means, Miles bought a regular supply of dollars. These were then 'clipped' and the silver shavings were melted down and re-cast into smaller denomination coins, including shillings. As well as their fund of freshly minted forgeries, the gang was also able to tender at face value the original dollars, though by then substantially diminished in size.

With English silver currency in short supply, the Government turned a blind eye to the increasing amount of Spanish and Portuguese coinage in circulation (in 1797 the Royal Mint regularised the situation to some extent by countermarking Spanish-American eight-reales, the fabled 'pieces of eight', and re-issuing them as Bank of England 'dollars'). What silver was in use was, for the most part, in pretty poor condition, of inferior quality and, as like as not, devalued by the attentions of the coin-clippers. The counterfeiters had become so skilled that it was now almost impossible for the untrained eye to distinguish the base coin from the genuine article. So a few dog-eared dollars more would easily have passed unnoticed.

But for that curious oversight with the bills of exchange, it was a racket that could have kept Miles & Co. in business for years. With the coining ring exposed, however, and Miles having flown the coop, the rest of the gang were rounded up and taken in for questioning. As well as Fleming, it included Peter Pickering, landlord of the Rose and Crown public house in Warrington – the man, as we shall see, who delivered Miles's last unsuccessful order for dollars to the silversmith's shop in Liverpool – William Oddy, Edward Lydiate and Thomas Case.

Lydiate, 26, was subsequently released. Although he was suspected of being involved in the Woolston robbery and murder, the evidence against him was insufficient to substantiate either charge. He had been one of the men named in the Post Office wanted posters of 30 September. Formerly employed by a Liverpool carrier, he had for the past five months been a driver for Miles, his brother-in-law.

The other gang members were not so lucky. Fleming was charged with the Hall robbery and, subsequently, with robbing and killing the Warrington post-boy. Pickering and Oddy were accused of 'assisting Edward Miles of Manchester in counterfeiting the current coin'. And Case was indicted with 'colouring and uttering silver coin' at Manchester.

All four appeared at the Lent assizes at Lancaster on 10 March 1792. After examining the evidence against Pickering and Oddy, the grand jury decided there was no case to answer and the pair were discharged.

Case was sent for trial on the coining charge and was convicted. And, although it was classed as treason and, therefore, a hanging offence, he was sentenced to six months in gaol – an unusual occurrence at a time when the prisons were used mainly as holding accommodation for offenders awaiting trial, convicts struggling to raise their discharge fees and debtors in need of more substantial financial aid to obtain their release.

For Fleming there was to be no leniency, however. He was found guilty of robbing the wine-merchant and was sentenced to death. As was the usual practice of the day, with one capital conviction secured, the court did not proceed to try him on the mail robbery and murder charges.

The Hall case indictment had accused Fleming, 'with divers other persons unknown', of assaulting the wine-merchant and stealing two bills of exchange, for £60 and £23 19s 0d, two guineas in cash, one hat valued at 5s and a penknife worth 3d. He pleaded not guilty.

Joseph Hall was attacked at about 8.30pm on Thursday 25 August 1791, as he was returning home to Liverpool on horseback. He was stopped on the Liverpool-Prescot road between Fairfield and Low Hill by five footpads 'armed with bludgeons and other weapons', according to a report in the *Liverpool Advertiser* of 29 August. When one of the men snatched hold of the horse's bridle, the animal shied and threw its rider to the ground. The robbers held him down 'with imprecations' and rifled his pockets. After dispossessing him of a number of papers, two bills and 17 guineas in cash, the men removed Mr Hall's saddle and set the horse loose, threatening to kill the terrified merchant if he made any attempt to raise the alarm. They then made off in the direction of Prescot.

In a reward notice in the same edition of the newspaper, the Mayor and Magistrates of Liverpool offered 100 guineas for information leading to a conviction and the prospect of a royal pardon to any of the offenders who turned King's evidence. They also appealed to people living on the outskirts of Liverpool to report 'all suspicious persons who may be seen lurking about their respective neighbourhoods', promising they would be handsomely rewarded.

But it appears only Fleming was ever brought to account for the crime. The 'divers other persons' involved (possibly other members of the Miles gang) remained unknown… officially at any rate.

The reward notices were repeated in subsequent issues of the *Advertiser*, including that of 19 September, in which the paper first revealed to its readers the shocking news of the post-boy's murder at Warrington.

Fleming was hanged at Lancaster on Saturday 7 April 1792. The *Manchester Mercury*, making brief reference to the event, reported three days later, 'Fleming declared himself innocent of the crimes laid to his charge, and altho' he had been charged both with the robbery and murder of the post-boy, near Warrington, he never was guilty of such Enormities, nor had ever associated with people of that Description.'

Miles, meanwhile, was still at liberty – though there was no let-up in the intensive manhunt that had begun the previous September. From the early days of the investigation, the Press, too, had conducted its own campaign to bring him, and his partners in crime, to justice.

The *Manchester Chronicle* of 8 October 1791, commented, 'Notwithstanding the strict and active search that has been made, the inhuman murderers of the post-man, near Warrington, are at present undiscovered. Many persons have been taken up on suspicion. A man who lived in this town is described as being very strongly suspected of a concern in the horrid transaction. It is hoped they will not long escape the arm of justice.'

A week later the paper revealed the name of the Manchester suspect, when it noted, somewhat impatiently, 'We are sorry to observe, that at present it does not appear that the real murderers of the post-boy, near Warrington, have been secured. Edward Miles, who lived at Knot-Mill in this town, and has absconded, is strongly suspected. It is imagined he is concealed, and public notice is given, that any person concealing him, will be considered as an accessary [*sic*] – it becomes, therefore, a matter of serious import to those who may be induced, from whatever motive, to favour the escape of such a criminal.'

Miles was to stay concealed, however, for another 20 months. On at least one occasion, he claimed later, he evaded detection by disguising himself as a woman. But in June 1793, despite wearing a black wig to hide his own distinctive light brown hair and bald patch, he was recognised in Manchester by Mr Nicholson, a Warrington attorney, and was arrested.

By this time the Post Office considered it had an unassailable case against Miles. But it was keen to put the rest of the mail robbers in the dock, too. In July 1793, therefore, the following notice was placed in the columns of the *Manchester Chronicle*,

GENERAL POST OFFICE
July 1st, 1793

Whereas Edward Miles, the person advertised in October, 1791, to be concerned in the horrid Murder of the Post-Boy, and the Robbery of the Mail, near Warrington, on the 15th September, 1791, was lately apprehended, and is committed to Lancaster Gaol for trial.

And whereas some persons, whose names are well-known, are strongly suspected of being accomplices in, or privy to, the said murder and robbery. If any of them will surrender his or herself to Thomas Lyon Esq., of Warrington, or any other Magistrate for the county of Lancaster, within one month from the date hereof, such persons will receive his Majesty's most gracious pardon, be admitted in evidence for the Crown, and be entitled to a reward of one hundred pounds, payable on conviction of the said Edward Miles.

And all persons acquainted with any circumstances respecting the said Edward Miles, are requested, for the sake of public justice, to communicate the same forthwith to Mr Lyon or to the Postmasters of Warrington, Liverpool or Manchester.
By Command of the Postmaster General
ANTHONY TODD, Sec.

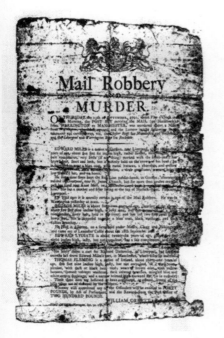

One of the Post Office notices giving details of the men wanted in connection with the Woolston mail robbery and offering a £200 reward for the apprehension of 'any of the Offenders'. From an original illustration in the archives of Warrington Library.

Whether the advertisement, repeated in the five following editions of the paper, had the desired effect is not clear. By the time Miles was brought to court, two other men had also been charged with the Woolston robbery and murder: Peter Pickering and William Oddy, the two members of the Miles gang who the previous year had been cleared of coin counterfeiting. But the main witness against these two seems to have been Miles himself.

On 10 August 1793 all three men appeared before the grand jury at the opening of the summer sessions at Lancaster Castle, an assize court venue since the first itinerant justices were sent out from Westminster in 1166. The evidence against Pickering and Oddy was considered to be too flimsy to proceed with and, once again, they were set free, leaving Miles to face the music alone. His trial on the lesser charge of robbing the Warrington post-boy took place four days later and lasted five hours. He pleaded not guilty.

Reporting the outcome to his bosses in London, GPO investigator George Western wrote on 15 August, 'Yesterday Edward Miles was fully convicted and received sentence, for robbing the mail near Warrington. He is to be hung in chains. The evidence was merely presumptive but of so strong a nature as to leave no doubt in the minds of the court.'

Main sign-posts on the trail of circumstances that led Edward Miles to the scaffold were that the accused was in Warrington earlier in the week in which the post-boy was attacked; he was in Hogworth's company on the day before his death; he was observed riding into Warrington at full gallop along the Manchester turnpike about an hour after the robbery and, later the same day, was seen by a coachman acquaintance of his at nearby Hollins Green. Then there was the evidence of Miles absconding immediately after the murder hunt began and the conflicting statements he made when he was eventually caught, first denying any knowledge of the crime then changing his story in an attempt to throw suspicion on others.

But the steel reinforcing the prosecution's otherwise rickety case was the cast-iron clue from the man of silver. Of the five bills of exchange sent by Miles to Jones, the Liverpool silversmith, to pay for his order for dollars on 19 September 1791, at least two – for £32 2s 8d and £9 7s 0d – were among the mail stolen from Hogworth.

The bills amounted to the most damaging evidence against Miles. And, although he denied sending them to Jones, he was unable to convince the jury, especially since there was ample proof that he had been doing regular business with the Liverpool trader.

According to the case file preserved in the archives at Post Office headquarters in London, a letter from Jones dated 28 March 1791, was uncovered during a search of Miles's last-known address, given as 12, Garton Row, Manchester. In it Jones noted receipt of 20 guineas and the despatch of the equivalent number of dollars Miles had ordered. He added, 'I will not disappoint you when you want your weekly allowance.' Miles was never able to explain satisfactorily how the letter came to be in his house.

Jones also confirmed that he received a letter on 1 September 1791, in which Miles requested that 40 guineas worth of dollars be sent to him at the Rose and Crown, the Warrington inn kept by Peter Pickering. And, wrote Miles, he would be placing a weekly order with Jones until further notice.

At first Miles said he knew nothing about the letter of the 11th, then he made a second statement in which he claimed Thomas Fleming had written it. But, the prosecution revealed, Pickering was at Miles's home on 10 and 11 September – and Miles spent the 13th and 14th at the Rose and Crown. Also, the order for dollars delivered by Pickering to Jones on 19 September, and containing the stolen bills, was 'exactly corresponding with the letter of the 11th', the Crown argued. And Miles turned up at Pickering's again on the 21st.

Jones testified that he had sold dollars to Miles on seven occasions, dating back to 24 January 1791. The first time, he said, he dealt with Miles himself. But in general some other person brought the orders; occasionally one of the Manchester-Liverpool coachmen would be the go-between.

'The dollars were for the purpose of coining, which the prisoner, and several other persons connected with him, carried on largely,' the prosecutor alleged.

Miles insisted he had only bought dollars off Jones once – 'nearly three years ago' – and had re-sold them to Thomas Case. Questioned further about his alleged counterfeiting activities, he denied giving William Oddy a quantity of shillings or 'pieces intended to resemble shillings', or sending eight guineas worth of such pieces to Pickering or anyone else. He claimed the £52 10s 6d he admitted he once gave Pickering was payment for horses he had purchased from his inn-keeper friend.

The prosecution also re-constructed a detailed picture of Miles's movements both before and after the mail robbery. He had arrived at the Rose and Crown in Warrington's Bridge Street (the inn survived until the west side of the street was extensively remodelled in the late 19th century) early on Tuesday 13 September. Later the same morning he and Thomas Fleming were seen together at the Griffin public house in nearby Horsemarket Street, sampling the locally brewed ale which, even in those days, had a reputation for being 'not inferior to the best in England'.

He left Pickering's early the next day, the 14th, and on his ride back to Manchester he overtook the post-boy Hogworth near Eccles. They stopped to take a glass or two of ale and continued their journey together, pausing for further refreshment at Pendleton. When they finally arrived in Manchester around mid-morning, the pair drank together again at the Woolpack in Deansgate, Miles no doubt taking advantage of each opportunity – and the tongue-loosening effect of the alcohol on his young companion – to elicit information about the post-boy's routine and some of the more interesting items to be found in his mail bags.

At that time Fleming was staying at the Woolpack and Miles was heard to inquire after him. That the two eventually met up with each other was evidenced, said the prosecution, by the testimony of one Ann Osbaldeston. Witness stated that she had seen the pair at 6am on the 15th – an hour after the estimated time of James Hogworth's death – galloping towards Warrington along the road on which the post-boy was stopped.

Later that day Miles was spotted in Hollins Green, some three miles outside Warrington, by Henry Livesley, driver of the Liverpool-Manchester stage-coach. Livesley, who knew Miles, was to say in evidence later that he had seen the prisoner a short time after the robbery and told him he was wanted for questioning about the crime.

Miles, said the coachman, declared he was innocent and that 'he did not care how soon he was taken up'. Asked why he had absconded, as had been reported, Miles insisted he had never left Manchester. And, by way of proof, he made the extraordinary statement that he had seen Livesley in a public house in Manchester but that the coach-driver would not have recognised him because he was dressed in women's clothing (he does not appear to have explained the reason for his unusual disguise).

Miles also denied being in Warrington on the day of the robbery. In his first statement he said he and Thomas Case went to Warrington on 13 September. The same day the two of them took a loaded cart to Parr, near Wigan, where they were joined by Edward Lydiate. That evening Case returned to Manchester by coach and Miles and his brother-in-law stayed overnight at the Rose and Crown.

Next morning he set off for Manchester alone. He admitted he accompanied, and drank with, the post-boy on the journey and that at the Woolpack he had sought out Fleming; he wanted the money owed to him for two shirts his friend had bought off him, he said. But he claimed he had remained in Manchester until mid-day on Friday the 16th, when he, his wife and young child went by horseback to Hollins Green. After spending the night there, Miles said he travelled to Antrobus, near Northwich, to look at a horse and later the same day went to Lymm, where he stayed until the following Wednesday 21 September. That day he dined at Pickering's and returned to Manchester in the evening.

After making this initial statement to a local magistrate, Miles had been committed to Lancaster Castle Gaol. By then conditions there were marginally better than in 1776, when prison reformer John Howard described the dungeons as being 'extremely close, dark, unwholesome and offensive' and their effect on those confined in them as 'pernicious'.

Nevertheless, the experience (to borrow from Samuel Johnson) would doubtless have concentrated Miles's mind wonderfully on his desperate position. And on 24 June 1793, he wrote a letter to Mr Nicholson, the Warrington attorney who, the prosecution brief recorded, 'had taken a very active part in apprehending the prisoner'. Miles asked the lawyer to come and see him. Mr Nicholson agreed and on 2 July he was present when Miles made a second statement.

In it Miles sought to save his own neck by incriminating other members of the gang. He now admitted giving Pickering the letter the publican delivered to Jones the silversmith on 11 September 1791, but said that the order for dollars had been written out by Fleming. He had approached the post-boy, he said, to ask him to take a message to Edward Lydiate in Warrington, instructing him to return to Manchester with Miles's team as soon as possible. This the post-boy had done. And, Miles claimed, when Lydiate arrived back in Manchester on the evening of the 15th, the day of the murder, he told him an interesting story.

Lydiate had spent a second night at the Rose and Crown and recounted how in the early hours of the following morning, he had been awoken by the arrival at the inn of two strangers. The men, who had apparently just ridden back from Newmarket Races, called Pickering from his bed, whereupon the inn-keeper dressed, saddled up his horse and rode off with them. He returned about an hour later alone and went back to bed. And, Miles added insinuatingly, when Pickering rose later in the morning he 'put on a different coat'.

Miles said he was at the Rose and Crown briefly on the Saturday (17 September), and Pickering's wife told him William Oddy had been there on the day the post-boy was robbed and murdered. Pickering asked Miles what he knew about the crime. Miles said he had heard a little about the affair when he was in Hollins Green. Pickering then described the manner in which the victim had been found with his hands and feet bound together behind him. And at this point, said Miles, the inn-keeper produced from his pocket a piece of thick cord and said, 'They were tied with such a cord as this.'

When he was re-examined, Edward Lydiate repeated his account of Pickering's early-morning foray with the two mystery men. Yet, while in custody earlier, he had made no mention of the incident; nor had Miles referred to it in his original statement. The omissions, said prosecuting counsel, were 'pretty remarkable'.

The jury thought so, too. Miles was convicted of robbing the mail and condemned to die. In keeping with the principle that a man cannot be executed twice, the second capital charge, that of murdering James Hogworth, was set aside. On this occasion, however, the Sword of Justice did turn out to be a double-edged weapon. In exercise of that long established prerogative of no mercy, an option most recently confirmed in the 1752 Murder Act, the judge ordered that, after the death sentence had been carried out, Miles's body should be hung in chains on a gibbet near the scene of the hold-up to act as a warning to others.

After his trial, Miles went back to Lancaster Castle Gaol, where he was to have plenty of time to reflect on his past deeds and prepare for his appointment with the hangman.

Saturday 7 September, was the date eventually fixed for his execution, but it was postponed for some reason.

A week later, on 14 September, however, Miles was taken from his cell and, along with the coffin in which he would make the return journey, he was loaded into a two-wheeled, horse-drawn cart and trundled out towards Lancaster Moor. As the pathetic procession, led by the county sheriff and his ceremonial entourage, made its way via Moor Lane and Moor Gate to Gallows Hill, the handful of relatives and friends bringing up the rear was swelled by the customary mob of rowdies and sensation-seekers come for their periodic ration of squalid excitement.

At the Golden Lion on the corner of Brewery Lane, the cart was halted while Miles availed himself of the condemned man's traditional last drink. In common with most of the motley cast that had previously acted out this odd little scene, he was inclined to spin it out as long as possible. He may well have been reminded of the sobering tale of the Yorkshire saddler who, declining the usual libation on temperance grounds, was executed only minutes before a messenger arrived with his reprieve. Had the abstemious artisan dallied long enough to take the proffered bowl of nerve-stiffening ale, his life would have been saved.

For Miles, however, there was no angel of mercy winging his way to Gallows Hill. With the noisy crowd growing impatient, he was finally returned to the waiting cart and hauled off to the place of execution. And there, on the same spot on which the legendary Lancashire witches had been hanged early in the previous century (see Chapter Eight), the law exacted payment in full from the small-time dealer in deficient money.

But if Edward Miles was prepared at the end to admit his part in the counterfeiting racket, he remained adamant that it was not he who had robbed and murdered the

Warrington post-boy. Typical of the Press reports of the hanging which appeared in the Manchester and Liverpool papers was this extract from the *Manchester Mercury* of 17 September, 'He acknowledged to have been concerned with a Set of Coiners, two of whom he believed were guilty, but declared his Innocence of the Crime for which he suffered.'

Miles was dead, but his judicial humiliation was not over. Two days later, on Monday 16 September 1793 – exactly two years and a day after the Woolston murder – his body was returned to the spot where the post-boy was attacked and killed and unceremoniously hung in chains. And there it remained, a grim reminder of the perils of interfering with the public mails, until well into the next century.

On display at Warrington Museum, the iron 'suit' in which the body of Edward Miles was reputedly hung on a gibbet in 1793 at the scene of the robbery and murder.

Although gibbeting was not formally abolished until 1861, there is no record of such a sentence after 1832, and even then the practice had been obsolete for many years. Ironically, the post-boys were among those who cheered loudest at its demise. For they more than most had to pass by the sinister structures. And on dark, stormy nights the sight of a blackened corpse swaying in the wind and the sounds of creaking scaffold timbers and rusty chains scraping eerily together, were enough to test the nerves of the boldest traveller.

The Warrington poet John Fitchett (1776–1838) appears to have had such a close encounter with the tarred and trussed Miles. The experience inspired both awe and lyricism. When a friend of his built a house on the former Woolston mossland on which the gibbet had stood, Fitchett sent him a poem he had written. In it, he referred to both the place's past claim to ill-fame and the more constructive achievements of its new occupant. Two of the stanzas ran,

> A spot of ground where late I knew
> A moss and scene of murder, too;
> Where a huge gibbet rose, and chains
> Swinging in air oft chilled my veins.
>
> Chang'd by some magic incantation
> Into a rich and gay plantation;
> Luxuriant set with willows tall,
> And in their midst a neat spruce hall.

A short distance across the River Mersey in Grappenhall, the tradition persists that Miles's 'suspended sentence' was carried out there; moreover, that he was executed in what is known locally as Gallows Croft, close to the Knutsford Road (A50). In 1978, when the ancient custom of walking the parish boundary was revived, an effigy of the highwayman was hung from a tree in the field in macabre memory of the alleged event.

Now, while it is a common mistake to confuse the roadside gibbeting of a criminal's body with the execution itself – some writers have claimed that convicted felons were occasionally fitted out with their iron suits while still alive and left to die in this hideous fashion – here history has been misplaced as well as misrepresented. It could well be that the Miles affair has, over the years, become mixed up with a case in 1592 in which one William Geaton, a servant of the Bishop of Chester, was executed for murdering a Scottish pedlar and hung in chains on Grappenhall Heath.

In 1845, long after Miles's mortal remains had crumbled to dust and the Woolston gibbet had collapsed and disappeared from view, the irons were dug up and stored for a time in the stables of Warrington's most celebrated historian William Beamont. And even there the shackles continued to exercise a certain restraining influence, it seems; servants, it was said, refused to go near the outbuilding until the offending item was removed.

3 ~ A Most Melancholy Circumstance

The iron cage, intact save for the part that enclosed the head, was later given to Warrington Museum, where it can be seen to this day: a metal skeleton from the murky closet of penal history…and an object of public attention still.

4

Last Stop on a Gruesome Highway

He was accordingly taken in a cart to Boughton...and on the road, and at the fatal tree, his behaviour convinced the beholders of his penitence. Never were the feelings of the multitude so much interested as they appeared to be when his wife and brother ascended the cart, to take a last, a long farewell! the sympathetic tear rushed from almost every eye, when the unhappy pair were taking their parting embraces! For a while his crimes were forgotten–the scene was too affecting; but then reason interfered, and it was considered that justice demanded that life, which it was evident he had made too criminal an use of...

Chester Courant, 26 April 1791

Part One: 'The Post Master'

SINCE no-one-knows-when the Old Man of Helsby has watched over the marshy hinterland of the Mersey estuary, commanding a magnificent panorama that rises out of the Irish Sea beyond Liverpool and stretches southwards across Wirral and into the Deeside fringe of North Wales, before vanishing into the mountain mists of Snowdonia.

Thrusting ahead of the smaller, less distinctive peak that overlooks neighbouring Frodsham, Old Stone Face – the unmistakable profile of a man can be seen etched into the rocky edge of the escarpment – maintains his vigil with unblinking eye: aloof, immutable, a silent sentinel guarding the entrance to the Mersey Valley and the changing landscape spread out below.

'The Old Man of Helsby', the rocky outcrop on which the body of William Lownds was hung in chains in 1791. The face of the man can clearly be seen in profile in the edge of the escarpment.

Nowadays, the view from atop this 464ft high crag is dominated by the more un-genial giants of industry – the smelly, fume-spouting petro-chemical installations of Ellesmere Port and Halton and the smoky towers of the Ince and Fiddler's Ferry power stations – by the concrete hive of Runcorn's Halton Lea shopping centre, with its swarming colonies of new town housing; the western sweep of the mighty Manchester Ship Canal and the neat, grey dividing line of the M56 motorway…a famous transport relic of the past alongside a communications landmark of the present.

But in April 1791 only the Mersey tributaries of the Weaver and Gowy intruded into the marshland and fields flanking the tiny settlements that nestled beneath the twin headlands of Cheshire's central sandstone ridge. And from miles around another, more sinister figure could be glimpsed on Helsby Hill.

The new 'top attraction' was the late William Lownds, whose body was hung on a gibbet on the highest point of the hill in customary fashion after he had been executed for robbing the mail. And that lofty scaffold was still there five years later when fellow highwaymen James Price and Thomas Smallman suffered the same fate – and for a similar reason – four miles away at Trafford Green.

Not long afterwards, a writer travelled the route of what is now the A56 and observed, 'The road from Warrington to Chester is a gruesome sight with three gibbets on it.' In fact, Price and Smallman – better known by his alias Thomas Brown – were hung on the same gibbet and it may have been that the author was including in his grim reckoning the convict Miles, then also on public display on the outskirts of Warrington (see Chapter Three).

Either way, there were enough rotting corpses consigned by judicial decree to the roadsides during the final decade of the 18th century to suggest that, in these parts at least, the 'deterrent' had long lost its powers of dissuasion. Alfred Ingham, in *Cheshire: Its Traditions and History*, published in 1920, claimed highway robberies were commonplace in the county at this time – an assertion fully supported by the evidence of local newspaper files and surviving assize court records.

Since 1635, when Charles I introduced the system of delivering letters by horseback (most went to local inns for collection before the countrywide network of post offices was established), the mails had been particularly vulnerable to attack. The post-'boys' (though many were very young there seems to have been a lot of older, less able-bodied men employed in the service as well) were unarmed; they travelled alone, often during the hours of darkness, and there was frequent collusion among inn-keepers, robbers and the messengers themselves.

The most scathing commentary on the situation was made by John Palmer (1742-1818) who, in October 1786, was appointed Comptroller General of Postal Revenue. Under his guidance the Post Office gradually won the war against the highwaymen by switching the mail to fast, well guarded stage-coaches. The first had begun operating on the London-Bristol run in 1784 and at the time of the inauguration Palmer declared, 'The post, at present, instead of being the swiftest, is almost the slowest conveyance in the country; and though, from the great improvements in our roads, other carriers have proportionately mended their speed, the post is as slow as ever. It is likewise very unsafe, as the frequent robberies of it testify. The mails are generally entrusted to some idle boy, without character, mounted on a worn-out hack, and who, so far from being able to defend himself or escape from a robber, is much more likely to be in league with him.'

A French view of the English post-boy, c.1774. Though some were very young, many post-boys were older, less able-bodied men. Note (right) the two corpses hanging from a roadside gibbet. By courtesy of HM Postmaster General.

Despite the remorselessness with which offenders were pursued, and the severity with which they were dealt, it seems there was no shortage of men willing to risk their lives for the chance of getting their hands on the post-boys' bags and the big money bills or other negotiable items they might contain. And, whereas James Price and Thomas Brown graduated respectively from picking pockets and stealing horses – and were caught after their first attempt at mail robbery – William Lownds was said to have been so successful at it that he was nicknamed 'The Post Master'.

Lownds, in fact, continued to prove himself the most resourceful of the trio even after his capture. And it was as much by his extraordinary escape attempts as his criminal escapades that he earned his reputation and his prominent place in the annals of Cheshire highwaymen…second only to the legendary Higgins (see Chapter One).

The details of this daring postscript to the story of the famous mail-robber, and of the careers of Price and Brown, are drawn largely from two remarkable documents, contemporary publications which not only boast virtually verbatim trial reports and eye-witness accounts of the executions, but also contain much revealing information about the operations of 18th century crime: of the methods of the mail thieves and the tricks of the horse-rustling trade, of fairground rackets and forgery and of the extent of the corruption pervading the sewer-like sub-culture of the prison system.

The man who was to go to great lengths to try to exploit the latter state of affairs, in what became an increasingly desperate bid to avoid the consequences of his crimes, came from Smallwood, a sparsely populated rural community in the Cheshire parish of Astbury, near Congleton. Though he later assumed so many different identities that he could be excused for forgetting his real name (even the official court records listed six aliases and still got it wrong), he was, according to the local parish registers, born William Lownds on 27 April 1755. The son of respectable parents, his father, also William, was a weaver whose character was said to be 'exemplary and industrious'. After receiving an education described as being 'somewhat superior to his situation in life', William Junior eventually joined the family business.

Congleton was then fast developing as a silk-manufacturing centre. But the woollen cloth industry – which, together with shoe-making, had previously provided the neighbourhood's chief source of employment – continued to flourish. Despite the liberating effect of the new industrial age, the work was still essentially domestic, with people producing the goods in their own living-rooms. For young William Lownds, however, the bonds of the weaving trade were not sufficiently strong to tie him to his home for too long.

At the age of 21 he seems to have been persuaded against his better judgment into marrying a local girl, Elizabeth (Betty) Hayes, with whom he had been carrying on rather shamelessly, by all accounts. Unusually, their union, in June 1776, was not 'blessed', however, until almost three years later, when a daughter, Alice, was born.

Lownds had by now developed itchy feet, a condition which his recently acquired part-time job as a dancing master was clearly not enough to remedy. The cure for his restlessness required more positive steps than that; so, shortly after the birth of his child, he waltzed off leaving his family, and the area, for good.

He appears to have landed first in Sunderland. There, judging by a somewhat hysterical letter delivered to him while he was in prison awaiting trial, he had a brief but passionate liaison with someone called Eliza. He soon moved on, however, and at Alfreton in Derbyshire he formed a more lasting friendship with one Amy Clarke, whom he married bigamously in July 1785.

Lownds's journey down the highway of crime had begun; over the next five years or so he was believed to have carried out a series of raids on the mails, all with Amy's knowledge. In fact, after bearing him two children, she herself took to travelling the country either with, or closely behind, her husband as he moved from place to place, always seeking to keep one jump ahead of the law.

The Post Master is thought to have served his apprenticeship by regularly robbing the Congleton-Macclesfield deliveries, with the connivance of the post-boy. The printed case history, compiled by John Poole, co-founder-proprietor of the *Chester Chronicle*, and published by his successor, John Fletcher, explained, 'Their practice was to examine the letters on the road, take out those which contained property to their liking, and alter the post-charges on the remaining letters, so as to correspond with the office-bill; this was continued till the alteration in the post-charge caused a suspicion, and the prevention of a repetition.'

After this, it was stated, several mail robberies were committed in the northern counties – 'most of which there is strong reason to believe were affected by Lownds'. The first offence known to have been committed by him, however – and the one for which he was eventually hanged – was the robbery of the Warrington-Northwich mail in 1788.

For two years he had been living under the name of Lewins in Chesterfield, where he had resumed his occupation of weaver; but, in March of that year, he turned up in Warrington. And early in the morning of the 11th, between Stretton and Antrobus, on what is now the A559, he attacked the post-boy and made off, on foot, with 'considerable property'.

Returning to Derbyshire, he set about capitalising his newly plundered assets. He negotiated one bill of exchange for £20 in Chesterfield a few days later; on 22 March he used another, for £69 5s 6d, to purchase cloth from a merchant in Leeds, endorsing it in the name of William Brown. Then, on 18 April, with a third stolen bill, value £111, which he again signed 'William Brown', he transacted some further unidentified business with a company in Hull. He had ordered the cloth to be delivered to an address in Wilston, near Matlock; but, on 20 May 1788, part of the consignment was found in a search of his Chesterfield home. Lownds, however, was by then long gone.

He had left on 7 May after learning of the authorities' growing interest in him, and for some months he seems to have lain low. Then, in the autumn of 1788, he and his wife and one of his children, a girl aged between two and three called Polly, boarded a boat for Ireland. They returned in the spring of the following year and that Easter went to live at the lodging house of a Mrs Ann Crow in Beaumaris, Anglesey. It was during an extended stay in North Wales that Lownds, now using the name Hutchinson, carried out his next mail robbery.

Around midnight on Sunday 29 June 1789, at Dunham-on-the-Hill, six miles north-east of Chester, he attacked and robbed the Chester-Frodsham post-boy. Within 48 hours he was back in Beaumaris, having journeyed by horseback and post-coach via a roundabout route through Barnhill, Wrexham, Mold and Bangor, a distance of well over 100 miles. The conduct of this impatient traveller attracted attention, however, and his description was soon being advertised in connection with the hold-up.

In early July, after seeing one of the wanted notices, a neighbour suggested to Ann Crow that her new boarder might be the hunted fugitive. And when she raised the matter with her 'Mr Hutchinson' – challenging him, she said, to 'either clear himself or take his chance' – he immediately packed his bag and fled, even though it was 10 o'clock at night and raining hard.

He managed to secure a passage over the Menai Straits, money and persuasion overcoming the boatman's fears of making the difficult crossing in the dark, and landed at Caernarfon.

But, the hue and cry having been raised, he was forced to make tracks again after being spotted at an inn. He was said to have narrowly escaped his pursuers by leaping out of a window and was last seen heading into the wild and storm-swept Welsh Mountains in his stockinged feet.

There was high drama, too, the next day when Lownds's wife Amy attempted to follow him. The Poole account told how she hired a boat to take her to the mainland (there was no mention of the child Polly) and, after reaching Bangor, she rewarded the three members of the crew generously. Too generously, as it turned out; for they all got drunk on the money and were drowned on the way back after their boat got into difficulties in the treacherous waters of the straits.

The Poole pamphlet recorded, 'Lamentable to relate, her favours were the cause of their deaths, as they were all lost on their return through excess of liquor.'

At this point there is another gap in the narrative; but by early 1790 Lownds and his family had been re-united and were living in Hexham in Northumberland, about 20 miles west of Newcastle upon Tyne. On 25 February he rode 50 miles across country to hold up the mail between Penrith and Keswick and on 3 June, at a bank in Newcastle, he negotiated a bill for £541 8s 0d, which had been in the stolen post-bags. Giving his name as William Hope, he received £441 8s 0d in cash and a note of hand for £100.

The following day the Lownds family were on the move again, travelling 40 miles south to Darlington. After settling Amy and the children into new accommodation, Lownds took the mail-coach to London, arriving in the capital on 7 June. His first port of call, naturally, was a bank; and with the firm of Smith, Wright and Gray he negotiated another stolen bill of exchange, this time endorsing it in his own name.

This was not as brazen or as risky an act as it might appear; for the advertisements that were now making widespread appeals for his apprehension consistently referred to him as William Lewins. So far as is known, however, the accompanying description was accurate enough.

It stated, 'The said William Lewins is about 35 or 36 years of age [he was 35], five feet eight or nine inches high, stout made…has remarkable good black hair, which he lately wore tied behind; has a florid complexion, large lips, is rather heavy limbed, and thick about the ankles.' The notices, put out by the General Post Office, offered rewards totalling £400, plus a royal pardon for any accomplice turning King's evidence, over and above the £200 automatically guaranteed by Parliament for information leading to the conviction of a highwayman.

From London, Lownds went directly to Exeter. And it was there, after being on the run for more than two years, that he was finally cornered on 7 August 1790. The manner of his capture is undocumented, but he was arrested by William Sarrell, Keeper of Exeter Castle Gaol, in the parish of St John, just outside the city gates, where he had been living under yet another alias (William Henry Clarke) in some style, apparently.

According to Poole, he 'entered into all the amusements and gaiety of that city' and was 'extremely active in the election of the place'.

The evening he was apprehended he had been preparing for his latest departure and had invited upwards of 20 local gentlemen to a farewell party. He was said to have behaved towards Mr Sarrell with 'the greatest coolness and intrepidity', even threatening the gaoler with prosecution for wrongful arrest. And he was so confident of his release that he sent a note from his prison cell bidding his guests to sit down to the supper provided and promising to join them later.

From this time on, however, there was to be no freedom for William Lownds. When he did finally leave Exeter in September, he did so in irons and under the escort of his erstwhile custodian.

He was being taken to Chester to stand trial, but on the way Mr Sarrell made a couple of major detours to conduct him on a kind of roving identity parade. He showed him first to three men at Oxford (using the name William Maule, Lownds had illegally obtained £7 worth of plate from a dealer in that city in August 1789) and then to four or five more potential witnesses the gaoler had arranged to meet in Derby – presumably the victims Lownds duped with forged bills of exchange following his robbery of the Warrington-Northwich mail.

Lownds claimed later that 'in most of the towns on the road', Mr Sarrell had brought people to look at him; and that the final indignity on this unusual tour of inspection was being told he had to pay his own travelling expenses.

Lownds continued to be 'made a public shew of', as he termed it, after his arrival at the Castle Gaol in Chester. The turnkey, Mr Thompson, explained that in encouraging as many witnesses as possible to identify the prisoner, he was merely carrying out the instructions of the Post Office. It was Thompson, too, who seems to have coined Lownds's nickname, invariably introducing him to visitors with the words, 'This is The Post Master: him which robbed the mail!'

While a steady procession of people trooped in to see the gaol's new-found celebrity, Lownds's own attentions were focussed firmly on getting out. And in an amazing four-month period, he concocted no fewer than five escape plans.

For the first, hatched out during November 1790, he needed the helping hands (or, rather, legs) of his wife Amy and the 'co-operation' of one of the warders. At the beginning of the month, freshly arrived from Exeter, Mrs Lownds visited her husband in gaol and, though closely examined on the orders of the gaoler, she managed to smuggle in two saws and a dozen files…bound in cloth and strapped to her thighs.

Lownds and two other prisoners were all set to break out on 26 November. They were to cut off their shackles, then attempt to hack their way through the window bars in one of the cells later that night, after having bribed the under-turnkey with a guinea to leave the cell door unlocked and to promise not to raise the alarm until morning. The iron grille defied all their efforts, however; and as dawn broke the three would-be escapers were forced to abandon their scheme, quickly dispose of their tools (they were handed to another inmate, a debtor named Booth, for safe-keeping) and return to their own cells before the under-turnkey reported his 'discovery' of their broken shackles to the gaoler.

In escape plot No. 2, Lownds sought to take advantage of the difficult circumstances under which the gaol was then operating. At this time Chester Castle, founded by William the Conqueror in 1069, was in the throes of its last great period of re-development; between 1788 and 1822 most of the surviving medieval buildings disappeared, to be replaced by the existing pillar-fronted shire hall (home, originally, to both local government administrators and the assizes, but now used mainly for crown court purposes) and, in its east wing, a new gaol and separate debtors' prison. New barracks, to maintain the castle's status as a garrison, were also included in the re-development scheme, designed in the Greek Revival style by noted Yorkshire architect Thomas Harrison (1744–1829), who also created the majestic Grosvenor Bridge over the River Dee nearby. Nowadays, only parts of the Agricola Tower, the Flag Tower, the Half-Moon Tower and a small section of the curtain wall of the inner bailey remain of the Norman fortifications.

The old county gaol was in the huge twin-towered main gatehouse, which stood near the site of the present Cheshire Regiment Museum. But long before 1790, when most of the buildings in the lower bailey were demolished, the gaol had been re-located on the east side of the castle. In his book, *Cheshire: Its Traditions and History*, Alfred Ingham presented this gaol-bird's-eye view of the castle lock-up.

[The] cells, or dungeons…were built in Saxon style with loopholes and gratings. At the main entrance was a high wall with a heavy oak and iron door bristling with nails, and of immense thickness, the whole having a forbidding and desolate appearance. Once inside, the poor wretch…could certainly abandon all hope of seeing the light of day again unless powerful interest was brought to bear in his favour. There was a hive of cells, narrow and contracted, and scarcely allowing of the poor prisoners stretching at length upon the damp and noisome ground. Of ventilation there was very little and the mortality amongst the prisoners was extremely great. Infection was frequently communicated to the inhabitants of the city with lamentable results. An inner room, generally on a level with the foundations, was the torture chamber, in which was a fireplace for heating the implements used. It was awful for prisoners to descend into these unknown depths. There was no loophole or grate.

That stark description almost certainly referred to the original gatehouse gaol. But when penal reformer John Howard made a series of visits to Chester Castle between 1774 and 1783, as part of his famous nationwide survey of prisons, he found the new accommodation little better.

Descending 39 steps into a dark passageway, he noted, 'No window; not a breath of fresh air: only two apertures (lately made) with grates in the ceiling into the pope's kitchen [the unlikely name given to the debtors' day-room] above.' It was on one side of this foul subterranean corridor that the main cells (Howard likened them to 'stalls') were ranged.

Six in number, they each measured 7½ft by 3ft, with an 8in by 4in opening above the door, and contained only a 'barrack-bedstead'.

Howard reported, 'In each of these are locked up at night, sometimes three or four felons. They pitch these dungeons two or three times a year; when I was in one of them, I ordered the door to be shut; and my situation brought to mind what I had heard about the *black hole* at Calcutta.'

In Cheshire's county gaol, as in similar institutions elsewhere, it was common, too, for untried prisoners to be lodged cheek by jowl with thieves and murderers in these underground chambers of horror; and, until a piece of Howard-inspired legislation of 1774, for innocents to be likewise detained after acquittal simply because they could not pay one of the numerous fees by which the gaoler was expected to earn his living.

Separate yards for felons and debtors had been formed by erecting a wooden partition down the middle of a small open court; but, said Howard, because of the 'high close pales', both sets of prisoners were 'deprived of the benefit of fresh air'. Off this court, down a flight of six steps, were two day-rooms in which the felons and debtors were also segregated–though in the felons' day-room, the so-called King's kitchen, men and women mingled freely (occasionally too freely, according to some accounts). The condemned cell was alongside the debtors' court.

Howard, whose report on the state of the nation's prisons was printed in Warrington by William Eyres, also discovered to his alarm that the gaol possessed neither infirmary nor bath.

Though the iniquities uncovered by Howard's researches led to some improvements, the indications are that conditions at the county gaol were substantially the same in Lownds's time there; clearly the need for a new prison had been recognised in the Castle re-modelling programme. The project was started in 1789 and took nine years to complete. Convict and other inmate labour was employed on the construction work... and it was in this little irony that Lownds saw his next opportunity to engineer his escape.

He first persuaded Charles Williamson, a fellow prisoner assigned to one of the work gangs, to fetch some clay from the building site and take impressions of the keys which the under-turnkey, negligent as well as corrupt, often apparently left on a stone near the door to the felons' yard. This done, Lownds then offered Williamson 10 guineas to take his chances and make a run for it on one of his work 'outings' and deliver the impressions to a locksmith friend of his in Wolverhampton. Again Williamson agreed and, about 11 December, he went successfully over the wall.

Unfortunately for Lownds, however, he had not chosen the brightest of allies; for Williamson, in discarding the distinctive yellow jacket that would have identified him as a convict, also left behind the key moulds in one of the pockets. Predictably, Williamson did not get far either: on 26 January 1791, he was re-taken and returned to the castle.

When, earlier the same month, Lownds had tried the old key ploy again, it was the amenable under-turnkey himself who took the impressions, thanks to another pay-off and a fresh supply of clay, both brought into the gaol by the ever faithful Amy. But once again it was to prove a costly failure.

For this plan, he enlisted the aid of a debtor called Peacock. Although certain parts of the gaol were set aside for felons and debtors, there were ample opportunities for them to consort with one another, especially during the twice-daily exercise periods in the castle yard and in the 'public hall', where visitors were received.

Peacock, using his visitor-son as the go-between, was to arrange for keys to be made from the impressions and also to hire two men to carry out the second stage of the operation. This involved a scaling-ladder which, at a pre-set time, was to be flung over the prison wall into the felons' yard where Lownds, having let himself out of his cell-block with the duplicate keys, would be waiting.

Phase one went smoothly enough; the impressions were duly smuggled out by the younger Peacock and the two 'getaway men', who had both spent time in the gaol up to their acquittal at the recent assizes, were recruited and put up at a nearby inn in readiness. But, after kicking their heels for a couple of weeks – during which all their expenses were paid by Lownds, through his wife – the outside help decided they wanted their 20 guinea fees in advance. Lownds, who had already settled the £29 5s 6d debt to secure old Peacock's release, refused their demands...and so, recounted chronicler Poole, 'this scheme was laid aside'.

Undeterred, Lownds switched to Plan D, a mass break-out through the gaoler's private quarters overlooking the felons' yard. It was timed for Saturday afternoon, 5 February, while two of the gaol's senior officers were away escorting a recently convicted transportee to the place of embarkation at Woolwich. In case they were frustrated and had to make their escape attempt at night, however, Lownds arranged for his wife to bring him a bottle of laudanum. This his guardian angel, the dependably disloyal under-turnkey, was to administer to the turnkey Thompson and also to the debtors (whose cells were directly above those of the felons) to ensure they all slept soundly, undisturbed by the activity going on down below.

As a sort of dry run, in fact, a quantity of the drug – Poole gave it as 42 drops – was given to Thompson in some wine 'to test the strength of his head'. Surprisingly, the turnkey does not appear to have suffered any immediate ill-effects from his overdose; though, in what was a strange sequel to this unusual tale, he died suddenly three weeks later. When word got out about his experiment with the laudanum, Lownds was suspected of poisoning the prison official, but a post mortem on the exhumed body failed to produce evidence to substantiate the charge.

As extra insurance, Amy also sent two loaded pistols to be delivered to her husband in a parcel labelled 'Tea and Sugar'. The servant girl she regularly employed to keep Lownds supplied with meat and other little luxuries, expressed doubts about the weight of the package to a neighbour, however, and the bag of tricks was exposed.

Despite the set-back, the escape plan went ahead. At about 3pm, with the under-turnkey turning a blind eye, Lownds and a group of other felons, who had been busy with their secret stockpile of saws and files, slipped out of their irons. Charles Williamson, back in favour after his recent botch-up with the key impressions, mounted the steps to the house part of the gaol – to all appearances still manacled – on the pretext of buying potatoes. When Thompson the turnkey answered his call, Williamson knocked him to the ground and threw off his shackles.

That was the signal for the others to rush the stairs; as he ran, Lownds shouted frantically to Williamson to grab the keys. But, once again, his henchman was a little slow on the uptake and Thompson, quickly recovering his wits, succeeded in throwing the keys through an open window into the castle yard below. There, alerted by the commotion inside, the gaoler's wife summoned the assistance of some of the more trustworthy 'trusties' and between them they were able to secure the outer doors before the felons could force their way through.

Thwarted at each devious turn, and with his court date looming ever nearer, Lownds now prepared for one last death-defying stunt. The aim, quite literally, was to go out with a bang. The idea: to blast open the outer door of the then unoccupied condemned cell with gunpowder. But the whole thing fizzled out when someone tipped off the gaoler.

As the Poole account explained, '...the felons hitherto in confederacy with Lownds, were not equal to such a daring outrage, and, by information, prevented the terrible event.'

There were no fireworks, either, when Lownds was eventually brought to trial; from the Poole testimony, it would appear that the hearing, on Monday 18 April 1791, was memorable only for an impassioned – and fairly eloquent – defence plea by the prisoner himself.

Lownds, indicted on several counts of mail robbery, all of which were deemed true bills by the grand jury, was convicted of attacking post-boy James Archer in the parish of Great Budworth on 11 March 1788, and stealing the bag containing the letters from Warrington bound for Northwich. He was charged in the name of Lewin and five other aliases (Clarke, Brown, Hutchinson, Maule and Hope) were also listed on the various indictments. But, if the court officials were confused about his true identity, the main prosecution witnesses had no doubt he was the culprit.

The post-boy Archer said Lownds had three times in the preceding two days approached him along the road on which the robbery took place, first to inquire about his travel schedule then, the next day, to offer him a guinea to let him hitch a ride to Northwich, finally claiming he had a letter for the boy to deliver. On each occasion, Archer said, he was suspicious and managed to fob the stranger off.

But some time between 4 and 5am on the 11th at a spot near the Wheatsheaf Inn at Antrobus (now re-named the Antrobus Arms) the same man ran up to him and, seizing his horse's bridle, ordered him to dismount. He was armed with a pistol and a club fashioned from a wooden stake with a nail through one end.

After hijacking Archer's horse, Lownds rode off towards Northwich; but only a short distance further on the animal pulled up at the roadside trough at which it was usually watered and stubbornly refused to go on. Before Archer and a local weaver, who had gone to the post-boy's assistance, could catch up with him, however, Lownds managed to grab the mail-bag and run off down a side-road.

Archer, it was revealed at the trial, had subsequently been dismissed by the Post Office and committed to the House of Correction at Middlewich for alleged involvement in another robbery of the mail he was carrying.

For even the most minor dereliction of duty, the post-boys risked the statutory sentence of one month's hard labour; at the start of their employment they were all issued with a printed caution, which warned of the consequences of such offences as giving lifts to unauthorised persons and loitering on the road, and which enjoined them not to 'wilfully mis-spend' their time.

Notice issued to post-boys in 1765 warning of the consequences of any dereliction of duty. By courtesy of HM Postmaster General.

CAUTION to POST-BOYS.

BY the Act of 5th of Geo. III. If any Post-Boy, or Rider, having taken any of His Majesty's Mails, or Bags of Letters, under his Care, to convey to the next Post Town or Stage, shall suffer any other Person (except a Guard) to ride on the Horse or Carriage, or shall Loiter on the Road, and wilfully misspend his Time, so as to retard the Arrival of the said Mails, or Bags of Letters, at the next Post Town or Stage.—Every such Offender shall, on Conviction before One Justice, be committed to the House of Correction, and confined to hard Labour for one Month. All Post-Boys and Riders are therefore desired to take Notice of this, and are hereby cautioned not to fail in the regular Performance of their Duty, otherwise they will most assuredly be punished as the Law directs. And it is hoped and requested, for the Benefit of public Correspondence, that all Persons, who may observe any Post-Boy or Rider, offending as aforesaid, will give immediate Notice to ___ *[signature]*
Surveyor of the General Post-Office, &c.

A carter who had been travelling the same road that morning said Lownds was the man who rode with him for part of the journey. And the Leeds merchant to whom Lownds tendered one of the bills stolen from Archer's bag, also recognised the prisoner; as did the merchant's clerk, who confirmed that the cloth Lownds bought with the forged bill in March 1788, was the same as that found at the defendant's home in Chesterfield and produced in court.

When the prosecution's case closed and the judge, the Chief Justice Edward Bearcroft, asked how his defence was to be conducted, Lownds, after some hesitation, took a piece of paper from his pocket and, in a voice that grew progressively more assured, read his prepared speech. It began, 'I, an unhappy prisoner, most humbly beg your Lordship and this jury, to take my most desperate case into consideration; desperate indeed to me, for I have been entirely deprived of making any defence for my safety; likewise very unjust advantages have been taken against me, contrary I think to law and justice.'

He denied he had ever been in many of the places in which he was accused of committing crimes and claimed the witnesses had perjured themselves for the reward money. He declared, sanctimoniously, 'The depravity of man is such, they will swear anything for money.'

After what Poole described as 'a very short consultation', however, the jury found him guilty. Mr Justice Bearcroft told him, 'You have been convicted upon as clear a chain of evidence as ever appeared in a court of justice, and of a crime so dreadful in its consequences that the legislature has very wisely thought fit to punish it with loss of life. For if it was otherwise, there would be an end to all commerce. The property of individuals, as well as of the public, must be protected.'

The judge ruled that, after the execution, Lownds's body should be gibbeted, a prospect which seemed to have an even greater effect on the prisoner.

The hanging was fixed for Thursday 21 April. On the Tuesday, Amy visited her husband in gaol for the last time and the following evening he wrote asking her to meet him at the place of execution.

She arrived at Boughton the next day accompanied by Lownds's brother and, as the cart carrying the condemned man halted before the gallows, they joined him and the officiating clergyman in prayers. It was with great difficulty that they eventually separated, but at last Lownds was left alone in the cart with the noose around his neck.

After standing silently for a short while, he finally dropped his handkerchief, the traditional signal that he was ready. The next second the cart lurched forward and the one-time dance tutor whose nifty footwork had kept the authorities on the hop for so long was left doing a mid-air jig of death.

The next day Lownds's body was hung in chains on Helsby Hill. It was some 10 miles as the crow flies from the place where he robbed the Warrington-Northwich mail, but the gibbet site had been chosen for maximum impact. As Poole explained, 'From whence it may be conspicuously seen, and, by means of glasses, is visible to the whole county [and] most part of Lancashire, Flintshire, Denbighshire, Shropshire, Derbyshire &c.'

Part Two: The second-class mail-robbers

As highwaymen went, few – if any – were hanged higher than William Lownds. But the lesson the dead 'Master' was intended to impart to the travelling public had no discouraging effect on James Price and Thomas Brown, two willing pupils who enrolled in the school of mail-robbery almost in the shadow of his hilltop perch.

Indeed, in taking this particular criminal path, they were following in Lownds's horse-tracks exactly. For their hold-up of a post-boy two miles away at Dunham-on-the-Hill in

January 1796 was a repeat of one of the crimes Lownds had committed seven years before. Compared to The Post Master, however, Price and Brown were very much second-class mail-robbers…and their first venture into the business was also their last.

The pair had known each other for about two years but had only teamed up together the previous month. Price, barely 20 when he went to the scaffold, had begun his lawless ways at the age of 15 when he fell in with a gang of thieves and pickpockets in his home town of Birmingham. Between December 1791, and the early months of 1793, in company with other members of the gang, he took part in a series of raids on houses, warehouses and shops in the Midlands.

In March 1792 at Stafford Assizes, Price, then aged about 16, and an older man were tried for stealing shoes from a shop in Wolverhampton. But he was found not guilty in what was the first in a remarkable run of court appearances in which he faced no fewer than five capital charges in the space of three and a half years…and got off on each occasion.

At Nottingham Assizes in March 1793, he was again acquitted, while a second man was convicted and only narrowly escaped the gallows, after they had been charged with breaking into a draper's shop in the city.

It was around this time that Price seems to have first tried his hand at picking pockets, eventually abandoning the burglary side of the gang's business for this more artful form of thieving. Working usually with one or two accomplices, he would travel miles to mingle with the crowds at fairs and race-meetings and turn a pretty penny lifting pocket-books and purses.

For the next three years, he was said to have confessed later, he did the rounds of most major fairgrounds and race-tracks in 10 counties, an area of operations stretching from Hereford to Preston, from North Wales to the Wash. Price, apparently, had a natural talent for this sort of work and quickly became so skilled at the dipper's art that, according to Brown, 'very few could exceed his dexterity'.

During this period he was arrested three times and tried for picking pockets, technically a capital offence until 1808. But not even these alarming experiences could deflect him from his chosen profession. The first occurred in August 1793, when he and his partner, David Jones, appeared at Worcester Assizes, following incidents at Bromsgrove fair. Jones was sentenced to transportation; but the case against Price was thrown out by the jury and he was discharged.

His next close call appears to have happened early in 1794 at Shrewsbury Assizes; this time he was found guilty of picking the pocket of a man at Drayton fair but evaded punishment (of the judicial sort, at any rate) by volunteering for military service. England was at that time at war with France and, taking advantage of this peculiar legal escape clause, Price, using the assumed name of Thomas Hillman, agreed to enlist in Lord Fielding's Regiment. But he was to serve King and country only briefly, deserting at the first opportunity.

During the winter of 1794–95, he lived in Manchester with several criminal associates, and from his new North West base he went on pocket-picking forays in various parts of the country. It was during this period, too, that Price and Brown became acquainted, meeting on at least two occasions while both men were going about their respective (unlawful) business on the fairground circuit. But it was to be another 12 months before they decided to go into partnership together.

Meanwhile, Price would stand trial for a fifth time. In August 1795, at Hereford Assizes he was charged in the name of Thomas Wood with picking pockets at Wigmore fair. But the evidence was insufficient and he was released once more.

He had another narrow squeak in November 1795, after he and James Berry had picked a man's pocket at Manchester Dirt Fair and stolen a draft for £144 5s 0d. When, in a curious echo of the Edward Miles case a few years earlier (see Chapter Three), Berry attempted to negotiate the money order at a silversmith's in Liverpool, he was arrested. Price, who had been on watch outside the shop, got away while Berry went for trial at the following spring assizes in Lancaster, where he was convicted and received the death penalty

It was a month later, at Christmas 1795, that Price cemented his ill-fated friendship with Brown, after the two met up again in Birmingham. The idea of joining forces to raise some fresh funds was particularly attractive to Brown, for whom a recent spell in gaol, and the means of securing his release, had left him desperately short of money. And for the former big-time horse dealer, this was a situation in which he had not found himself for some considerable time...as Price was to learn as he got to know his new partner better.

Brown, aged 26, was born Thomas Smallman a few miles from Willenhall, near Wolverhampton. He was a sawyer by trade, having been bound apprentice by an uncle. But before he was 20 he had become a 'hawker of Manchester and Birmingham goods', touring the fairgrounds of the Midlands and the North in a caravan.

Then he started buying and selling horses; at first his dealings seem to have been strictly above board, but in 1792 an accidental meeting – and a revealing conversation – with the leader of a gang of rustlers and receivers persuaded him that, while honesty may be the best policy, it was not necessarily the most profitable. And over the next three years or so, aided by a hand-picked band of helpers, he boosted his earnings considerably from the sale of stolen horses. He was said to have admitted later that the transactions brought in at least £1,000, a small fortune in 18th century terms.

In June 1790, in Manchester, Brown had married a girl from Knutsford whose step-brother, John Hewitt (alias Smith and, occasionally, Jones), was one of the members of his gang. Like Brown and Price, Hewitt was also to finish up swinging from the end of a rope in the Spring of 1796; he was executed, along with Price's old thieving mate Berry, at Lancaster for horse-stealing. But up to the end of 1795, he and Brown prospered.

From December 1793 to the following May, the Browns lived in the ancient Cheshire parish of Over, now a suburb of Winsford; and while he peddled horse-flesh, stolen mainly from farms around the county, she worked at keeping her husband's hardware business going.

In the middle of 1794, still with Hewitt in tow, they moved to Royston in Hertfordshire, where Brown's horse-stealing activities (by now he was operating successfully in both legitimate and black markets, it seems) expanded to such an extent that he eventually employed a couple of stable hands, kept a gig and built up a substantial reputation in the community.

The techniques of the horse racketeers were revealed by Brown in a confession he was said to have dictated to the Reverend Peploe Ward, Chaplain of Chester Castle Gaol, and reproduced in a comprehensive account of the Price-Brown case published after the trial by Mr Edmund Monk, proprietor and printer of the *Chester Courant*.

Brown said it was usual for the thief and the receiver to settle on the target and draw up plans for the snatch between them. The former would then take a surreptitious look at the animal shortly beforehand to confirm its worth and ensure it was properly shod and fit to travel. After the raid, the stolen horse was always delivered by side-roads to the receiver, who generally paid about a third of its value to the thief.

Stolen horses were difficult to track down, said Brown, because they were 'mostly lodged in secrecy, and in the hands of men of apparent good character'. The most effective way of combating the problem, he offered helpfully, was to keep a regular watch on the premises of suspected dealers and, in particular, to 'examine...what they style their sick-stables'.

Receivers not in at the planning stage of the operation always inquired as to where the horse had been stolen to avoid an accidental meeting with its owner later. And where a stolen animal had been re-sold to an unsuspecting buyer at a particularly good price, the fence would often let the rustlers know the address of its new owner so that it might be re-taken and the whole lucrative process could begin all over again. Some thoroughbreds changed hands several times in this manner.

The gang invariably disposed of the horses at one of the many traditional livestock fairs, which were held regularly in towns and cities throughout the country. There the racketeers would first establish ownership – to safeguard their interests should anything go wrong later – by a simple ruse. A formal registration procedure, involving an official toll-book, existed at the fairs to discourage dishonest trading; but there was a way of circumventing the system.

As Brown explained, 'The receivers of stolen horses frequently with two of the gang, go to the toll-book, on their entrance into a fair; when the receiver, the apparent purchaser, pays down the money, the accomplice receives it as the seller, and the other man is the voucher as to the character and credit of the seller. That is done to protect the receiver, if the horses should happen to be claimed by their owners.'

Brown also disclosed that 'in the traffic of horses, a large quantity of forged five-guinea country bank notes are circulated, as well as a considerable quantity of base coin'. But while he admitted he had been closely acquainted with many counterfeiters, he denied any personal involvement in the dud money racket. Price, on the other hand, in his alleged confession, also taken down by the Revd Ward and included in Monk's case study, claimed that during 1793 and 1794 his erstwhile partner had 'passed a great number of forged Leicester and Newcastle upon Tyne five-guinea bills', which he had purchased for 10s 6d each – one-tenth of their face value.

It was not horses, counterfeit money or pockets that Price and Brown picked on as the basis for their new working relationship, however. Having pooled their meagre resources to obtain pistols from a gunsmith on Snow Hill, Birmingham, they decided to take a shot at highway robbery. But it was a move doomed to failure from the start.

In early January 1796, after being forced for various reasons to abort plans to hit targets at Bromsgrove and Droitwich, they headed north. First they were to see what pickings could be had at Preston fair; then they intended to hold up the Warrington-Chester mail and after that, possibly, the Birmingham mail as well.

At the fair, the dab-handed Price proved he had lost none of his old touch by lifting a pocket-book containing a five-guinea bill and a purse with three guineas and some silver in it. And when the two friends arrived in Manchester later, Brown made his contribution to their joint funds by selling his horse (a six-year-old grey mare he had stolen from outside Birmingham on the way up) to the landlord of the Bear Inn for eight guineas. They stayed at the inn (it stood opposite the old infirmary in what is now Piccadilly) for about a week before making their mail-robbery move.

On Monday 18 January, they took the turnpike road to Warrington, Brown riding a chestnut mare stolen from a field on the outskirts of Manchester, and Price mounted on a cropped bay he had bought for eight guineas from a corn-factor in the city earlier in the day. Reaching Warrington at about 7 o'clock the next morning, they split up, Price stopping for refreshment at the Bridge Inn (now demolished) at Bridge Foot and Brown continuing on to Daresbury, where he breakfasted at the Ring o' Bells beside the Warrington-Chester road.

They met up in mid-morning near Preston-on-the-Hill; but, to avoid suspicion, they separated again until, shortly after noon, they arrived at the Nag's Head at Bridge Trafford, about a mile further on from the spot where they had determined to attack the post-boy. After lunch, Brown sent for the local blacksmith to have his mare re-shod and gave instructions, rather unwisely, under the circumstances, that the fore-feet should be fitted with special double-channelled shoes…a distinctive 'tread pattern' that would leave some clearly recognisable tracks at the robbery scene later.

The two of them left the Nag's Head at 4.30 in the afternoon to go first to Tarvin, from where, when it got dark, they would set off for Dunham-on-the-Hill (now more usually abbreviated to Dunham Hill). After their earlier concern about being seen together, they now seem to have abandoned all caution. On the way to Tarvin they asked at least two people for directions and were observed by a third person, while on the return journey a gate-keeper made a particular note of their appearance after they had galloped past his toll-bar without paying. All four witnesses would give evidence against them at their trial.

At about 8.30pm, three-quarters of a mile on the Chester side of Dunham Hill on the Warrington-Chester road, post-boy Peter Yoxall, aged 15, came upon two men riding up ahead. As he attempted to pass between them, they turned their horses into him. With the taller of the two (Brown) waving what he was to describe in court as a 'smallish bright pistol' under his nose and threatening to blow his brains out, he was made to dismount and led into a field off Morley Lane. There, out of consideration for his health, apparently, he was placed on his upturned saddle; it was still warm from his horse and would, therefore, 'secure him from catching cold', Brown explained later. He was tied to a tree, with his feet bound inside one of his leather mail-bags and his hat pulled down over his eyes.

The highwaymen were both masked: Brown had a handkerchief covering the lower half of his face, while Price's features were similarly hidden beneath a piece cut from an old horse-blanket. But it was a bright moonlit night and Yoxall had seen enough to be able later to give his employers accurate descriptions of his attackers. He also gave them another important clue: as his legs were being buckled together with a coat-strap, he had complained to the bigger man that it was too tight and was hurting him. But the man did not appear to hear him. Brown, it emerged later, was deaf.

After selecting the most valuable items from the mail-bags, including two bills, one for £150 and the other for £8, and a little over £1 in cash, the robbers left, Price warning the post-boy that two guards had been posted to watch him and that, if he moved, they would 'cut off his arm'. It was an hour-and-a-half before he broke loose and reported the incident to the parish constable at nearby Mickle Trafford.

Price and Brown, meanwhile, were making for Birmingham, where they eventually arrived at about eight 'clock on the night of Wednesday 20 January, after a gruelling journey that had taken in brief stops at inns at Tarporley, Nantwich, Woore and Wolverhampton. They rode hard and their hectic progress did not go unnoticed; at one point, around three in the morning of the 20th, they put up their horses at the Swan Inn at Woore and collapsed exhausted in the stable. For the final part of the trip, from Wolverhampton to Birmingham, they took the post-chaise, leaving instructions for their tired-out mounts to be delivered later to stables in Livery Street, Birmingham.

News of the Dunham robbery was also travelling fast; and soon descriptions of the two wanted men were circulating. The Post Office hand-bills stated,

One…is about eighteen or twenty years of age, five feet four or five inches high, slender made, short light-coloured hair, long thin smooth face; wore a light-coloured ash coat, striped green Manchester waistcoat, boots and long-necked spurs, round hat, has a drab-coloured top-coat buckled to the crupper of his saddle; rode a cropt dark-bay or brown horse…

The other man is about twenty-five or thirty-five years of age, five feet seven or eight inches high, stout made, black short hair powdered…pitted with the small-pox, and pimpled face; had on a black coat, and a kind of half pantaloons made of thickset…boots and long-necked spurs, round hat, had an ash-coloured top-coat, rode a light chestnut blood mare…(shod) on her fore-feet with double groved or channeled (*sic*) shoes.

But it was the lure of the obligatory £200 reward, attached to the bottom of the bills, that eventually led to the capture of the two robbers. Brown had entrusted the job of collecting their horses from Livery Street to a carter friend, but the man's brother learned of the arrangement; and on Friday 22 January, having first extracted a promise of payment for the information, he told Joseph Tart, Constable of Aston, of the whereabouts of the hunted men.

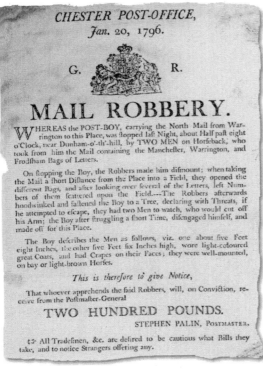

CHESTER POST-OFFICE,
Jan. 20, 1796.

G.   R.

MAIL ROBBERY.

WHEREAS the POST-BOY, carrying the North Mail from Warrington to this Place, was stopped last Night, about Half past eight
o'Clock, near Dunham-o'-th'-hill, by TWO MEN on Horseback, who
took from him the Mail containing the Manchester, Warrington, and
Frodsham Bags of Letters.

On stopping the Boy, the Robbers made him dismount; when taking
the Mail a short Distance from the Place into a Field, they opened the
different Bags, and after looking over several of the Letters, left Numbers of them scattered upon the Field.---The Robbers afterwards
hoodwinked and fastened the Boy to a Tree, declaring with Threats, if
he attempted to escape, they had two Men to watch, who would cut off
his Arm; the Boy after struggling a short Time, disengaged himself, and
made off for this Place.

The Boy describes the Men as follows, viz. one about five Feet
eight Inches, the other five Feet six Inches high, wore light-coloured
great Coats, and had Crapes on their Faces; they were well-mounted,
on bay or light-brown Horses.

This is therefore to give Notice,

That whoever apprehends the said Robbers, will, on Conviction, receive from the Postmaster-General

TWO HUNDRED POUNDS.

STEPHEN PALIN, Postmaster.

☞ All Tradesmen, &c. are desired to be cautious what Bills they
take, and to notice Strangers offering any.

Reward notice issued by Chester Post Office in the hunt for the two men who robbed the post-boy at Dunham Hill on the evening of 19 January 1796.

According to the Monk account, the tip-off took Tart and his son, William, to a public house at Gosta Green, where they found Price and Brown playing cards with two other men in the parlour. They were arrested and handcuffed without a struggle, despite the fact that Price had no fewer than three loaded pistols concealed in various pockets at the time. Brown, too, had been well armed; but he had left his pair of loaded handguns in his room.

It was, said Monk, a stroke of providence – 'otherwise he certainly should have shot Tart, having resolved never to be apprehended by anyone'.

One of the weapons Peter Yoxall later identified as the 'smallish bright pistol' Brown had used in the hold-up.

The two prisoners spent their first few days in custody at the constable's house. And it was there, on 26 January, that the landlord of the Nag's Head and the smith who had fitted the special double-grooved shoes on Brown's horse, confirmed that they were the two men who had been in Bridge Trafford on the afternoon of the mail robbery. They identified Price straight away but, at first, they had some difficulty in placing Brown who, it appeared, had attempted to disguise his face by wearing rouge. It was only when Tart ordered him to wash off the colouring that the witnesses were able to say positively that he was the other man.

All told, 20 people who noted the progress of the prisoners on their near-100 mile journey from Manchester to Birmingham gave evidence to that effect when, on 6 April

1796, James Price and Thomas Brown were tried before Mr Justice Burton at Chester Assizes.

In a statement made to a magistrate in Birmingham and read to the jury by the Attorney-General, Mr Leycester, Brown claimed he was a surgeon and came from London. He declared he did not know Price; he said the two of them had met by accident on 19 January, the day of the mail robbery, on the road between Warrington and Bridge Trafford.

In court Price made a similar claim; he explained that the two travellers had struck up a conversation and, discovering they were both going to Birmingham, had agreed to keep each other company the rest of the way. He had been in Manchester selling hardware, he said. And both defendants insisted they knew nothing about the robbery.

As was the usual practice, the jury sat through a number of trials before retiring to consider the evidence; consequently Price and Brown had some time to wait before the guilty verdict was announced. It was not until Saturday 9 April, that they were ushered back into the crowded courtroom to hear the judge pass sentence of death on them.

For reasons undisclosed, their executions were also delayed. During his extended confinement, Brown seems to have suffered some feelings of remorse and got a lot of his thieving activities off his chest, even offering to reveal the possible whereabouts of all the stolen horses he had ever handled should their rightful owners choose to visit him in Chester Castle Gaol. Whether anyone took up his invitation is not recorded.

Monk also claimed that Brown composed his own epitaph while languishing in prison. On the wall of his cell, underneath a crudely drawn coffin complete with corpse, he was said to have written,

Behold the corpse within the coffin lies,
With stretch'd out limbs and closed eyes;
But ah, poor Brown! No coffin thou shalt have,
Nor yet a shroud, nor yet a peaceful grave.
Prisoners all a warning by me take,
Repent in time, before it is too late;
Repent in time, leave off your thieving ways,
Then thou shall all see happier days.

The two feckless highwaymen were executed on Saturday 30 April, three weeks after conviction, at Boughton. The old gallows, though by then obsolete, still stood on the high embankment overlooking the River Dee five years after being replaced by a new structure on the opposite side of the road. The latter had been erected 'temporarily' in apparent anticipation of the early reform of the hanging laws but, wearily, it was to remain in regular use until 1801.

Illustrations from the contemporary account of the Dunham Hill robbery showing (above) the post-boy watching helplessly as the two robbers rifle his bags and (left) the 'Road the mail robbers went' and the double gibbet that was to be their final destination. From an original document in the archives of the Wariington Library.

Price and Brown were hanged side by side; afterwards their bodies were suspended in similar fashion on a gibbet by the Warrington-Chester road at Trafford Green, about two miles from the robbery spot. The area was enclosed in 1820 and, though the remnants of the scaffold and its occupants were removed at the same time, the place where it stood (believed to be the piece of land opposite the end of the little road that leads to Plemstall Church) continued to be known locally as Gibbet Field. It is said that a robin's nest was found inside Price's skull.

Though the rapidly expanding network of coach routes brought economy, speed and safety to the business of delivering the mail, post-boys were still being exposed to the perils of the highway in Cheshire up to the coming of the railways. For it was not until 1837 that the county's last remaining relay of post-horses – they ran between Chester and Northwich – was finally turned out to grass.

By that time even the mail-coaches were beginning to be replaced by trains on some of the main inter-urban routes; Cheshire's first railway, the Grand Junction line connecting Warrington with Birmingham, via Crewe, was opened the same year.

And stealing from the Post Office was no longer a hanging matter. It had been expunged from the book of capital offences earlier in the decade, along with half a dozen or so other heinous crimes like rick-burning and sacrilege.

5

Losers in a 'Dreadful' Gamble

> On Saturday week, one of those awful scenes which consigns the perpetrator of crime to a death of ignominy, was exhibited at the east front of the city gaol. The unhappy victim was Thomas Brierley, who with two others... was convicted at the last assizes for highway robbery...There was a great aggravation in the crime, from the violence that was used; but Brierley was manifestly the most daring and sanguinary...

Manchester Mercury, 24 September 1822

SOLDIERS returning from military service overseas swelled the ranks of the lawless in the crime-dogged decade-and-a-half following the end of the Napoleonic Wars. Among the criminals who lost their lives battling against the forces of law and order in Cheshire in those post-war years, was at least one ex-Army man. Thomas Brierley fought against the French in Spain, was wounded in two historic battles...and met his Waterloo in a wheat field just outside Congleton.

By his own account his army record was honourable; during the Peninsular War (1808-1814) he was wounded in the temple at the Battle of Albuera in south-west Spain (16 May 1811) and again during the Siege of Bajadoz (March–April 1812). But he was one of the lucky ones; a great many of his comrades did not survive what were two of the bloodiest engagements of the whole campaign. Of the 6,000 British troops who took part in the former, 4,500 were either killed or wounded in the fierce hand-to-hand combat, while the Duke of Wellington's recapture of the key fortress on the Spain-Portugal border almost a year later came at a cost of 5,000 British casualties.

Brierley was under arms for nine years and – a claim that would go unchallenged in court later – maintained that he 'had a good character in [his] regiment'.

His movements immediately after the war are unknown; but at some point he got a job as a dyer for what was described in the *Chester Chronicle* as 'a very respectable concern' in his home city of Manchester. In comparison to his adventures as an enlisted man, he must have found the work dull and uninteresting...and clearly felt the need to put some excitement back into his life.

Some time in 1821 his thirst for action seems to have landed him in gaol; according to the same *Chronicle* report, he served six months (probably in Manchester's New Bailey prison) after being convicted of 'a felony'. Then, in the summer of 1822, the restless ex-soldier and a couple of friends sallied forth in search of fresh opportunities in the wealthy, farming region of Cheshire, even then very much a land of milk and money.

The 34-year-old Brierley and his two pals, Robert Ellis and Samuel Rowe (all of whom were described as 'labourers' in the court files), met up at a lodging house in Congleton on Saturday 27 July. Ellis also claimed to have served in the army, for eight years; and, while he volunteered no further information about his service record, it is possible that he and Brierley fought together in the Napoleonic Wars. When they arrived at 'the widow Britain's house' that day they might not have had robbery in mind, particularly as Ellis had his wife in tow. But the idea could well have presented itself when another guest in the house, William June, a pedlar from Manchester, gave them a shilling from his expensive-looking red leather pocket-book to buy themselves a meal and accidentally dropped a sovereign on the floor. Brierley, at least, saw it fall and noticed it was not the only gold piece in the pedlar's purse.

June, who had booked into the lodging house the day after the others, also had a military background: he had served in the Marines before being pensioned off. Now he had a stall at Manchester market, though what he sold is not recorded. It was also alleged that he had another lucrative sideline...as a pick-pocket.

In depositions filed with the case papers in the National Archives, Brierley, Ellis and Rowe all insisted that June persuaded them to stay in Congleton until the following Tuesday (30 July) when, on his way home to Manchester, he planned to stop off at Knutsford Races. Brierley stated, '[June] said he did not fear but that he could make £50 at any races and would give us a share of it, for he could get it out of any person's pocket.' Rowe's version was that June had boasted, 'I can make £40 or £50 a day and these are the hands (holding out his own hands) that can do it'. In his deposition, Ellis put the figure at £70.

The three friends agreed to accompany June to Knutsford and, together with Mrs Ellis, they all set off around 7.30 on that Tuesday morning. Though the evidence is far from clear on the point, it seems they took the northbound road out of town (the route of the present A34); then, after about two miles, they headed west and struck out across country. The short-cut was Brierley's idea, June would say later. He went along with it not realising he was being led into a trap. In what was described as 'a little bye-lane' the travellers came upon the New Pool public house and June, who was not feeling too well, apparently, decided to stop for a pint of ale (part of the pub's original frontage is still discernible in the large private residence that was later built on the site in what is now Giantswood Lane, Somerford Booths).

Once recovered, and refreshed, he and his travelling companions continued on their way. It was now a little before 9am. They had gone only a short way around a bend in the road, however, when Brierley gave the signal and the three men fell upon the startled hawker. He was pushed into the roadside hedge, then dragged into the ditch beneath, where Rowe held him down and Brierley tore open his waistcoat and snatched his pocket-book. How much money it contained would later be disputed by the three robbers; and

June himself doesn't seem to have been entirely sure. The official indictment, presumably based on his information, lists 'ten sovereigns, 10 sixpences, four half-crowns [and] one crown piece' (and then confuses the issue still further by computing that as '£10 10s in monies'); while in court later June would swear only to the 10 sovereigns.

This large private residence was built around the remnants of the old New Pool pub at Somerford Booths. After stopping for refreshment there in July 1822, Manchester pedlar William June was attacked and robbed by his three travelling companions just beyond the bend in this photograph.

It was at this point that the anonymous Mrs Ellis played what June would later accept was her only part in the robbery, urging the three men to 'Run, lads, run!' With their booty secured, Brierley, Ellis and Rowe duly took to their heels and disappeared in the direction of Congleton, leaving the woman behind. She was taken by June back to the New Pool pub and remained in his custody while a concerted effort was made to hunt down the robbers.

It began when farmer John Durbar, travelling on horseback from his home in Kermincham to Congleton, overtook June as he escorted his reluctant charge to the New Pool and learned what had just happened. As it was still only about 9.30am, he realised the robbers could not be far away, so he set off in pursuit. Meanwhile, a messenger was on his way to fetch Somerford's constable Richard Stanyer. He, in turn, deputised a local farm labourer, David Hall, and they were also quickly on the robbers' trail.

The search ended less than a mile away on the Somerford Booths Hall estate of Charles Watkin John Shakerley Esq., Lord of the Manors of Somerford and Congleton, former Sheriff of Chester (1791) and head of one of Cheshire's oldest and most respected families whose lineage stretches back to pre-Conquest times. In what was an amazing climax to the morning's drama, the three pursuers converged at Radnor Bridge, over the River Dane, where two men had been spotted running into the parkland of the 17th-century manor house. The posse was enlarged to five when farmer John Hulme and his servant Randle Bradbury, who had first seen the fleeing men and raised the alarm, also arrived to join in the round-up.

Somerford Booths Hall, the 17th-century manor house built on the north bank of the River Dane near Radnor Bridge, where, in the estate parkland, the search for the three highway robbers had its dramatic ending.

Bradbury eventually caught Rowe, who cried out, 'I haven't got the money. The other man in the wood has it.' This proved to be Ellis, who, seeing that he was outnumbered, sensibly decided to give himself up. All he had of June's money, however, was a single sovereign, which he had hidden in the lining of his coat.

In the subsequent search of the surrounding estate land, Constable Stanyer discovered Brierley who, he would say later, was in a wheat field 'lying down in a wet ditch, flat on his belly'. His pockets were turned out but no money was found on him. Constable Stanyer's assistant, Hall, returned to the field later and found June's red leather pocket-book, but the rest of the stolen cash was never recovered.

The three prisoners were taken to the 'Lock-up House' in Congleton (actually dungeons, or temporary holding cells, in the basement of the Town Hall in High Street). On the way there, Ellis was alleged to have told another constable, Richard Davenport, that June 'had no business showing them the money, for money was very tempting'.

At the Chester Summer Assizes, beginning on 26 August 1822, Brierley, Ellis and Rowe all pleaded not guilty to assault and highway robbery. Prosecutor June, who gave his address as 34, Withy Grove, Manchester, told the court how he had treated the three men to a meal at the Congleton lodging house. 'I gave them a shilling,' he was quoted as saying in the *Chester Chronicle*'s trial report of 30 August, 'as they complained of being short of money. I said it was a pity anyone should starve for want of meat.' As he reached in his pocket-book, he dropped a sovereign on the floor, which, he said, 'Brierley saw'.

He then recalled the moment on the journey to Knutsford when he realised he was going to be robbed, 'About 300 or 400 yards from the [New Pool] public house, Brierley said "Now's the time" to the other two men and I looked round to see what was the matter, when Brierley suddenly seized me by the throat, and I fell back on the hedge-cop. He held one hand over my mouth. Rowe then came up and kicked me in the stomach violently several times. Brierley then took the pocket-book from my side pocket and said "Now

I have it". After Rowe had seized me, Brierley said "Kill him, kill him, for if we are taken we shall all be hung". Rowe then drew a knife from his right-hand waistcoat pocket and opened it, as I lay in the ditch.'

When he saw the knife, June said he 'gave a start' and screamed, 'Murder! If you have robbed me, spare my life.' He admitted, however, that Rowe made no move to hurt him with the blade. In court he unhesitatingly identified the three men as his attackers.

In their preliminary examinations, conducted by Congleton magistrate Holland Watson, Brierley and Ellis had admitted their involvement in the robbery. Brierley conceded that he had grabbed the pocket-book after Ellis had pushed June over and Rowe had held him down. Ellis, in his statement to the magistrate, agreed with that version of events. But Rowe, who said he had known William June 'several years', made it look as if Brierley and Ellis had committed the robbery while he simply looked on.

As to the amount of money in the pocket-book, Brierley deposed that he 'found no more than two sovereigns and some silver'. Rowe said Brierley had told him the same thing.

All three were found guilty – 'on evidence that could not be questioned', said the Judge, the Honourable Charles Warren – and sentenced to death. Warren, at that time Chester's Chief Justice, told them, '[The] law has provided that in cases like yours, the punishment should be the severest that can be passed by an earthly tribunal.' Rowe, in particular, 'seemed deeply affected,' the *Chronicle* reported.

At this point, the Prosecutor, June, approached the bench. After requesting the return of a sovereign which, he said, had been seized as evidence by a constable (the coin found on Ellis, presumably, and no doubt handed to officer Stanyer), he looked up at the Judge, who was sitting with Mr Justice Marshall, and commented, 'I hope, Gentlemen, you'll not take the men's lives. Let them be transported and have time to prepare for another world.'

Mr Justice Warren dismissed him, apparently, with an impatient 'Very well, very well' – but later went some way towards acceding to the robbery victim's plea. It is evident from contemporary Press reports that it was normal practice at this time for the presiding judges to review the cases of at least some of the capital convicts in private after the close of court business and announce their findings 'before they left the city' (as the local papers usually put it). On this occasion Judges Warren and Marshall reprieved Ellis and Rowe and their sentences were commuted to transportation for life. But Brierley, they announced, would be 'left for execution'.

When 'several most respectable Chester gentlemen' (in the words of the *Chester Chronicle*) subsequently raised a petition to try to save the condemned man, Judge Warren wrote them a letter in which, referring to the imposition of the death penalty, he pointed out that there was 'no part of the duty cast on me as a Judge which I exercise with greater reluctance'. And he explained, 'Mr Justice Marshall and myself very fully considered the case of Thomas Brierley and of the two others convicted together with him…we thought it was a case of aggravated criminality, and that the unfortunate man now left for execution was the foremost, and worst, of the three. After having given the greatest attention to the grounds of the present application, I very much regret that I cannot see sufficient cause to alter my opinion of the propriety of the sentence which has been passed.'

Chester's notorious hangman Samuel Burrows put the sentence into effect on Saturday 14 September 1822. Thomas Brierley was ushered into 'the world of spirits' loaded down with a heavy pair of leg irons – 'for the purpose of accelerating his death, Brierley being but a short man,' as the *Chronicle* felt the need to explain (20 April). Even so, his body was 'much convulsed for about a minute and a half after being turned off, when all motion ceased'. In the same meticulously detailed vein, the paper continued, 'Convulsive struggles again ensued – the hands were closely gripped – the chest heaved several times, and the knees were bent upwards.'

The length of time it took Brierley to die caused a not-untypical disagreement between the two city newspapers. The *Chester Courant*, which never missed an opportunity to deride hangman Burrows, commented, 'Whether the rope had not been properly adjusted, or from whatever cause we know not, but the malefactor was agonised for some considerable time – his convulsive motion did not cease for at least four minutes.'

According to the *Chronicle*, however, it was all over in less than three minutes (which seems to have been about the norm on these far-from-normal occasions) and obviously felt Burrows could not be faulted. 'The executioner,' said the paper as if responding to its rival's interpretation of events published three days earlier, 'gave a fall to the rope of at least 20 inches, previously fixing, as he always does, the end of the noose in the nape, or back part, of the neck,'

On his arrival at the City Gaol, Brierley had told officials there that 'June had sworn falsely against him'. He repeated his claim that the pocket-book had contained only two sovereigns and some silver and denied he had ever urged Rowe to kill the pedlar or said anything about being 'taken [up] and hung'. When the *Chronicle* dispatched a representative to the Castle to quiz Brierley's two accomplices on the issue, he reported back that both men also denied that any such words were spoken or that anyone had threatened June with a knife.

Before shuffling off to his death, Brierley was heard to say to the City Gaol officials, 'It was a hard thing for the Judge to pick from three of us; but it's all very well, for the Lord has thought proper to save my soul. If I had lived longer and gone on in the same way, I would most likely have gone to hell.'

Finally, the *Chronicle* disclosed that, for commendably humanitarian reasons, it had been withholding one piece of information about Brierley. The paper explained, 'It was not generally known that some time ago, he was convicted at the Manchester [New] Bailey of a Felony and received six months' imprisonment. We did not mention this before, being fearful that, had any hopes been entertained of saving him, this fact may have thwarted all expectations.'

Born in Salford, where his mother still lived, Brierley, who had a brother living in Wilmslow, had 'spent a most abandoned life for several years,' said the *Chronicle*.

His partners in crime, Rowe and Ellis, were to be transported 'beyond the Seas for the Term of their Natural Lives' (in the words of the official Home Office orders). But first, it appears, they had to spend time on the notorious 'hulks', the old worn-out warships moored on the River Thames and at the south coast naval ports that had been converted into floating prisons when transportation to America ended in 1775. For, as the same Home Office records confirm, it wasn't until 22 April 1823, that, together with 169 other convicts, they finally embarked on the transport ship *Ocean* bound for New South Wales. Ellis, the *Chronicle* had noted somewhat unnecessarily, had 'every appearance of being an ideot [*sic*]'.

*   *   *

Thomas Brierley was one of a new breed of highwaymen – footpads and street hustlers all of them – whose villainies produced a significant crime wave in Cheshire in the third decade of the 19th century, causing widespread fear and panic among the populace. And, despite the deadly determination with which Cheshire's judges responded to this outbreak of lawlessness, there were still men who were willing to gamble with their lives, often for little reward, to follow Brierley down this dangerous road.

Of the 22 convicts hanged at Chester between 1819 and 1829 eight had been charged with highway robbery – curiously at a time when this particular offence was in decline nationally. And many other members of this criminal coterie narrowly escaped death only to be banished forever to the other side of the world.

It was a fate that befell three young men from Stockport in the summer of 1823. James Boon and James Brooks, both aged 19, and William Sumner (18), together with 17-year-old Edward Clarke and another gang member, attacked a man in a back street in their home town and robbed him of the princely sum of 12 shillings.

It had happened around midnight on 14 December the previous year as James Robinson, a butcher's assistant, was returning home from his regular Saturday evening stint helping man a stall at Stockport Market. At the bottom of Hillgate he was confronted by five young men. One of them, Clarke, knocked out the lighted candle he carried to guide him through

the darkened streets and the others began jostling him. He took temporary refuge in the Bishop Blaize public house in Lower Hillgate, but Sumner followed him inside (30 years later the pub would also figure in another shameful episode in Stockport's history, when it was the scene of the brawl that sparked the infamous anti-Irish riots of June 1852).

Stockport's Market Place where, on Saturday 14 December 1822, butcher's assistant James Robinson had been working on a stall in he market when he was confronted by a gang of five young roughs.

Robinson was to say five days later in a deposition contained in the case files in the National Archives that he 'had a noggin of gin'. Sumner had the gall, apparently, to suggested Robinson might like to buy him a drink. Robinson told him he did not like his company and declined the invitation. When he left the pub – the 200-year-old hostelry only closed its doors in 2011, when it was converted into offices – to resume his journey, however, Sumner again followed him and in 'a bye-street near the Waterloo Road' he was joined by his four companions. Robinson stated, 'They suddenly rushed me, one seized me by the breast and pressed me up to some garden rails and they began to rifle my pockets.'

Left: Robinson sought refuge in the Bishop Blaize public house in Lower Hillgate (pictured here when it figured in another shameful episode in Stockport's history: the infamous anti-Irish riots of 1852), but was afterwards pursued by the gang and robbed in 'a bye-street near the Waterloo Road'. Right: The Bishop Blaze photographed in more recent times. The 200-year-old pub only closed its doors in 2011, when it was converted into offices.

They took from him 10 shillings in silver, two shillings in copper, a tobacco box, a penknife and his house key. He entreated them not to take the box as it had been a gift from his wife. To which one his assailants replied, 'Damn you, and your tobacco box.' At the sound of approaching footsteps the thieves ran off in the direction of Rosemary Lane. Robinson said he had managed to grab hold of one of them around the head and shoulders, and persuaded him to return his house key. But after crying out 'Boatsman!' to one of his fleeing friends the man broke free and escaped. He left his hat behind in the brief struggle.

It so happened that the young man with the nickname 'Boatsman' was known to the authorities and on the following Monday, 16 December, Stockport Constable William Booth took Edward Clarke into custody and charged him with the robbery. Clarke, while admitting he was 'commonly called 'The Boatsman', at first denied he knew anything about the matter.

As a result of 'certain information' given to him, Booth said in his court deposition, he also went with Deputy Constable John Stapeley Barratt to arrest Sumner. His informant, no doubt, was James Robinson who, though unable to identify his other attackers with any certainty, had had a good opportunity to study Sumner's features while they were in the Bishop Blaize together.

Told he and Clarke were to be charged with highway robbery, Sumner began to weep, claiming, 'Boatsman led me into it'. As well as Clarke, he named Brooks and Boon as his accomplices along with a man who, he said, he only knew as 'Samuel'. This, apparently, was William Prussia, also known as Samuel, who was the fifth defendant listed on the formal indictment but stated to be 'not in custody' at that time. Brooks, said Sumner, had given him sixpence from the three shillings that had been his share of the proceeds.

The following day, Tuesday, Booth and another Constable, Francis Donovan, apprehended Brooks and Boon in Manchester. Both men said they knew nothing about the robbery. Boon admitted he had been in Stockport on the 14th but, when the officers questioned him about the new hat he was wearing, he denied losing his old one that night.

However, when Donovan took Clarke and Sumner to a local magistrate to obtain an order for their remand in custody, he deposed that Sumner confirmed it *had* been Boon's hat that had been left behind in the robbery. Of his own involvement in the crime, he said he had merely 'stood by' while Robinson was relieved of his cash and possessions. Donovan's deposition went on, 'He said Brooks got all the 'Blunt' (money) and gave him sixpence, and Clarke had sixpence and Boon a shilling because he had lost his hat.'

Edward Clarke eventually confessed to his part in the robbery but the charge against him was later dropped in exchange for his turning King's Evidence and testifying against his fellow accused. And it was largely on the strength of his evidence, that Brooks, Boon and Sumner were convicted when they appeared at Chester Assizes beginning on 7 April 1823. They were each sentenced to death, though the sitting judges reprieved them at the close of the sessions and ordered them for transportation instead.

Clarke's piece of good fortune was a warning he failed to heed, however. And when on 12 May, just five weeks after his court discharge, he committed a similar offence, he was not allowed to wriggle off the hook a second time. At the Spring Assizes at the end of August that year it was alleged that he and two friends robbed a weaver named James Shawcross from Heaton Norris in Bamford Street off Lower Hillgate, Stockport, and stole from him 5s 8d in cash and a cotton handkerchief. Clarke, who had turned 18 in May, was found guilty and received the death penalty (the other robbers had not been traced).

He was executed at Chester City Gaol, on Saturday 13 September 1823. According to the *Chester Chronicle* (19 September), 'no young man ever left the world with less concern'. The prisoner, said the paper, 'betrayed a sullen indifference to his approaching end, and talked with heartless levity of the arrival of that hour which would number him with the dead'.

His cut from the robbery was probably less than two shillings, worth about £6 today.

In an odd twist of fate Clarke's latest arrest landed him in Chester's Castle Gaol at the same time as James Brooks, James Boon and William Sumner, the former gang-mates he had 'shopped', were awaiting the arrival of the Home Office orders detailing the arrangements for their transportation. What their feelings towards him were, we can only imagine; yet, according to the *Chester Chronicle*, Clarke insisted that, along with Brooks and Boon, he had been in on the plot that, on Friday 23 May, led to six prisoners making a daring early evening break-out...through the prison drains.

They first sawed through an iron grating underneath the wooden seat of a privy in one of the felons' exercise yards and, with the aid of ropes made from torn-up strips of clothing, dropped five feet to the first level of the drainage system. Then, after scrambling 30 yards along a four-foot high, brick-lined tunnel and hacking through a second grating, the escapees descended another 10 feet to the lower level, where the main sewer outfall carried the prison waste under the city walls and into the River Dee. Between the line of the wall and the river, they somehow managed to punch an 18-inch hole through the tunnel roof and the pavement above (it was in a narrow thoroughfare called Skinner's Lane). Boon, the last one out, was seized as he emerged, covered in excreta, from the hole. Brookes remained at large only until the following morning, when he was recaptured some eight miles away at Handley.

Clarke later claimed he had been 'found out' and caught just as he was about to follow the others into the privy and down into the stinking, rat-infested sewers.

The three highway robbers were eventually removed from the Castle and delivered to the hulks, Boon and Brooks to the *Ganymede* moored at Chatham and Sumner to the *Justitia* on the Medway. The former pair embarked for Van Dieman's Land (the old name for Tasmania) aboard the transport ship *Sir Godfrey Webster* on 4 August; but it wasn't until 16 March 1824 that Sumner was finally shipped out to Australia on the *Countess of Harcourt*.

*   *   *

Samuel Mealey was another young chancer who tempted fortune once too often. In trouble with the law since his mid-teens, he continued to ignore court warnings until, like Edward Clarke, his luck finally ran out on the violent streets of early-19th century Stockport.

Baby-faced Mealey, by this time aged 21 but looking a lot younger, was one of a gang of four men who carried out a determined assault on Thomas Pollitt in Lower Hillgate on the night of 5 March 1821. It was a frighteningly familiar occurrence in a town already famous for its burgeoning cotton industry but which was also developing a reputation for lawlessness.

Pollitt, a land surveyor, was returning home shortly before midnight after drinking at the Bulls Head public house in Market Place when the robbers pounced. After a brief struggle, he managed to break free of them and ran off up Hillgate. But he got no more than 50 yards before they caught up with him and one of them sent him staggering with a heavy blow on the right cheek. Fighting back, Pollitt again escaped but was eventually over-powered at the foot of a flight of steps. As he lay on his back, two of the robbers held his arms while the others stole his pocket-book containing a Bank of England 'post bill' for £10 and a £1 banknote.

In the darkness he could barely make out his attackers; then his hat was knocked off and one of them exclaimed, 'By God, it's Pollitt of the Dog and Partridge!' He immediately recognised the speaker as Samuel Mealey, a local man who had worked part-time for him when he was landlord of the inn of that name (it was formerly situated in Churchgate directly opposite St Mary's Church).

When, a month later, Mealey appeared at the Chester Spring Assizes charged with assault and highway robbery, Pollitt told the jury, 'I had frequently seen the prisoner in my house when I kept the Dog and Partridge. He assisted [my] ostler on market days.'

A working publican also identified Mealey...as the young man who had knocked on the front door of his pub, little more than half an hour after the robbery, and asked if he could buy a pint of rum. William Whittaker was described in court as the licensee of 'the Pack Horse'. Contemporary street maps indicate there were at that time two similarly named pubs, the Lower Pack Horse and the Higher Pack Horse, occupying adjoining blocks in the short stretch of Middle Hillgate between Bamford Street and Mottram Street. Whichever one Whittaker ran, he said he was there clearing up at about 12.30am when his late-night visitor called. Although it was past closing time, he said he served the man, who handed over what the witness described as 'a £10 note' in payment for the two-shillings'-worth of liquor.

It was obvious from his conversation, however, that the after-hours customer believed it to be only a £1 note. Whittaker decided there was something fishy about this confused stranger (both Pack Horse pubs were only a few hundred yards from the crime scene, but he had clearly not heard about the robbery at that stage). Witness went on, 'I gave him only 18s in change. I had a suspicion it [the note] was not honestly come by and I kept it.' The young man, he added, thanked him for the change and left.

Whittaker's suspicions proved to be well-founded: the £10 'note' was the same bank post bill, endorsed with the name 'J.B. Clarke' and the letters 'T.S.', that had been stolen from Thomas Pollitt earlier. And Whittaker said he had no doubt that the young man who had used it to buy rum was the prisoner at the bar.

Pollitt and Whittaker were the only prosecution witnesses; in his defence, Mealey, a cotton-spinner, explained that he had been helping out that night at 'the Pack Horse' (the other one, presumably) and going home along Middle Hillgate he had met a man and a woman, and the man asked him whether he could 'get him some rum anywhere?'

Mealey stated, 'I said perhaps I could. He gave me a note and, seeing a light at Mr Whittaker's vaults, I went there, got the rum and the change, and gave it to the man. That is all I know about it.'

The jury did not believe his story; they found him guilty 'without hesitation' (the two Chester papers described it in identical terms) and the Judge, Second Justice Samuel

Marshall, concurred. Addressing the prisoner, he is quoted in the *Chronicle*'s trial report of 13 April as saying, 'Of this indictment the Jury have found you guilty; from such clear evidence [of which] no doubt could be entertained by any rational mind.

'Your offence is much aggravated, and accompanied by circumstances of great violence. You did not alone attempt to waylay the prosecutor [Pollitt] – you formed part of a desperate gang; you followed him and beat him to the ground and rifled his pockets of property which…is traced to your hands half an hour after the transaction.

'Under such circumstances, it becomes the painful duty of the Court to attempt to put a stop to such desperate acts. The public must be protected against them, and a dreadful example must be made. We therefore feel it necessary now to inform you that you will certainly be left for execution.'

Mealey, said the *Chronicle*, 'seemed not at all moved by his situation, and left the Bar with great composure'. The *Courant* noted that 'we have not heard that any of his associates in the crime have been taken up'.

It was after his conviction that the local papers referred to Mealey's previous court appearances, though not all the Press claims can be substantiated from the official records. The *Courant* (8 May) confined itself to commenting, 'Mealey…had for a long time been suspected of being connected with men of notoriously bad character; and, if our information be correct, had more than once been charged with criminal offences.'

The *Chronicle*, on the other hand, alleged on 11 May that 'he had been in custody nearly a dozen times on different charges'. And the paper revealed, 'The last time he was imprisoned in Chester Castle, he was cautioned not to persevere in the paths of wickedness, and the fatal consequences of crime were pointed out to him; but he treated the humane exhortation slightly, observing that he would not go far enough to get hung, meaning that he would not commit any offence which would subject him to death – but he has paid the melancholy forfeit of his temerity!'

That 'last time' may have been in April 1817. Assize court files show that Mealey, then a 16-year-old labourer, and two older men had all pleaded guilty at the Spring sessions to stealing 'eighty herrings of the value of 2s and ten lemons (10d)' from Daniel Bancroft at Stockport on 27 January that year. The indictment does not record the court's findings; but an assize news-in-brief round-up in the *Chester Courant* indicated that, while his two co-defendants were each transported for seven years, Mealey somehow escaped punishment and was discharged.

One other charge against him can also be verified: in early September 1816, he appeared at Cheshire's Summer Assizes with William Wilson, a 20-year-old weaver, also from Stockport, jointly accused of stealing 20 yards of Irish linen from the shop of William Chatterton on 10 August. Wilson was one of the two men with whom Mealey was tried for the theft of Daniel Bancroft's fish and fruit. According to a report in the *Chronicle*, counter assistant John Booth testified that Mealey and Wilson had come into the Stockport shop between 9pm and 10pm and that Mealey took the piece of cloth off the top of a bundle and left. He and a young shop lad followed Mealey outside and stopped him. The boy corroborated Booth's account.

However, the teenaged Mealey put up a game defence. He was reported to have told Chief Justice Sir William Garrow that Booth was 'as great a scoundrel and blackguard as any in Stockport', that 'he would swear anybody's life away to gain by it' and that what he had said was false. He also pointed out that his accuser had recently been in the same dock charged with a felony (he was acquitted of stealing a watch). The Judge recalled the case with evident distaste.

The jury, said the *Chronicle*, 'did not give the evidence for the Prosecution much credit' and found the two defendants not guilty. The theft was still classified as a capital offence (the so-called 'Bloody Code' listed more than 200 crimes for which the death penalty could be imposed, though many of them were minor variations of the same offence) and had Samuel Mealey been convicted, he would probably have been hanged or transported. But neither that alarming thought, nor the wake-up call of his subsequent courtroom let-off, was sufficient to persuade this 'determined offender' (as the *Chronicle* characterised him) to mend his ways.

Reporting his execution on Saturday 5 May 1821, the paper reflected that Mealey 'might, had he received the benefits of education, have been a useful member of society'. 'Unfortunately,' the *Chronicle* went on, 'he had not the advantage of learning or of parental care and solicitude,' adding, 'His mother, we are told, keeps a house of common reception in Stockport, and neither she nor his sister visited him in his last moments.' There were many different kinds of common lodging house in the expanding urban areas of 19th century England; some were highly respectable, while others were cheap doss-houses whose proprietors were not too fussy about the habits, background and morals of the 'guests'. It was obvious into which category the *Chronicle* believed Mrs Mealey's establishment belonged.

Mealey was hanged 'in view of an immense concourse of spectators,' according to the *Courant*'s report (8 May), which ended with the observation, 'Being a light man, his convulsive struggles were strong; and several minutes elapsed before his dying agonies appeared to terminate'. The paper described Mealey as a young man of 'boyish appearance', who, though 21, 'did not seem to be more than 18'.

*   *   *

Joseph Walker was the first of the eight who suffered the full force of the crackdown on highway robbery in Cheshire during this period. He was young; it was his first offence. But the crime was bound up with strands of personal revenge and extreme violence that made him an odds-on candidate for the rope.

Walker, then aged 20, and another man, robbed his former employer three weeks after he had been sacked for laziness. John Collins, a Northwich carrier, was half-strangled, almost choked and so badly beaten his attackers probably believed they had left him for dead.

But the elderly haulage boss, a man in his 70s, apparently, survived his bloody roadside ordeal; and at Chester Assizes in April 1819, he was the 'Prosecutor' – until well into the century the vast majority of criminal prosecutions were initiated and conducted by the victim of the crime – in the case against the ex-employee to whom he had not only given a job but a roof over his head as well.

Walker, whose family lived in Baguley, near Altrincham, worked for Mr Collins as a carter. How long he was in his employment is not known; but latterly he also lived in with the Collinses. Then, about the middle of September 1818 he was fired. As Mr Collins explained at Walker's trial, 'I had parted with him because I could not get him to work.' Nevertheless, Walker seems to have been allowed to stay on at the house for about a week after his dismissal, presumably while he found alternative employment.

This was how he repaid the old man's generosity...

A little after 7pm on Tuesday 6 October, as Mr Collins travelled back to Northwich from Manchester with his horse-and-cart (a business trip he made regularly each Tuesday, Thursday and Saturday), he was ambushed by two men in what was described in court as 'a narrow bye-lane' at Bowdon, about a mile beyond Altrincham. On these trips – a fact that would have been well-known to Walker – he appears to have been in the habit of leaving the turnpike road to Northwich at Altrincham (for refreshment, possibly) and then heading for Bowdon, most likely along the route of present-day Bowdon Road, The Firs and Church Brow, before re-joining the main road (now the A56) at the western end of Park Road. One of his assailants (Walker) grabbed hold of his horse's reins and pulled him to the ground. Snatching a silk handkerchief from his pocket, the two men tied it around his neck with such force it ripped in two. Collins would later claim, 'If it had not broken [*sic*], they certainly would have hung me.'

These old cottages on Church Brow, Bowdon, were on the route that elderly Northwich carrier John Collins seems to have favoured when returning in his horse and cart from his regular business trips to Manchester and would have been close to the spot on which he was robbed in 1818

The robbers then stuffed his mouth full of soil to prevent him from crying out, and continued to beat him 'in a very violent manner'. Finally, they cut open the inside pocket of his coat and took his pocket-book containing £17 in banknotes. As they started to leave, Walker turned around, rushed at the gagging, gore-soaked figure in the roadway and landed a last ferocious kick on the side of his body. The old man was lying unconscious beneath one of the high hedges that overhung the lane, bleeding profusely, when his attackers finally ran off in the direction of Altrincham.

Mr Collins told the jury, 'When he [Walker] left me, I think he did not believe I was alive.' Of the extent of his injuries, he said, 'I received many dreadful blows; two of my ribs were broken, or put out of their places, and my eyes were swelled up so that I could scarcely see. I lost a great deal of blood.'

Although the night was misty and overcast and the light was fading fast, the Prosecutor recognised Walker as the chief aggressor. 'I know him very well and do positively swear that [he] is the man,' he declared.

He was also able to say that Walker was wearing 'a round dress...like a smock-frock' when he stopped him. He also had on a velvet hat. Both items of clothing were to help the prosecution fashion a conclusive case against the defendant.

Walker's hat had come off in the struggle and was lying on the ground nearby when Mr Collins finally recovered consciousness. In the gathering gloom, he picked it up believing it to be his own and threw it into his cart. As he made his painful way home he was totally unaware of the valuable piece of evidence lying on the seat beside him (Walker appears to have made off with Mr Collins's hat under a similar misapprehension).

His wife recognised the headgear immediately she saw it. Seventy-one-year-old Mrs Margaret Collins recalled, 'I remember him coming home on the night of the robbery. He was in a very shocking state, and had been very ill-abused. There was a great deal of blood about him.'

Her husband dropped the hat on to the floor and, she said, she knew it was Walker's even before she knew he was one of the alleged robbers. 'I knew it very particularly, and will swear to it as Walker's,' she testified. 'I know it from the velvet being loose, and a hole next [to] the crown. The prisoner only had one hat.'

The carter's smock that Walker had been wearing that night was confiscated by Altrincham constable Nathaniel Pass after he had arrested Walker as he worked for his new employer in a potato field at Sale Moor. Walker was in his shirt sleeves and the smock was 'at the end of a butt' a short distance away. It was three days after the robbery but, said Pass, there were 'marks of blood' visible on the garment.

Asked how they had got on to his clothing, Walker told the constable they were 'from his master's child, who had cut his thumb the day before'. The blood-stained smock and the hat ('very much torn') were shown to the members of the jury by the officer (this was a time, it should be remembered, when medical science had not yet come up with a test to differentiate between human and animal bloodstains, let alone blood grouping and DNA profiling).

Evidence was also give by Henry Gresty, who said that about 6.30 on the night of the robbery he was walking along the road from Bowdon towards Altrincham when, just outside the town, he met two men hurrying in the opposite direction. He hailed them with a cheery 'Hello! Good night, gentlemen', whereupon one of them, he said, 'slipped [by] rather sideways'. Gresty heard the second man ask why his companion 'went out of his way' and receive the reply, 'It's Henry Gresty and he would know me.'

It was. And he did. Said the witness, 'I am sure it was Walker. He had a carter's frock wrapped around him and had a hat on.'

As the two men carried on 'at a sharp pace', he also heard one of them, though he did not know which one, exclaim, 'Look sharp, or he'll be before us!' – meaning if they didn't hurry Mr Collins would have passed by the spot at which they planned to waylay him.

After doing business in Altrincham, Gresty said he saw Walker and the other man again; this time they were running back towards the town and both of them were 'out of wind'.

At the close of the prosecution case, Walker, when asked if he had anything to say in response to the charge, declared, 'I am not guilty. I am innocent of the crime altogether.' It was a denial he would continue to repeat, even with his dying breath.

Called up in his defence, John Holt said that, like Walker, he was 'a servant of Mr Hickson'. The two of them had been at Sale Moor 'getting potatoes' on the day of the robbery and finished in the field at dusk. Returning to their employer's house, where they both lodged, they were met by their mistress, who expressed concern that her husband had not yet returned from Stretford, where he had been conducting some business. Walker, said Holt, was sent to look for him.

Cross-examined by the Attorney General (Samuel Yate Benyon), the witness claimed that Walker had set out as his master's clock was striking seven – about the time John Collins was being robbed at Bowdon, some five miles away. However, when Constable Pass was recalled, he pointed out that there was a significant time difference between Sale and Bowdon. Bowdon time 'generally agreed with the Altrincham town clock', he said; but he had checked the Hicksons' clock and found it to be 62 minutes 'before' (i.e. ahead of) Altrincham time. It seemed Walker had left Sale about an hour *before* the robbery, leaving him just enough time to get to Bowdon for 7 o'clock.

Moreover, he doesn't appear to have caught up with his master, either. Holt said Mr Hickson came home alone at around 9 o'clock (8pm Bowdon time?), but it wasn't until three hours later that Walker returned. The house was locked up for the night and he had to get a ladder and climb in through his first-floor bedroom window.

In his summing up, the Chief Justice, the Honourable John Singleton Copley, drew the jury's attention to the bloodstains on Walker's smock, observing, 'If they had been really caused by the circumstances stated by the prisoner, it would have been very easy for him to have produced the child to corroborate his story.' And he wondered, 'Why did he not also call his mistress to speak to the fact of her having sent him to Stretford?'

In its trial report, the *Chester Chronicle* of 16 April, stated, 'The Jury, after a few seconds consideration, found the prisoner – GUILTY.' On the same page, the newspaper revealed that a bill against John Hooley, a 19-year-old labourer from Hale, near Altrincham, alleging he was the second man in the robbery, had earlier been thrown out by the Grand Jury for lack of evidence.

When, at the end of the sessions, Walker was 'called up for Judgment', the *Chronicle* reported him as saying, 'It is a hard case to suffer for another man's crime.' But Mr Justice

Copley told him, 'You have been tried and convicted of the crime of highway robbery, by a patient and attentive Jury, on evidence the most clear and conclusive.' And he left him in no doubt that, by taking revenge on his former employer in such a brutal manner, the late farm worker had dug his own grave.

He said, 'Your offence is one of great aggravation and considerable atrocity. Knowing the route of your former Master, you stopped him on the highway and, not content with taking from him his property, you added extreme violence and brutality to the crime, and left him weltering in his blood and apparently dead. It would be doing injustice to the public not to make a signal example in your case; and we should be deluding you also were we to suffer you to hope for the slightest amelioration of the awful sentence which the law awards.'

'His Lordship, who was greatly affected, passed judgment of death on the unhappy man in the usual form,' the *Chronicle* added.

On Saturday 8 May Joseph Walker was executed outside Chester City Gaol, his final words another bitter declaration of his innocence. What he actually said, according to the *Chronicle*, was 'I am as innocent as the child unborn', though the *Courant* had it as the slightly more eloquent 'I am as innocent as the babe in its mother's womb'. Judging by the Press reports of the day, this, or some other variant on the same theme, was a popular disclaimer among departing malefactors (though it just might, of course, have been a product of the journalistic licence that seems to have been given fairly free rein on these occasions).

The *Courant*'s coverage, published as it was three days ahead of its city rival, was the more extensive of the two local newspaper accounts. It began with a comment about Walker's parents, who were described as 'poor but honest and industrious people'. They had a 'large family' – Walker appears to have been one of nine children – and lived 'in the parish of Bowdon'.

The *Courant*'s enterprising correspondent appears to have gained access to the County Gaol to see the condemned man bid farewell to his fellow inmates and then accompanied him all the way from the Castle to the scaffold.

He was able to report, for instance, that several prisoners wept as Walker said his goodbyes; that on leaving one of the exercise yards he cried out, 'Farewell, brothers and sisters! I shall soon be out of this world of trouble.' He also told how Walker had shared a glass of wine with the prison Governor (Matthew Hudson) and recounted an incident in the Turnkey's Lodge just before he was handed over to the city sheriffs.

['There'], said the *Courant*, 'a fetter was put on one foot and hand. While the men appointed to perform this painful duty were executing it, Walker said to Mr Hudson, "I wish you would not put this thing (pointing to the fetter) upon me. I would go as well without it."'

When Hudson explained that he had been given orders to 'bind him', Walker replied, 'Well, well, I am going to a better place.' He seemed eager to get there, too. When he was led to the waiting cart, 'he sprung into it with considerable agility'; and, once at the City Gaol, he 'bounded from the cart with great activity'.

Later, standing on the gallows high above the heads of the crowd, he presented a 'very juvenile and prepossessing' appearance, the *Courant* added. His hair was light and curly and his complexion 'remarkably fair'. He was about 5ft 5in tall, his physique 'lusty and well-proportioned'.

The two Chester papers also referred to something else that happened on the way to the gallows. As he set off from the Castle, Walker spotted someone he knew in the press of people following the cart . The *Courant* said it was 'a constable from his neighbourhood' (Pass, possibly?). The condemned man leaned over the edge of the cart and begged him to call on his parents and ask them to come to Chester to claim his body and 'bury it in Bowdon Churchyard'. It was a matter the family already had in hand.

Later that day the coffin containing the mortal remains of Joseph Walker was conveyed to Baguley on the back of a horse-drawn cart, in part along the same route he had travelled the day he extracted bloody revenge on his disapproving boss – possibly even passing the spot at which he carried out the brutal crime. Four days later, on 12 May, in accordance with his dying wishes, Walker was interred in the graveyard of the Parish Church of St Mary's, Bowdon, in a committal ceremony conducted by the Curate, the Revd John Jackson.

Curiously, in the burial entry in the church registers, there is an exclamation mark after his name. The worthy cleric's way, perhaps, of drawing attention to another young life so emphatically ended by the hangman's noose?

6

An Old Country Recipe...for Murder

Seldom have the awful solemnities of public justice presented a more affecting scene...The nature and strength of the evidence against the unhappy prisoner, his decent and reputable appearance, and the very solemn and pathetic manner in which the learned judge pronounced the awful sentence of the law, left scarcely a dry eye in the court. The prisoner indeed seemed but little affected...May he have found that mercy with the eternal Judge which the laws of this country could not, consistently with the peace and welfare of society, afford him...

Chester Chronicle, 28 April 1786

THE OLD North Country method of making furmetry was to first steep the whole-wheat grain in water overnight then boil it in a mixture of milk, flour, currants and butter, seasoning with sugar, spices and, preferably, a few bracing drops of rum. Result: a pungent porridge-like dish that, according to custom, was particularly popular around Christmas time.

To the traditional contents of Phoebe Steer's breakfast bowl one late November morning in 1785, however, someone had added an unscheduled ingredient...a generous helping of arsenic. Result: mother-of-four Mrs Steer was consigned to a slow and agonising death, and her husband Peter almost got away with murder. Almost.

He may well have got away with it had it not been for his own callous behaviour and a series of foolish indiscretions that were bound to set tongues wagging in the tiny, close-knit community in which he lived. As it was, his wife had not been in the ground three weeks before the doubts and suspicions gained sufficient currency to prompt a more thorough investigation into recent happenings in and around the Cheshire hamlet of Morley, near Mobberley.

A post mortem on the exhumed body of Phoebe Steer revealed she had received a massive overdose of arsenic: enough, incredibly, to have killed her more than 40 times over. In his haste to be rid of her, Steer also 'doctored' the drinks and other preparations he administered to his wife after she had taken to her bed – under the pretence of helping ease her suffering. Rather than get better, however, Phoebe grew steadily worse until, after three days of increasing pain and misery, she finally succumbed.

In the inquiries that followed in the wake of this sensational discovery, a surgeon in a neighbouring town remembered selling a quantity of the poison to a man answering Steer's description. And the word among the predominantly Quaker folk of Morley was that Phoebe Steer's husband had a particularly strong personal reason for wishing her out of the way.

Peter Steer's motive for murder was his infatuation with a girl young enough to be his daughter, and the equally consuming desire to remove the one obstacle standing between him and the future he mistakenly believed she was keen to share with him. It was the old, old story...with one notable difference. Sarah Barrow, the third party in this tragic affair, was just 14 years old when she first turned the head of the lovelorn Steer.

The pair met in the early months of 1784 when she went as servant to Mrs Steer's brother, corn merchant Thomas Cash, who lived with his other sister Mary at the farmstead in Morley (mid-way between Knutsford and Wilmslow) where Steer was employed as a casual worker. He was then 39 years of age and had been married to Phoebe, three years his senior, for 17 apparently contented years. Though in his seasonal employment as a day labourer his earnings would have averaged no more than 10 shillings a week, he had married well and lived in a comfortable house. And, like most people in his position, he and his family would have augmented their income from the produce of their few acres of land and livestock and, possibly, from some domestic industry, too: wool or cotton-spinning or button-making, for instance.

Within 12 months of their meeting, however, Steer had seduced the pretty young serving girl and vowed to make her his wife. And Sarah Barrow, a precocious child of yeoman stock whose family lived four miles away in Mere, seems to have done little to discourage him.

His passion aroused, Steer pursued the winsome Sarah at every opportunity. Their first sexual encounter occurred in a cowshed; she afterwards claimed he had raped her and that she was too terrified to put up more than token resistance. But she appears to have been a noticeably less unwilling partner when, a short time later, there were further steamy sessions in a hay-loft. And the couple were often alone together on Sunday mornings, either at his home or in her master's house, after the Cashes and Phoebe Steer and her children had all gone to the Quaker meeting.

Thomas and Mary Cash were 'convinced' Quakers, as were a lot of families living in Morley and the surrounding areas of Mobberley and Wilmslow at that time; Morley, in fact, was one of the two earliest Quaker communities in the county. The Steers and the Barrows, on the other hand, were among those regular, but as yet uncommitted, members of the congregation known as 'attenders'. All, however, were expected to live by the strict, almost puritanical Quaker code which set great store by moral education, rigid discipline and the preservation of virtue.

That Peter Steer and Sarah Barrow were behaving together in a manner that appeared to be immoral, ill-disciplined and un-virtuous did not long escape the notice of the sober, gentle and well-intentioned people who gathered weekly at the old Meeting House in

Altrincham Road – in fact, two buildings that had been a focus of Quakerism since 1694 and which can still be picked out among the more substantial lines of the handsome pair of private dwellings that now occupy the site. And, although a predisposition towards silence was, and is, an integral part of the Quakers' informal style of worship – and scandal, along with politics, was one of the two taboo subjects of conversation – there was undoubtedly some talk of this unholy alliance in their midst.

The old Meeting House in Altrincham Road in Morley, one of the two earliest Quaker communities in the county, where murderer Peter Steer and his young paramour Sarah Barrow were both regular 'attenders'. Photograph courtesy of Mr and Mrs N.J. Pearson.

What they could not know, as that Autumn of 1785 drew to a close, however, was that Peter Steer, having long since forsaken the Seventh Commandment, was now ready to break the Sixth as well.

Having cooked up the plot to poison his wife's food, Steer seems to have made his final plans on Friday 18 November. When he came home from work at noon he announced he felt ill and would go into Knutsford the following day to see the doctor if he had not improved by then.

This he duly did; but the real purpose of his trip was to obtain the means by which to put his evil scheme into operation. He completed his lethal shopping expedition late that Saturday afternoon and returned home with the arsenic just as his wife was about to prepare the hulled wheat for next day's breakfast.

Old-fashioned furmetry, also known as 'furmety' or 'frumenty' in other parts of the region, was a seasonal favourite throughout the rural North, where its warming, wholesome and nourishing qualities were much appreciated, particularly on cold back-end mornings. But on Sunday 20 November 1785, it was to be the chilling recipe for Phoebe Steer's murder.

After making the furmetry, Mrs Steer divided it up into six helpings, one for herself and one each for her husband and the couple's four children: Alice, less than two weeks away from her 14th birthday; Sarah, just turned nine; Thomas, aged six, and Elizabeth (three). While she busied herself with the rest of the breakfast preparations, she left the furmetry cooling on the back-kitchen table.

It was at this point that Steer slipped some of the arsenic into his wife's distinctive cup, an all-purpose utensil which she apparently used at most meal-times. Then, from across the table, he watched her carefully as she began to eat.

The woman noticed the poison's slight but characteristically sweet and metallic taste immediately, but suspected nothing sinister – even when, after she had given some of her furmetry to her youngest daughter, her husband snatched it from the child and poured it back into his wife's dish, muttering disapprovingly.

The *Chester Chronicle*, in a detailed report on the case published five months later, said of the incident at the breakfast table, 'She expressed astonishment at his action without appreciating the cause of it.'

At mid-day on the Sunday, when the bouts of sickness began, Mrs Steer simply put it down to the bad quality of the wheat in the breakfast cereal. It was not until the following Tuesday, when Mary Cash called to find her sister considerably worse, that Phoebe Steer's deteriorating condition became cause for concern, and the question of medical attention was first raised. By then it was too late, however. At 11pm that same day, 22 November, she died.

Steer, seemingly insensitive to his wife's suffering during her final hours, continued to act suspiciously after her death, an occurrence which, in the days when people were dying all the time from uncertain disorders, and formal medical certification was unknown, would not in itself have been regarded as exceptional. Indeed, Mrs Steer's symptoms could quite easily have been mistaken for those of cholera, endemic throughout 18th-century Europe, dysentery or some other abdominal disease. However, the poor woman's body was scarcely cold before Steer was pressing for a quick burial – and failing to hide his disappointment when told the arrangements could not be hurried.

But his biggest mistake was to openly declare his love for Sarah Barrow – and his intention to marry her – only a little over a week after Phoebe's funeral. Pretty soon, other hitherto unconnected events were assuming a new significance among the rustic folk of Morley in the light of this unexpected announcement. And in conversations everywhere, the hands that hid the whispered accusations increasingly pointed the finger at Peter Steer. The murmurings around the village grew into a swelling chorus until, eventually, the authorities were compelled to dig a little deeper into the Steer family's sudden bereavement.

Phoebe Steer had been interred, with the same absence of ceremony and priestly intonations that characterises the sect's entire religious philosophy, in the old Quaker burial ground in the adjacent parish of Mobberley. The Quakers, or Religious Society of Friends, as they are more properly called, had acquired this isolated plot on the edge of Lindow Moss in 1669 from a group of land-owners which included Edward Alcock. Four years earlier, Alcock had become one of an estimated 21,000 Friends who suffered imprisonment or fines in the 30 years or so up to the passing of the 1689 Act of Toleration, which effectively ended the widespread and persistent persecution of dissenters. During this period at least 450 Quakers died for their beliefs.

The little walled cemetery, its dead elms giving it an appropriate atmosphere of decay, is to be found today, disused but still periodically tended, half a mile down a rambling track known as Graveyard Lane, which runs eastwards from Newton Hall Lane.

The old Quaker burial ground at Mobberley, last resting place of Phoebe Steer, whose husband Peter poisoned her by putting arsenic in her breakfast bowl of 'furmetry' in the late autumn of 1785.

Two of her children, John, aged 15, and Mary (nine), had already been buried there (in 1783 and 1784 respectively) when Mrs Steer went to join them on Friday 25 November 1785. It was to be an interrupted 'reunion', however. For 15 days later, on Saturday 10 December, amid mounting local speculation, her body was exhumed in a bid to get at the truth behind the murder rumours.

That Mrs Steer had been poisoned was fairly quickly established by the post mortem examination. And from this and other evidence presented at the inquest into her death, held on Thursday 15 December, coroner John Hollins had no hesitation in recording a verdict of wilful murder.

Peter Steer was arrested and imprisoned in Chester Castle Gaol, where he was to remain for the next four months. He was finally brought to the bar on the penultimate day of the county's Spring assizes on Friday 21 April 1786.

The official court dossier, containing the inquest papers together with the subsequent statements of other Crown witnesses, stands as a comprehensive record of the case and provides important insight into the crime and its many contrasting aspects. It tells a story of violently conflicting emotions – of hot passion and cold hatred – of calculated cruelty and monumental carelessness…and of the two teenaged girls who were the opposites that attracted most attention at Steer's trial.

Sarah Barrow and Alice Steer, the two chief prosecution witnesses, were friends (if not strictly Friends, with a capital 'F'). But they could not have been more different: the one, articulate and worldly-wise, now still only 16 but possessing a maturity beyond her years; the other, barely 18 months younger but totally without guile, an innocent child burdened with the awesome responsibility of giving evidence against her own father. In their separate ways, however, the girls were to share a common destiny: reluctantly, they both helped send Peter Steer to the gallows.

If Sarah Barrow's intimate revelations about her relationship with Steer caused the biggest sensation in the crowded gallery, the appearance and testimony of Alice Steer ('a melancholy witness', as the *Chester Chronicle* described her) produced the trial's most poignant moment.

The *Chronicle* reporter, in a lengthy article headed 'Some interesting particulars of the singular detection, trial and conviction of Peter Steer', printed on 28 April, noted, 'The tears of some of the audience and the deeply-fetched sighs of others, when this part of the evidence was given…sufficiently spoke of their feelings on hearing a pretty young creature of 14, with all the artless simplicity of truth and innocence, relate such a series of circumstances, as were at once indubitable proofs of her father's guilt and decisive of his fate.'

Alice, the prisoner's eldest daughter who had had her 14th birthday on 1 December, exactly a week after her mother's funeral, first recalled the scene in the Steer household on that fateful Sunday morning in November. She said her mother, having steeped the wheat the previous evening, made the furmetry in the back-kitchen, filling five cups and a can for her father. Mrs Steer's cup, Alice explained, 'she usually ate out of and was larger than the rest'. The children were each given a cup and the family sat down to breakfast together.

Her statement went on, 'Mother said the furmetry was not so good as it used to be. She did not like it and ate but a few spoonfuls and set the cup by on the dresser in the kitchen.' Alice said she had eaten all her furmetry and had not noticed anything unusual about it.

Between 10 and 11am she left to go to Morley Meeting House. Although her mother stayed at home on this occasion, she was at that time all right. When Alice returned some three hours later, however, Mrs Steer told her daughter that she had been sick and felt unwell.

'She continued sick and vomiting all that day,' Alice stated. 'She said the furmetry had made her ill.'

On the Monday the sickness became more acute, Mrs Steer complaining incessantly about 'great pains in her stomach and bowels'. Then the following day, at about 11 o'clock at night, Alice's statement added, her mother died.

The unhappy girl's deposition contained one more crucial piece of evidence: a reference to the incident two weeks later which first raised questions about Phoebe Steer's death and sparked off a murder inquiry. We shall return to that presently; but first a more detailed look at events before and immediately after Mrs Steer's death as told by other trial witnesses.

Mary Cash – the deposition description of her as 'one of the people called Quaker' perhaps reflecting the prejudice that still lingered more than 130 years after the Society's formation – had gone to see her sister on the Sunday afternoon, immediately on hearing she was ill. Phoebe was upstairs lying on her bed and when she declared herself to be 'very sick', Mary went downstairs to get her 'something warm'. Phoebe followed and 'vomited much by the fireside'. Mary said to her, 'Let me get thee a sup of tea. I think it might take that sickness off.'

After drinking some of the tea, Phoebe got up and walked across the room and, placing her head against the window, moaned, 'Oh, dear, dear!' Then she again vomited 'to a great degree', fetching up what Mary described as 'a greenish water'. By now it was late afternoon and almost dark, so Mary returned home, leaving her sister in the care of her husband and daughter Alice.

Mary did not visit her sister again until the following Tuesday, when she said she found her in bed 'very ill indeed'. In a weak voice, Phoebe told her, 'I got up yesterday and dressed myself but today I cannot.'

Since the onset of her illness, Phoebe had developed an insatiable thirst – one of the effects of the arsenic in her system – and in the course of the morning she drank various quantities of camomile tea, buttermilk and water gruel. And, though the drinks Mary Cash prepared for her sister were innocuous enough, those served up by Steer on the Sunday and Monday had been laced with further doses of the poison.

Mary went back after lunch on the Tuesday to learn that Phoebe had passed 'many loose stools consisting of greenish matter'. Her sister's colour also 'appeared much changed', Mary stated. At this time, she said, Steer was in an adjoining room 'shilling' (shelling) peas, 'seemingly unconcerned and without being affected with sorrow'.

Before she left her sister's bedside later that evening, Mary told Phoebe that if she was not better by morning she should 'have someone in who understood her complaint'. Repeating her opinion to Steer, Mary said he simply 'gave her some short answer'. But at that stage she does not appear to have made any connection between Steer's unnatural behaviour and his wife's baffling illness.

About 11 o'clock that night, a neighbour, Elizabeth (Betty) Pearson, called to tell Mary that Phoebe was 'either dying or going into a fit'. By the time she arrived at the Steer house, however, her sister was already dead. Peter Steer, she said, was in the room, apparently grief-stricken. But, Mary observed, 'His sorrow appeared more affectation than real.' A disturbing thought, perhaps, was at last beginning to insinuate itself into Mary Cash's troubled mind.

The widow Pearson deposed that she had looked in on Mrs Steer on the Monday and also on the day of her death. On Tuesday, Phoebe had managed to get downstairs but was 'not able to talk much'. As the evening wore on, she 'appeared fainty' and, said Mrs Pearson, Steer remarked to her, 'I think she's going.' It was at that point that she hurried over to the Cashes' house to inform them of the seriousness of the situation.

Tabitha, the wife of Betty Pearson's shoemaker son Samuel, was sent for to lay out the corpse. When she arrived, at about 1am, she said she was surprised to find Mrs Steer's body 'swelled to a great degree in so much as a woman great with child'.

Shortly after 4am, Tabitha Pearson and her mother-in-law went to knock up Samuel Goodyear to come and measure up for the coffin. When they returned with the village carpenter, Steer said that 'it would be as well to have her buried on Thursday morning'. However, because of the distance some of Phoebe's relations would have to travel to attend, Steer had to accept, rather grudgingly, that the funeral could not take place before Friday. When they placed the body in the casket, Tabitha said, she noticed it was 'much swelled about the neck'.

Sam Goodyear was also struck by Steer's haste to have his wife interred, and by the condition of the body. He asked Steer why he was in such a hurry and received the curious reply, 'I am afraid she might swell and be troublesome.'

With the evidence of his contemptible crime right under their noses, Peter Steer had good reason to be afraid, though it was some days before anyone smelled a rat and his wife's body did, indeed, prove 'troublesome'.

Goodyear's reaction was to dismiss Steer's fears as, he said, Phoebe had not been ill long and had not taken much 'physic' (medicine). And he began lifting the body into the coffin.

As he did so, the woman's head fell back and, said the carpenter, 'immediately there came up a large quantity of a green or yellowish matter from the mouth, nostrils and ears of the deceased'.

Hannah Strettell, another neighbour in the house at the time, got a cloth to wipe around the dead woman's face and head, whereupon they both saw the right side of Mrs Steer's neck was 'quite black'. Hannah asked Goodyear what he thought might have caused it but he was unable to offer any explanation. She said she had 'never seen the like before except in one man who was strangled'.

She asked Steer what his wife had eaten last, repeating the question several times before receiving the answer 'a little small beer with sugar in it'. And all the while Steer 'did not appear concerned for the loss of his wife' – something which Goodyear, in the statement he made more than four months later, said he 'wondered at'.

In the 'chain of circumstantial evidence' the *Chester Chronicle* referred to in its report of 28 April, the three vital links the prosecution had to connect to Steer were: motive, means and opportunity. That he had the latter there could be no doubt; the evidence concerning motive will be examined shortly. As to proof that he possessed the means, the jury was asked to consider the unusual events of Saturday 19 November 1785…launch date of Steer's timetable for murder.

After setting out to go to Knutsford, ostensibly to see Dr Howard, at about 9 o'clock that morning, Steer stopped off en route at the home of a shopkeeper friend, John Howarth, in Mobberley.

Howarth's deposition contains an intriguing reference to Steer having called at his house 'with a paper for him [Howarth] to carry to Knutsford to buy some harmless powder' for a sick sister-in-law who was then staying with the Howarths. Perhaps, in a previous conversation, the pair had discussed the woman's illness and Steer had suggested a palliative and was now bringing his friend a wrap of paper, of the kind in which apothecaries routinely dispensed small quantities of the medicinal powders they sold to treat a variety of minor complaints.

Whatever the 'paper' was, that Steer chose this particular day on which to deliver it cannot have been coincidence. And the use of the word 'harmless' in the statement was surely not without significance. It seems likely that the visit to the shopkeeper, and Steer's subsequent offer to accompany Howarth to Knutsford, were part of an elaborate attempt by the murderer to establish some sort of alibi to cover his poison-buying mission planned for later in the day. At any rate, Steer spent most of that Saturday with Howarth.

Having travelled to Knutsford together, probably in the shopkeeper's cart, their first port of call was an apothecary called Penny, from whom Howarth purchased the 'harmless powder' and some sweet oil for 4d. Steer did not buy anything. Afterwards they went to the George Hotel, where they each had two or three pints of ale.

Steer then left the inn, telling Howarth he wanted to look out for a man 'coming from about Mere Town'. He evidently did not meet up with the mystery man, for a short while later he rejoined Howarth, who had by this time moved on to the Red Lion. There they had a few more drinks (beer was about 1d a pint in those days) before Steer disappeared again.

Howarth said Steer had earlier complained of being troubled with a cold and that he had gone to see Dr Howard but he had not been in. When, some considerable time later, Steer had not returned, Howarth assumed he had gone once more to seek out the good doctor. But, for some reason, he decided to go and make sure. Satisfying himself that his friend was, indeed, at the physician's house, Howarth went back to the Red Lion to await his somewhat restless companion. When Steer eventually turned up, he explained that the doctor had 'taken some of his mad blood' and had 'let him bleed' (blood-letting was the treatment routinely administered by medical practitioners for a multitude of ills at this time and, indeed, well into the 19th century). The two men remained at the pub until after dark – though, claimed Howarth, Steer went missing on at least one more occasion during the course of the afternoon.

On the following Monday, Howarth's statement added, he was in Morley on business and, as he passed Steer's house, his friend came out to tell him that Mrs Steer had been 'taken very poorly'. And, said Howarth, Steer remarked that he thought she would 'go off this time or not mend again or words to the same effect'.

It was during one of his Saturday afternoon vanishing acts, as we shall see in due course, that Steer obtained the arsenic. And on his way back to the Red Lion, he bumped into Josiah Barrow, father of Sarah and a man with whom he was obviously well acquainted.

Now, whether due to the unexpectedness of the encounter, coupled with the guilty knowledge of what he had in his pocket, or the emboldening effect of the large amount of alcohol he had consumed that day, Steer was apparently thrown off his guard by his meeting with Barrow, who was in Knutsford selling butter at the weekly market. For, after inviting the farmer to join him and Howarth for a 'cup of ale' at the Red Lion, Steer made some particularly incautious (though at the time largely incoherent) comments.

At one point, Barrow testified, the defendant clapped him on the knee and said, 'Josiah, thou art a widower and I think I shall be one soon.' Barrow said he asked whether Phoebe was 'bad', but could not recollect Steer's reply. He had since heard she was in perfect health at that time.

Steer also seems to have hinted at his feelings for Sarah, surprising Barrow by blurting out, 'I have a great respect for your family!' When asked what had brought him to Knutsford, he repeated his claim about seeing Dr Howard 'to be let blood'. When he left the other two men's company at about 5pm, Barrow said Steer seemed 'cheerful and merry'.

Just as Barrow was about to depart, Steer made one more odd statement. He suddenly remembered he had a message for the farmer from another of his daughters, Hannah. He said Hannah, who had by then replaced Sarah as domestic servant to Thomas Cash, had asked Steer to tell her father she wished to see him. But the girl said later she had given him no such message.

Could it have been that Steer, overcome by last-minute doubts, had decided to call on his way home for a final re-assuring reunion with Sarah Barrow before embarking on his murder plan, and sent her widowed father on a wild-goose chase to be sure of finding her at home alone? If that was so, the evidence of his teenaged sweetheart suggests he changed his mind. For Sarah made no reference to such a meeting in her deposition.

Steer eventually arrived home at around 9pm, a fact confirmed by John Ardern, a tailor who lived in Dean Row on the east side of Wilmslow. Ardern had spent all day Thursday and Friday working at his trade at the Steers' home and was still there on the Saturday night when the head of the household returned.

It had rained heavily throughout the six-mile journey from Knutsford and Steer was soaking wet. According to Ardern, he was also 'stupid with liquor'. Phoebe, oblivious of the murderous resolve now set firm in her husband's heart, fretted over him as she helped him out of his sodden clothing.

Ardern it was who revealed Friday's conversation in which Steer first mentioned his proposed trip to Knutsford and described the mood in the house the following morning. Phoebe, he said, 'rather objected' to Steer's going to Knutsford and tried to persuade him to go instead to see Dr Jeffs in Wilmslow. 'He can bleed you just as well,' she told her husband. 'But,' stated Ardern, 'Steer said Dr Jeffs knew nothing of the matter and seemed determined to go to Knutsford.' The tailor said he thought it was only an excuse for Steer to go to Knutsford to meet Sarah Barrow, between whom he had heard there were 'some connections'.

The reason for Steer's journey, of course, was the procurement of the powder (of a certain far-from-harmless variety, in this case) with which he planned to remedy his current marital handicap and, he hoped, smooth the way to more lasting 'connections' with his young paramour. He seems to have made his deadly purchase on the last of his Saturday afternoon excursions. The source of his supply may not, however, have been his original choice.

The *Chester Chronicle* surmised that 'probably his first intentions were to have purchased the fatal dose' from Dr Howard. But, 'thinking the knowledge he had of him might lead too directly to a discovery', Steer went instead to surgeon William Billingham at Nether Knutsford on the northern outskirts of the town.

Billingham said in his statement that between 3 and 4pm a man unknown to him, 'seemingly about the age of 40 years', entered his shop and asked for two-pennyworth of white arsenic. The surgeon, showing commendable caution in dispensing so dangerous a drug, inquired as to the reason for the purchase and the man replied, 'To kill rats or otherwise lice on cattle.'

Though this was 60-odd years before the first statutory controls on the sale of arsenic were introduced, and the obligatory maintenance of a poisons register was still more than 80 years away, Billingham then asked his customer to identify himself. 'Heald of Mobberley' came the reply.

Now Billingham knew several families of that name in the neighbourhood of Mobberley and Morley but he did not recognise this man as being a member of one of them, so he took particular notice of his appearance. He was later able to describe the stranger as wearing a round hat, darkish-grey coat with black buttons, a lightish-brown waistcoat, leather breeches, blue and white stockings and black shoes. When he was subsequently shown the coat Steer was wearing on that Saturday, Billingham confirmed, to the best of his recollections, that it was the same as the one worn by the man in the shop. And in court, according to the *Chester Chronicle*, he identified Steer 'in the clearest and most satisfactory manner'.

By an ironic twist of fate, the two medical men who figured in Steer's scheme to dispose of his burdensome wife, were to be instrumental in his own demise. For it was Dr Howard, assisted by Billingham, who performed the post mortem that proved Phoebe Steer had been poisoned.

Dr Howard presented their report to the court. Although putrefaction was well advanced, he said, he immediately noted the 'highly inflamed' state of the abdomen and the 'gangrenous appearance' of the stomach lining. In the stomach he found a quantity of granulated white powder and further grains of the same substance adhering to the upper portion of the small intestine. Some of the powder had also found its way into the cavity of the abdomen, apparently through a perforation in the lower stomach. The material, stated Dr Howard, 'appeared very much like white arsenic, from its colour, its roughness and grittiness and from the dreadful symptoms with which the deceased was afflicted'.

A feature of arsenic poisoning is that quite harmless amounts can accumulate in the body to produce a fatal dose, and a build-up of 130 milligrams is normally reckoned enough to kill. In Mrs Steer's case, Dr Howard estimated a total intake of two drachms – nearly eight grams.

He went on, 'There was not a sufficient quantity for the usual experiment, which is generally clear and affords a satisfactory decision.' But the doctor and the surgeon concurred, 'From the appearance of the body and other circumstances we have but too much reason to believe she was poisoned.'

Mrs Steer's body had been disinterred on a rising tide of suspicion whipped up, apparently, by another Sunday meal-time incident in the Steer family home. It involved a conversation in which Peter Steer's motive for murder was finally brought out into the open...by the killer himself. The details were first revealed at the trial, however, by the sad-looking Alice.

In an atmosphere already highly charged by her distressing recollections of her mother's death, she spoke of the afternoon of Sunday 4 December...and an unexpected visit by Sarah Barrow.

Sarah, on horseback, was passing the Steer house (it must have been situated in the area of what is now Morley Green Road) when Fanny Jackson, a friend or relative who seems to have been acting as housekeeper or nanny to Steer's motherless children, went out and invited her in. Alice said her father was upstairs at the time and Sarah 'went up to him and stayed there for half an hour'. Afterwards, they had tea with the three Steer girls, Steer seated on a high-backed wooden settle and Sarah on a chair beside him.

In handing round the refreshments, said Alice, Fanny Jackson had used 'Japanned tea-tongs'. And, commenting on the fact, Steer turned to Sarah and declared, 'Sally, when we are married we will have silver tea-tongs!' Alice Steer's deposition added only that 'after tea Sarah went home', leaving unsaid the astonishment she and the rest of the tea-table gathering must have felt at Steer's sudden pronouncement.

Sarah Barrow provided a fuller version of her Sunday afternoon visit to the Steers. She said she had met Steer earlier at the Quaker meeting. It was the first time she had been in Morley since the beginning of November when she left Thomas Cash's employment to nurse a sister, who was dying.

Steer inquired how she was and Sarah said she 'answered indifferent'. He asked her to call at his house later if she was passing that way, but again she was non-committal. When she did eventually arrive at the house, she said she had not really intended to stop as it was getting late, but Fanny Jackson had insisted. And, following Steer's 'silver tongs' remark, she said she 'gave him no answer'.

If Sarah's general unresponsiveness had not already started alarm bells ringing in Steer's head, what followed would have come as quite a shock to him.

After tea, he beckoned her into the parlour and, her statement added, he asked her if she could make use of any of his wife's numerous clothes. She said she was surprised that he could think of such a thing, whereupon he said he would 'make her a good husband and would have her to have him' (*sic*). But Sarah told him she 'did not intend it to be so', and left the room.

The disquieting fears which must now have assailed him – that he had badly misjudged Sarah's feelings towards him and risked his neck for nothing – would not have been allayed much, either, by her subsequent demeanour. On leaving the house, she ignored Steer, standing watching her departure from the shippon doorway, and rode off in the direction of Morley Green. As she turned into Burleyhurst Lane a few minutes later, however, Steer, having taken a short-cut across the fields, caught up with her and told her he 'wanted to say something more to her'. He again offered her marriage and, according to her deposition, Sarah replied off-handedly that she would 'think at it'.

In the gathering gloom, Steer walked with her for about half a mile then left her to continue on alone to her uncle's at nearby Mobberley (Old) Hall, where she was to spend the night before returning to Mere the following morning. She did not see Peter Steer again until the trial.

It seems likely, in fact, that Steer had been deluding himself all along about his prospects with the youthful Sarah, though it is difficult to resist the conclusion that she led him on to a large extent. The Quaker principle of equality, which they both embraced, presumably, would, in theory at least, have removed any social barrier to their betrothal at some future date. And as a friend of her father, Steer might reasonably have imagined that Josiah Barrow would give the parental consent which, since an Act of 1753, had been required for the marriage of a minor.

But, in spite of his living in surroundings which would have been considered substantial by most working-class standards – and notwithstanding the *Chronicle*'s trial remarks about his 'decent and reputable' appearance – Peter Steer was still a simple labouring man, while Sarah Barrow was educated and manifestly middle-class. There was also the not inconsiderable matter of the 25-year difference in their ages.

If, however, Sarah had unwisely gone along with Steer's romantic fancies earlier, she had clearly had second thoughts by the time of their last meeting on that Sunday afternoon in December.

It was the end of a torrid affair that had begun some time in the Spring of 1785…as Sarah had revealed when she opened her evidence. As she stepped into the witness-box, a buzz of anticipation spread through the public benches. And the 'thoughtless young creature' (the *Chronicle*'s description) did not disappoint the thrill-seekers in the gallery. As far as the jury were concerned, however, the most significant effect of Sarah Barrow's courtroom confessions was to provide vivid confirmation of the reasons why Phoebe Steer was murdered.

She began by recalling the first time Steer had made known his feelings for her. It happened about a year after she started working for Thomas Cash and her first meeting with Steer. She was turning the cornflour in the barn in which he was winnowing when, her deposition stated, 'he took hold of her and clasped her in his arms and gave her several kisses and wished she was his wife'. Then, about a week later (to use the *Chronicle*'s words again), 'an intimacy, criminal in its nature and fatal in its consequences, took place'.

Sarah said that one evening, as she and Steer were in the shippon together milking cows, he 'took her round by her neck in the cow boozey [cattle stall] and laid her down'. Sarah said she tried to break free from him but could not, and he forced her to have intercourse – or, rather, he 'had carnal knowledge of her', as she more delicately put it.

The extent to which the girl resisted, however, can perhaps be gauged from the next sentence in her deposition. It read, 'She was obliged to cry out, but not very loud, when he said to her, if she would not be quiet he would do the same to her as he had done, and if she persisted in shouting out he said his master would hear.'

The deposition added, nonchalantly, 'He then suffered her to get up and they finished milking the cows.' Sarah would have been 15 at the time.

A few weeks later, in May, as she recalled, the pair were again working together in Cash's barn. Steer was pitch-forking straw up off the barn floor into the 'balks' (the open loft area above), where Sarah was storing it away for winter feed for the animals.

The deposition stated, 'He came up to her when he had finished and, by violence, seized her and threw her down and had carnal knowledge of her.' Shortly afterwards, she said, Steer 'lay with her a second time', apparently without protest on this occasion. The age of consent in 18th century England was 12.

By now Steer seems to have become totally besotted with the girl. And, though he may not yet have contemplated murder seriously, Sarah claimed that in the weeks that followed he paid frequent Sunday morning visits to her master's farm, when she was alone in the house, and in their conversations he 'many times wished his wife dead for sake of her'.

What finally influenced Steer to kill his wife when he did is possibly explained by a seemingly unrelated reference in the brief, and otherwise corroborative, statement of Thomas Cash. In it the corn-dealer mentioned calling to see his sister Phoebe on the Sunday on which she was first taken ill. He said she told him that her husband 'frequently went out with a neighbouring man and stayed unreasonably with him'. And, in line with Quaker thinking which held that encouraging good behaviour was a shared responsibility, Mrs Steer said she had threatened him she would have words about it with her brother and with the mother of the other man.

Had Steer covered up his assignations with Sarah Barrow by claiming to have been out with this unidentified neighbour, perhaps? That being so, Phoebe's confrontation with the man's mother would have exposed the deception and, doubtless, the real cause of Steer's 'unreasonable' absences. It was a denouement Steer would have clearly wanted to prevent… and quickly.

That he chose poison, a 'weapon' more traditionally associated with women murderers, as the solution to his problem seems particularly appropriate in his case. Secretive, deceitful, treacherous…the nature of the crime matched perfectly the conduct of the man in the months that led up to it. Some indication of the determined and methodical way in which he administered the arsenic can be gleaned from two separate 'confessions' he was alleged to have made after his eventual conviction and the ending of a trial that lasted six hours.

The *Chester Chronicle*'s report of 28 April, referring to Steer's final hours in the county gaol, claimed, 'To the reverend gentleman who attended him, he made a full confession of his guilt, but solemnly disavowed the charge of having accelerated her death by strangulation [a suspicion raised by the marks observed on Phoebe Steer's neck shortly after her death]. He, however, declared (such was his resolution and impatience to destroy her) that he actually gave her three doses of arsenic on the night previous to the day of her dissolution.'

The second admission was contained in a broadside printed after Steer's execution. Bearing a woodcut depicting the execution cart and the ritualistic scene at 'the fatal tree', the broadside purported to contain the murderer's 'last dying speech and confession' and included a copy of a letter he was said to have written to his brother from the condemned cell.

Dated 21 April 1786, it included this passage, 'I now inform you of the truth, and nothing but the truth: And first, I gave her a small quantity of arsenic in some furmenty [sic]. Secondly, I gave her some more arsenic the same night in buttermilk and water.'

In the alleged letter, Steer also spoke of his affair with Sarah and begged his brother to look after his soon-to-be orphaned children, 'Sarah Barrow, she is the girl I was concerned with, and knows all these things, and would have gone with me out of the country. We went on very wickedly for twelve months together. She very frequently came to my bed, when she could pick an opportunity, to lie with me.'

The letter went on, 'Pray tell my dear Daughter to keep from Sarah Barrow's company, and shew her this letter, and tell her to take all the care she can of my youngest Daughter;

adding no more, but beg you will accept of this small acknowledgement of your unfortunate Brother. I beg you will take care of my fatherless and motherless children; and now, I leave you (in hope) as a father to them.' And it ended with the suspiciously familiar hope that 'my ignominious fate will be a sufficient warning to all'.

Ignoring for a moment its questionable origin, the letter suggests strongly that Peter Steer still believed he and Sarah could have had a future together. If, as seems likely, he was wrong, the same fatal delusion that cost Phoebe Steer her life was about to claim its second victim.

The broadside – judging by its sermonising tone, its author was a religious enthusiast of some sort: a local Quaker preacher, perhaps – also claimed that Steer tried to hang himself in prison.

He was executed at Boughton on Monday 24 April 1786. After noting that he was 'clearly convicted', the *Chronicle*'s report of the proceedings went on, 'Accordingly, at the time appointed, this unfortunate man was taken to the place of execution, amidst a prodigious concourse of spectators, where, after due time spent in prayer, the judgment of the law was put in execution, and his remains were afterwards delivered to an eminent surgeon for dissection. His behaviour, after condemnation, was marked with every appearance of penitence and resignation; and in his last moments he evinced a becoming sensibility of his unhappy situation.'

A more colourful description of public justice 18th-century style had appeared in the *Chronicle* two weeks earlier, on 14 April. The article, headed 'Executions – a fragment', was primarily an attack on the severity of the hanging laws, prompted by the record number of convicts condemned to die that spring at the various assizes up and down the country. The writer, the newspaper's Editor William Cowdroy, observed,

Tis true, the avenue of this mode of going out of life, is inconceivably ignominious and awful: the terror-striking bell – the officers of justice in their habiliments – the admonitory clergyman – the fabled cart – preceded by a squalid figure in the shape of a man, called the executioner – all environed by a multitude of sympathising spectators – among whom are females at intervals bursting into tears, and praising the 'cumliness [*sic*] of his person!' – the whole moving, as one body, in slow and silent pace towards the fatal tree – present a picture of solemnity and horror, indescribable...The curtain of eternal night having dropped upon the last scene of the culprit's life or (in other words) the execution being over, the multitude return to their several avocations, till evening arrives, when they again assemble, in little groups to recapitulate the dying words and actions of the deceased; another day passes and you do not hear him mentioned – save that a few hirelings had, late in the preceding night, with rude hands, lodged his body in an obscure corner of an unfrequented churchyard or probably in unhallowed earth – where his memory and his crimes are interred with his bones!

Part of the 1786 broadside relating the sensational details revealed at Peter Steer's trial about his seduction of a 15-year-old girl and the murder of his wife.

Cowdroy's message was that the deterrent value of capital punishment was being rendered ineffective by constant public exposure to what he saw as 'deplorable scenes of human carnage'. And he called on the legislators to devise, for certain types of felony, a mode of punishment, short of death, that was 'nearly, if not equally, replete with ignominy and horror' and possessed 'the salutary advantage of being permanent and lasting'.

He presumably had in mind imprisonment for life; however, in making his eloquent plea for humanitarian reform, the newspaper chief almost certainly did not have Peter Steer in mind. The *Chronicle* would later describe him as a 'remorseless wretch' who had committed a 'horrid and diabolical' murder. And popular opinion, very probably, was that he got what he deserved.

Cowdroy was more likely to have been thinking of the three other prisoners who were ordered to be executed at Chester Assizes that April: two for burglary and one for horse-stealing. But, if it was for these sorts of crimes that he was advocating new and less severe sentences, his campaigning was to be in vain.

Transportation – though in its own way undoubtedly ignominious, often horrific and sometimes permanent – continued as the only substantial alternative to hanging for more than half a century before being replaced by penal servitude in the 1850s. Horse-stealing remained a capital offence until 1806. And it was not until 1861, and the passing of the Criminal Law Consolidation Act, that the death penalty was officially reserved for murder and treason.

The latter change of law came distressingly too late to save Martin Doyle, who inadvertently assured Cheshire of a place in the criminal record books as the last county in Britain in which someone was executed for attempted murder. He was hanged at Chester on 27 August…just three months before the act came into force.

7

A Mother's Deadly Premonition

Persuant to his sentence [he] was launched into eternity from the drop at the back of the new gaol in this city. We are informed that the unhappy man persisted to the last in declaring his innocence of the murder and whilst conveying from the Castle he evinced the greatest fortitude. But when approaching the fatal platform he appeared very weak. It was the general opinion of spectators, on the curtain which enveloped the scaffold being drawn, that he was absolutely dead, but his immediately throwing down the handkerchief and the subsequent falling of the drop convinced them of their mistake...

Chester Chronicle, 4 May 1810

TO JAMES BOWDEN, making his usual early-morning journey to work along the canal towpath, the dirty brown shape floating near the water's edge looked like the bloated carcase of a drowned animal. At first. As he hurried by, however, he shot a second glance at the half-submerged object just below him. And what he saw stopped him in his tracks.

Reaching over and hauling the ragged bundle on to the bank, Bowden – employed in the local manufacture of the mixed linen and cotton cloth know as fustian – found himself staring down at the coarser texture of sacking…and the trussed-up corpse of a young woman.

The murder victim had been bound in the sack, with her head and shoulders and feet protruding, by means of a length of rope (a particularly distinctive kind of rope, as it turned out), which also secured a large stone. The intended weight, however, had failed in its purpose, and the body had been brought to the surface by the combined effect of abdominal gas and the movements of vessels on the then busy Bridgewater Canal.

The dumped remains were fished out of the Duke of Bridgewater's famous waterway on an Autumn day in 1809 in the little north Cheshire village of Lymm as, 15 miles 'upstream' in Manchester, a mother waited anxiously for news of her missing daughter.

The previous day, Mrs Betty Eckersley had suddenly been struck by a terrible foreboding, some sort of premonition, apparently, that the girl, also called Betty, was dead. Now, less than 24 hours later, her worst fears were about to be confirmed.

The body of the younger Betty Eckersley had been in the water for a little over a week. She had died from a broken neck sustained, it seemed, in the course of a severe beating. It did not take long to find a murder suspect.

Thomas Done, a young Runcorn boatmaster and former steady boyfriend of Betty, had been with the woman shortly before she disappeared. On that occasion he was observed late at night carrying her, protesting, into the cabin of his vessel, the *Six Brothers,* a 'flat' type barge which regularly plied the Bridgewater route between Manchester and the River Mersey. And Betty had told friends that Done had once threatened her after accusing her of cheating on him.

Picturesque Lymm Bridge on the Bridgewater Canal, from where the body of murder victim Betty Eckersley was recovered in September 1809. In the background: the Bull's Head pub.

The Bridgewater Canal during its busy heyday. The barges on the right are similar to the 'flat' boat that convicted murderer Thomas Done skippered and on which Betty Eckersley was killed.

Added to that, canal boatmen generally were looked upon as a rough, disreputable lot: waterway gypsies who invariably found release from their hard work in hard drinking, brawling and womanising. And Thomas Done, it appeared, was not untypical of the breed.

Such was the overwhelming strength of the *prima facie* evidence, in fact, that just one day after the recovery of Betty Eckersley's body, an inquest jury was sufficiently impressed to return a verdict of wilful murder and to name Done as the alleged killer.

When, seven months later, the 20-year-old boatman was manoeuvred into a dock that for once was grimly unfamiliar, however, he was not alone. For, as the story of the dead woman's final hours unfolded, a second man was implicated in the crime.

Robert Holroyd, aged 28, was also a 'flatman' and Done's assistant on the *Six Brothers* at the time. After making two statements which conflicted in one particularly significant detail, he, too, was charged with murder.

Without the benefit of a transcript of the trial, it is not even possible now to say for certain where or when, never mind how or why, Betty Eckersley was killed. From most of the surviving evidence it seems more than probable that she died aboard the *Six*

Brothers as it lay at its moorings after an overnight stay in Manchester…the fatal sequel to a quarrel following some drunken horseplay the previous evening.

But, as we shall see, at least two of the witnesses' depositions suggest another interesting, not to say bizarre, alternative.

What the court record does show is that the deadly course of events which ended with the discovery of the body in the Bridgewater, had its source on the connecting Rochdale Canal, the spectacular trans-Pennine waterway that climbs westwards into the hills above Sowerby Bridge then plunges 500ft into the heart of Manchester. Opened fully in 1804, the canal was the first of three to scale England's backbone, its 92 broad locks taking it in giant steps across the rugged borderlands of Yorkshire and Lancashire for a distance of 33 miles.

It was at the terminus of the short branch into Rochdale, however, that the *Six Brothers* began its tragic journey on Sunday 27 August 1809. Holroyd, who came from Elland in Yorkshire, had set off navigating the horse-drawn craft single-handedly while Done stayed behind trying to sort out some problem over waybills with the canal company clerks. The flat, so-called because of the shape of its hull, was probably a square-sterned Rochdale 'cutter', a variant of the Mersey flat, measuring approximately 70ft by 14ft beam, with a maximum capacity of 90 tons on a 5ft draught, though somewhat less on the fairly shallow Rochdale Canal.

The vessel was owned by a Littleborough carrier, Job Cogswell, but appears to have been on regular contract to the Bridgewater Canal Company. What she was hauling is not revealed, though it seems to have been merchandise of a less bulky nature than, say, coal, roadstone, timber, lime, corn or wood, which were the principle cargoes on this route at the time.

After negotiating the half-mile branch and pulling on to the main line of the canal south-east of the town, Holroyd led the flat south-westwards into the final 12-mile descent into Manchester; under Gorrell's and March Barn (reputedly the first two skew-type bridges ever built), past the fields and scattered communities of places with evocative names like Royal Barn, Mount Pleasant, Stake Hill and Slacks, then on through the increasingly urbanised environs of Failsworth, Newton Heath and Ancoats, before being swallowed up in the city's below-street-level warren of tunnels, wharves and basins.

The *Six Brothers* arrived in Manchester at about 6pm and was already tied up close to the Rochdale Canal Company's impressive warehouses off Dale Street when Done, following on by foot, caught up with her. Holroyd, by this time, had stabled the horse, washed and gone to the Bull's Head in Shude Hill with William Brookes and another boatman he knew only as 'Old David'. Around 8 o'clock Done joined them.

Betty Eckersley, who lived in Manchester, was also in the pub drinking at a separate table with two friends, Sarah Rigby and Martha Hancock. She was clearly in a happy mood. As Done entered she shouted out a greeting to him; and when he sat down she went over and perched playfully on his knee. The two other women also joined the men's company and they all drank together for an hour or so, getting through about a gallon of beer, paid for by Done.

When they all staggered out of the pub and around the corner into Thomas Street, Betty was on Done's arm. They were both fairly drunk. After standing about chatting for half an hour, the party dispersed, Holroyd and William Brookes going off together in the direction of the canal basin and Done, Betty and Sarah Rigby following close behind.

The Bull's Head in Shude Hill, Manchester, about 1900. After drinking here in the company of Thomas Done and others, Betty Eckersley accompanied him, somewhat reluctantly, back to his boat lying in the Dale Street basin. She never got out of it alive. Courtesy of Manchester Libraries, Information and Archives, Manchester City Council.

Reaching the end of Dale Street, a distance of almost half a mile, Holroyd went straight aboard the *Six Brothers* and to his bed in the cramped mate's quarters in the bows of the boat. Betty eventually went with Done into the more spacious captain's cabin aft.

She and Done had been friends for about three years, though for some reason his regular visits to her home had dropped off a year or so before. She seems to have asked Sarah Rigby to accompany her from the Bull's Head as a chaperon; and was less than enthusiastic about going aboard Done's boat without her.

As Sarah hesitated, however, Done took matters firmly in hand by sweeping up the reluctant Betty into his arms and carrying her off across the road towards the wharf. Sarah's last sight of her friend was of her silhouette disappearing through a darkened hatchway into the bowels of the flat.

The manner of the young woman's departure from the boat – and exactly what happened in the confines of that frowzy, ill-lit cabin in the intervening period – are similarly shadowy areas. In the trial depositions, the defendants gave contrasting accounts of events aboard the *Six Brothers*. Holroyd told two versions, both of which differed from Done's. And another witness provided a fourth slant on the perplexing affair.

In his first statement, Holroyd claimed he knew nothing about Betty's death. He said that about 6am the next day, Monday 28 August, he was awoken by Done and he went aft to the main cabin. The Eckersley woman, whom he had met for the first time the night before, apparently, was on one of the wooden lockers which, in the limited space below deck, doubled as seats. She was dressed and 'appeared in [good] health', said Holroyd.

For the next six hours or so, the two men occupied themselves with the orderly routine of a busy cargo boat: unloading the vessel, completing the necessary paperwork, securing a fresh horse for the next stage of the journey and negotiating the congested waterway traffic and the nine locks that lay between the Dale Street arm and the Rochdale Canal's junction with the Bridgewater.

Though it was only a one-and-a-quarter mile stretch of water, they made slow progress; and it was early afternoon before the now unladen *Six Brothers* eventually emerged from the Knott Mill Tunnel under Deansgate (at that time over 330 yards long) and arrived at Castlefield. This was the distribution centre for the Worsley coal trade that had inspired the youthful 3rd Duke of Bridgewater's grand canal venture and by then the main terminal of central Manchester's booming inland docks complex.

After passing through Duke's Lock into the Bridgewater, said Holroyd, Done told him he had 'put the woman ashore at Oxford Road end' while his assistant had been busy elsewhere.

Between 2 and 3pm at Cornbrook, on the south-western outskirts of Manchester, they were overtaken by a long-boat, an open-holded barge not unlike the flat but a couple of feet longer. As the long-boat went by, a woman poked her head through the cabin's hatch and, said Holroyd, Done remarked that it was the same woman who had been aboard the *Six Brothers* with him the night before.

The two men stopped for refreshment at Altrincham and, at about 7pm, arrived in Lymm, where they spent the night. Around 5 o'clock the next morning, Tuesday the 29th, they started out on the last leg of the haul to Runcorn, the expanding canal port at the western terminus of the Bridgewater.

Holroyd said he was with Done for the rest of the week and saw his skipper last on Saturday 2 September. Two days later Betty Eckersley's discarded body was retrieved from the canal near picturesque Lymm Bridge.

On Saturday 9 September, just 24 hours after making that statement, Robert Holroyd changed his story. By then two other witnesses had told of the time when, in a jealous outburst, Done had threatened Betty. Now Holroyd admitted he had seen the woman dead in Done's cabin; the business about putting her ashore in Manchester and then seeing her in the passing long-boat, he explained, had been a fiction invented by Done. They had agreed it should be their answer to anyone who came asking awkward questions about the missing Betty.

Knowing he, too, was under suspicion, Holroyd claimed he had had no involvement whatsoever in the murder or the disposal of the body. And, though he stopped short of accusing Done, he ensured that the balance of guilt tilted perceptibly in the other man's direction.

Holroyd's second deposition was an altogether more detailed diary of the vital hours surrounding Betty Eckersley's murder. He began by repeating his recollections of Sunday night – of what occurred both in the Bull's Head and at the Dale Street basin – and his claim that he had seen the woman alive and well at 6 o'clock on the Monday morning. Six hours later, however, she was dead, Holroyd now revealed.

Although it was a bit vague on times, if this new evidence was to be believed, the murder was committed, amid the clamour of canalside activity, either as the *Six Brothers* lay alongside the Rochdale Company's wharf or as she began her halting passage through the crowded network of city centre locks.

At some point during mid-morning, after the flat had moved the short distance from its overnight berth to a position directly in front of the warehouses, the job of unloading the vessel's unidentified cargo began. Later Holroyd left Done to it while he went to collect the horse from the nearby stables. He said he was gone for about an hour only. But when he returned, he found Done had completed the unloading operation and manhandled the flat to the head of the Dale Street lock. It would seem from Holroyd's testimony that by this time, too, Betty Eckersley was already dead.

Soon afterwards, Done disappeared; he told his mate he was going first to see about a bill of lading for the flat's next cargo (to be taken on board, presumably, at Castlefield) and that he would then be adjourning for a midday drink in the Woodman pub in Clowes Street (now lower Dale Street). It was while his captain was away that Holroyd said he learned of the woman's death.

The *Six Brothers* had by now passed through two locks and was 'parked' in the pound below Piccadilly awaiting its turn to lock down to the Chorlton Street level. A number of boats were already jammed together in the 300yd long pool, and on one of them Holroyd recognised Thomas Chadwick.

Chadwick, an owner-captain who was also from Elland, saw his friend was alone so he went to help him tie up in the queue. By way of thanks, Holroyd invited Chadwick below for a glass of rum and they went into Done's cabin. The time was about noon.

Holroyd said that while he was searching for the liquor, Chadwick discovered the woman in the 'bedhole', the cabin's boxed-in sleeping compartment. She was lying on her side on top of the bed-clothes, fully dressed.

Holroyd stated, 'Thomas Chadwick took hold of her hand and found her to be dead.' The woman's face and one side of her neck were said by Holroyd to be 'as black as his hat'.

The two men left the cabin immediately. Holroyd said Chadwick made some remark about it being 'a pity' and promptly returned to his previous employment 'discharging stones' (limestone, probably) a vessel's length away.

Holroyd walked the few hundred yards to the Woodman, where he found Done drinking with two canal employees. He said curtly, 'Come Tom, let us go.' But if Done wondered at his crewman's air of urgency, he does not appear to have questioned it. And for the next couple of hours Holroyd kept quiet about the body in the bunk.

In the end, he said, it was Done who broke the uneasy silence. Just below Oxford Street he went to his cabin for the first time since rejoining the flat at Piccadilly. Holroyd's deposition went on, 'He immediately returned and said "This woman is dead, we must keep our own counsel or we shall both be hanged".' Holroyd said he protested his innocence and told Done that Thomas Chadwick had also seen the lifeless Betty, but Done made no reply.

There was no further conversation about the matter, either, until the flat had cleared the city limits and was heading south into the relative peace and tranquillity of the Cheshire countryside. Then, said Holroyd, Done told him he had put the body into a sack, to which the other man again responded with a plaintive 'I am innocent.'

At Altrincham the flat made its customary half-hour halt at the Bridgewater Canal Company's warehouse. It was a regular refreshment break, but Done said he was not hungry and remained in his cabin. Holroyd insisted he went nowhere near his captain's quarters during the stop-over. From there they travelled on to Lymm. Holroyd rode the horse and the two men barely spoke to each other.

When they arrived in Lymm in the early evening, Holroyd took the horse to John Wrigley's stable at the Bull's Head in the village, leaving Done with the vessel. After paying the landlord the 1s 8d stabling charge, he had several drinks with two other flatmen and returned to the *Six Brothers* at about 9 o'clock to find the captain had already gone to bed. Done, he said, slept until five the next morning.

But Holroyd, despite the soporific effect of the alcohol, 'did not sleep very well'; the events of the day, it seems, were weighing heavily on his mind. Consequently, he said, he 'knew Done had not got up in the night' – the inference being that he must have got rid of Betty Eckersley's body while Holroyd was at the pub.

The *Six Brothers* continued on its way the following morning via Preston Brook, the important trans-shipment port at the Bridgewater's junction with the Trent and Mersey Canal, and thence on to Done's home-town of Runcorn.

In 1809 Runcorn was a town of around 2,000 people. Seven years earlier it had been described in a trade directory as 'an astonishing place of business', with stone-quarrying and boat-building adding considerably to the commercial activity that had been generated by the completion in 1776 of the Bridgewater Canal, the first modern industrial navigation in England and the feat of engineering that launched the great canal age. At Runcorn the canal terminated at the Top Locks basin, from where a flight of 10 locks provided access to the River Mersey tideway and the lucrative trade route between Liverpool on the north bank of the estuary and Manchester, the North West and the Midlands.

The end of the Line: Top Locks, Runcorn, the western terminus of the Bridgewater Canal and a familiar sight to Thomas Done on his travels to and from his home town.

The opening in 1804 of the Old Quay Canal, built by the Mersey and Irwell Navigation Company from Latchford to Runcorn, brought more dockside business to the town and helped boost population further. But it was over the next four decades, when competition between the Bridgewater and Mersey and Irwell companies reached a peak of intensity (ending only when, in 1844, Lord Francis Egerton, the Duke of Bridgewater's heir, bought out the rival navigation for £550,800), that the real growth in Runcorn occurred. In that time the town's population rose to almost 10,000 as a direct result of its expanding role as a major canal port.

The mushrooming community was centred on the old village of Lower Runcorn, situated just east of Top Locks and close to the ancient Mersey Ferry that had operated over the quarter-mile narrows at Runcorn Gap since the 12th century and which remained the only means of crossing the river thereabouts until the London and North Western Railway Company's bridge, with its iron spans and massive battlemented stone piers, was opened for both rail and foot passengers in 1869. From a town of 320 dwellings in 1801, Runcorn began to spread out in three main tentacles of development along the lines of what were to become Bridge Street, Church Street and High Street, and by 1851 the number of households had increased by eight-fold.

The town in which Thomas Done grew up – he was born the son of James and Mary Done in the parish of All Saints on 28 December 1789 – was also a popular spa. John Aikin, in *A Description of the Country from Thirty to Forty Miles Around Manchester*, published in 1795, said Runcorn was 'a place of some resort for salt-water bathing [where] the agreeable situation and the good air…are useful auxiliaries to the effects of the bath'. Its salubrious climate later earned it the title of 'the Montpelier of Manchester…[to] where the invalids of that town resort for their health'.

All this, of course, was before the chemical industry took up permanent residence on both sides of the river in the middle of the 19th century, transforming Runcorn's sparkling waters into a huge open sewer and darkening its skies with clouds of pollution.

It was, however, to the resort town of Runcorn, its summer bathing season now drawing to a close, that Done returned on that Tuesday in August 1809. Arriving at the Top Locks basin, end-of-the-line on the Bridgewater route, he repeated his warning to Holroyd that they must 'keep their counsel' or they would both hang. Holroyd's only reaction, it seems, was to plead his innocence for the third time.

For the rest of the week the two men travelled the Rochdale and Bridgewater canalways together without, apparently, saying another word about the late Miss Eckersley. Finally, on the Saturday after they had arrived in Manchester, Holroyd could contain his curiosity no longer, and he asked Done what he had done with the body. Done, he said, refused to tell him, and instead persuaded him that, if he was questioned about her disappearance, he would go along with the lie about the woman leaving the flat at Oxford Road and their having seen her last in another boat at Cornbrook.

Holroyd's final statement, before appending his cross to this second deposition, was to identify the piece of rope tied around the body in the canal. He said he recognised it as having come from Done's vessel by the special way it was 'whipp'd at the ends'.

On 8 September Thomas Done, already in custody, was taken before the examining magistrate to be confronted with Robert Holroyd's first statement and the testimony of

Sarah Rigby, the companion who had witnessed the deceased's rather undignified arrival aboard the *Six Brothers* after the Sunday night drinking session. When he had read the depositions, Done commented, 'I am innocent of the death of Betty Eckersley.'

The following day he, too, made a full statement in which he again denied he was a murderer, but admitted he had helped dispose of the body – an act in which, he alleged, Robert Holroyd had been a willing accomplice.

Done also laid the foundation for what was to become, apparently, his persistent defence to the charge of murder, which was that Betty Eckersley had drunk herself to death, that she had received her injuries after being dumped overboard – presumably by being struck by the keels of passing canal craft – and that he had been panicked into attempting to do away with the body by the fear of being accused of her murder.

The deposition, its scrawled X 'signature' indicating that, like his mate, Done was also illiterate, began by tracing the events of Sunday 27 August, including the fact that Betty had accompanied him back to his boat, though there was no mention of her reluctance to go aboard the flat. It merely stated, 'Betty Eckersley went with him and stayed all night.'

At around 7 o'clock the next morning, Done said, he gave her a glass of rum and put the bottle back in the cupboard of his cabin. About a pint of liquor remained. Soon afterwards he went up on deck to begin the day's work, leaving her below 'alive and hearty'. He did not see her again, he said, until the vessel had passed through the fifth lock from the Dale Street basin (Oxford Road).

The deposition went on, 'He went into the cabin and found her lying on the bed dead. Her knees were drawn up towards her face and her face was bent towards her knees.'

Done went back up on deck and on to the towpath, where Holroyd was tending the horse. He told his assistant that the woman was dead and asked him if he 'knew the cause of it'. Holroyd said he did not. Done said he had not examined the body to try to ascertain the cause of death, but that he and Holroyd then 'talked about what should be done with her'. He told Holroyd he had noticed some rum was missing and said that the mate replied, 'I suppose she has drunk to an excess to kill herself' (a claim Holroyd strongly rejected in his second statement).

It was as the flat neared Lymm that they finally decided what to do with the body, Done revealed. He stated, 'Holroyd proposed she should be put into a sack and thrown into the old river' (presumably the River Bollin, which the Bridgewater Canal crosses on a small aqueduct three miles outside the village). But Done said, 'No. She shall be put into the canal where she may be found and get interred.'

He admitted getting a large stone from the canal bank and tying it to the sack-bound Betty with a rope off the vessel. And he said Holroyd helped him jettison the body overboard at a place called Clambrook, halfway between Oughtrington and Lymm.

It was a story Done stuck to, apparently, until he died. And, significantly, he at no time appears to have attempted to implicate his crewman in Betty Eckersley's death, whereas Holroyd in his re-examination had made a number of damaging insinuations about Done.

If it was now obvious that one of the suspects was lying, the subsequent evidence of Thomas Chadwick was to indicate that both men knew more about the murder than they were letting on. Much more.

Chadwick, it will be remembered, was the flatman friend Holroyd said had been with him when they discovered Betty, while the *Six Brothers* was held up in the Manchester locks. Holroyd had stated that the woman was already dead; but now his fellow Yorkshireman claimed otherwise.

In a deposition made to a magistrate at Knutsford on 14 September, Chadwick said he had come across the woman in the dimly lit cabin when he accidentally brushed against her hand hanging over the edge of the bed. The statement went on, 'He looked upon the bed and saw the face of a woman which was very pale, and which shocked him.'

But he made it clear he did not believe her to be dead. For he allegedly asked Holroyd, 'What does the woman ail, think you Robert?' The mate, stated Chadwick, said he did not know; and, when asked whether Done had given her anything to drink, said that he thought he had.

When he returned to his own vessel, Chadwick said, he told his wife and their hand Benjamin Crowder that he had just seen a woman 'so ill he had been frightened'. He denied telling Holroyd she was dead or saying anything about it being a pity.

If Thomas Chadwick was telling the truth, Betty Eckersley may still have been alive when the *Six Brothers* left Manchester. Now it was, of course, perfectly understandable that Holroyd's boat-owner friend would not have wanted to admit he had knowledge of a suspicious death and had done nothing about it. But statements were subsequently obtained from two other witnesses who seemed to be offering information in support of his inference that Betty Eckersley did not die until much later.

John Wrigley, the publican who had stabled the tow-horse during the *Six Brothers'* lay-over in Lymm, stated that just after 12 o'clock the same night he was in his backyard when he heard a woman's agonised cries coming from the direction of the canal bank. The Bull's Head is only a matter of yards from the towpath and, said Wrigley, he distinctly heard her call out 'Lord Jesus! Oh my God!'…'as if in the last extremity'. The woman cried out again but this time her voice was much weaker and he was unable to make out the words. He said at first he had assumed it was his neighbour's wife in labour, but he learned later that it could not have been as she was not at home that night.

Another neighbour, Ann Middlebrook, appeared to give partial corroboration to the inn-keeper's intriguing testimony. Though unsure about the date, she, too, remembered a recent midnight disturbance on the canal bank and hearing 'the voice of a woman in great distress'. The cries eventually 'got fainter or appeared farther off', she recalled.

Looking at the case papers now, these two latter depositions seem disconcertingly out of place. But, taken with Chadwick's statement, they suggest only one possibility: that Betty Eckersley, after lying unconscious from the effects of alcohol or a beating, or both, came to at some point and was finally silenced in a midnight assault at Lymm. And, if it did happen that way, they are persuasive evidence that Holroyd (who admitted he had been aboard the flat with Done at the time and that he had been lying awake) not only knew about the murder...but may have had some part in it.

By inferring in his 'second thoughts' statement that the crime had been committed on board the *Six Brothers* in Manchester – while he was (conveniently) away from the boat – Holroyd had shown no obvious inclination to protect Done; so why, unless it was to cover up his own involvement, would he disagree with two seemingly independent witnesses and insist the girl died long before they got to Lymm?

A more plausible explanation, of course, is that the midnight screams were unconnected with the murder and that Chadwick lied to excuse his own irresponsible behaviour after finding the body. But the fact that Ann Middlebrook's deposition was dated 8 January 1810, would seem to suggest that, even four months after the murder inquiry began, there was still uncertainty about the precise circumstances of Betty Eckersley's death.

That the investigation should flounder in a cross-current of doubts and deceit was not altogether surprising, however, given the murky waters into which it had strayed. For the domain of the early 19th century canal boatmen, it seems, was a distinctly unsavoury place: a sort of parallel world in which, long before the excesses of their dissolute lifestyle were exposed to Parliamentary censure – at the Select Committee hearings on the Observance of the Sabbath (1831) and Sunday Trading on Canals and Navigable Rivers and Railways (1841) – the floating population had acquired a reputation for dishonesty, violence, drunkenness and immorality.

In 1818 one carrying company agent tarred the whole of this new nomad-like generation of workers as 'a vile set of rogues'. And there was a major public outcry in June 1839, after a Liverpool woman in her early 30s was raped and killed while travelling alone on a passenger boat on the Trent and Mersey Canal.

The body of Mrs Christina Collins, who had joined the London-bound fly-boat at Preston Brook, was thrown overboard at Brindley's Bank near Rugeley in Staffordshire by the three drunken boatmen responsible for her murder. The 39-year-old captain and one of the crew were sentenced to death for their parts in the crime and the third man was transported for life.

While the image was doubtless distorted, it was certainly true that the canals did attract a lot of the wrong sort. The rapidly developing system of water transport – between 1790 and 1794, when the first wave of canal mania swept the country, Parliament authorised no fewer than 81 navigations – brought wage levels unheard of before. With generous bonuses available, too, a captain of a Weaver Navigation flat, for instance, was said to be able to earn £80 a year in 1795. And, two years later, following a strike threat, the new basic rates for Mersey and Irwell flatmen were fixed at 16s a week for captains, 13s for mates and 6s to 9s for hands.

Root cause of the problem, however, was that between 1790 and 1815 England was at war with France and many able-bodied men were in military service. As a result, in the words of Harry Hanson in his book *Canal People* (David and Charles, 1978), 'disreputable characters found their way on to the waterways to taint them for the remainder of their existence'.

How Thomas Done and Robert Holroyd fitted into this somewhat grimy picture is impossible to say; but another of Hanson's sketches seems particularly appropriate to the two Eckersley murder suspects and, indeed, to the case itself. In *The Canal Boatmen, 1760-1914* (Manchester University Press, 1975), he concludes, 'There were many young, undisciplined, unmarried men, cut off from civilising influences, who were to be found letting off steam after five days or more "on the cut" with little rest, preparing themselves for a similar period of abstinence'. And heavy drinking and fornication seem to have been their main sources of recreation.

Boatmen also had to be strong to cope with the physical demands of the job; and, as Harry Hanson points out, to get their boats through they had to be pretty forceful people, too. It was quite common, for instance, for a dispute over who had precedence at a lock to be settled by a fist-fight on the towpath. On the densely trafficked routes of the North, such 'strength of character' would have been a particularly essential pre-requisite. And to have attained the rank of captain by the age of 20 – even in a labour market depleted by the manpower calls of the Napoleonic Wars – Thomas Done must have had to display more than an average amount of that quality of tough determination. The relevant witnesses' statements in the case file, flawed though some of them undoubtedly are, underpin the impression that he had just that kind of dominant personality.

That his were the powerful hands that had slain Betty Eckersley soon became apparent, too, when the two flatmen were tried at Chester Assizes on Monday 30 April 1810. Whether, by then, the apparent conflict over the time and location of the murder had been resolved, and what line the prosecution's case eventually took, the surviving records do not tell us, unfortunately. The only certainty is that the jury decided that Done – and he alone – was the killer. Holroyd, probably as much by the testimony of Done himself as anything else, was acquitted.

Key witnesses at the trial were the three women closest to the victim: her widowed mother, her sister Ellen and friend Sarah Rigby. Between them they supplied the important background details of Done's relationship with Betty, about his threatening her and about the Sunday night binge that had a hangover of horror. And from Mrs Eckersley came the dramatic account of her foretaste of fear...

She told the jury that Betty had lived with her and her other daughter, Mrs Ellen (Tess) Walker, at their Manchester home until January 1809. Why she left, or where she went, was not explained in the witnesses' statements, though she apparently remained in Manchester. Then, during the summer, unbeknown to her mother, she moved in with Sarah Rigby.

Mrs Eckersley said her daughter had 'kept company' with Thomas Done for some time and he had often called at the house to see her. At the time of Betty's death, though, he had not been for more than a year. After he became 'slack in his visits', Betty quit her job as a cotton weaver and became 'very low and uneasy' and complained of being 'unhappy in her mind', said Mrs Eckersley.

At one stage she told her mother glumly, 'I fear Tom Done is got married [*sic*].' This proved not to be so; and shortly afterwards it was his turn to be jealous, it seems. For when Betty next spoke of Done she said he had threatened her.

Mrs Eckersley explained, 'He told her he would be an enemy to her by night and by day for having kept company with another man.'

It was on Sunday 3 September, that Mrs Eckersley had her premonition. Since January she had had only occasional contact with her daughter and was unaware that she had not been seen for a week. Had she known of her daughter's absence, she might not have attached too much significance to it; Sarah Rigby and the young woman's other close friends obviously did not. After all, Betty had been friendly with Done for three years and had no doubt accompanied her boatman boyfriend on his travels before.

But in the middle of the day, Mrs Eckersley said she was 'all at once struck with fear' and, her deposition went on, 'Betty Eckersley came into her mind'.

Unable to shake off her unaccountable feeling of anxiety, the widow Eckersley went in search of Tess Walker to see if she knew of Betty's whereabouts. She found her at a neighbour's house with two other young women, one of whom, by coincidence, was Sarah Rigby. Sarah confessed she had not heard from Betty for a week and recounted details of their last meeting and of the Sunday night antics at the canal basin.

Mrs Eckersley listened with a deepening sense of alarm, then she revealed her own private fears. Now, for the first time, apparently, there was genuine concern for the missing woman's safety.

It seems likely that the worrying disclosures would have jolted the family into some kind of action, starting, probably, with inquiries at the Bull's Head, then at other nearby haunts of the canal workers and, ultimately perhaps, a visit to one of the local constables. That the authorities had already been notified of the circumstances of Betty Eckersley's disappearance by the time she was found dead would certainly help explain how, in the days when no co-ordinated system of law enforcement existed and the horse was still the speediest means of communication, there was sufficient information available to enable the inquest jury to reach such an emphatic verdict within little more than 24 hours of the discovery of Betty Eckersley's body.

An 18th-century view of the Dee basin, part of what had once been the thriving port of Chester, overlooked by the city walls and, on the extreme right, the City Gaol, Cheshire's new place of execution, where Thomas Done was among the first to be hanged.

Tess Walker's trial statement supported her mother's evidence, though her account of her sister's friendship with Done differed in a couple of minor details: the man's visits to their home had ceased about 18 months ago, she said. And Done's threat to Betty had been that he would 'haunt her by night and by day'. As a result of the latter, Tess said, she had warned her sister to keep away from him.

The deposition of Sarah Rigby, whose address was also given simply as Manchester, revealed she had known Betty for some years and that they had lived in the same house for the previous three months. She said she had seen Betty and Done together many times. On that last occasion, after leaving the Bull's Head, she said she had stayed with Betty at her friend's insistence. They reached the Dale Street basin and, before she knew what was happening, she said Done 'took Betty in his arms and carried her off across the street'.

Betty, she said, begged, 'Tom, let me go!' But Done replied, 'No, thou shalt go aboard with me.' And he lifted her on to the deck of the *Six Brothers* and into his cabin.

Sarah returned home alone, clearly believing that, despite her protests, her friend and house-mate was in no danger. It must have come as a particular shock to her, therefore, when she eventually learned of Betty's murder.

James Bowden, the Lymm fustian-cutter whose canal bank discovery broke the news of the tragedy, said in his statement that the object he had seen floating in the Bridgewater on 4 September had been about 40 yards from Lymm Bridge. His deposition went on, 'He thought it was a dead dog or a sheep, but on drawing it to the side discovered it was the body of a woman.' He said she 'had no cap or hat or shoes on' and he also noticed that 'her toes were poking out of her stockings'.

The body was removed to a nearby building where it was examined by Dr Thomas Grundy, a local apothecary and surgeon. Dr Grundy deposed that the woman was dressed in a red and white bedgown, a pair of stays, a black skirt, white underskirt, a calico shift and coarse black stockings. In one of her pockets he found a red ribbon and a penny-piece. Cause of death, said the doctor, was dislocation of the neck. There were bruises on the woman's arms and back, but no wounds on the head or body.

His somewhat brief trial testimony does not convey the extent of the injuries which the doctor seems to have reported to the coroner's court on 5 September, the day after he examined the body. For, in the intimidating legal language of the day, the official inquest record alleged that Done 'not having the Fear of God before his Eyes, but wooed and seduced by the Instigation of the Devil…did beat, strike and kick Betty Eckersley about the belly, breast, arms, back and sides' before delivering the fatal blow to the neck.

The result, however, was the same: the jury found Done guilty of murder after a trial lasting nearly five hours. The case attracted considerable interest, of course, and, said the *Chester Courant* on 1 May the court was 'excessively crowded' as Chief Justice Robert Dallas 'pronounced the awful sentence of the law'.

Done was hanged on Wednesday 2 May 1810, at the new city gaol in Chester. Opened two years earlier in City Walls Road, it was built to replace the old and dilapidated

Northgate Gaol, which had briefly taken over as the county's place of execution in 1801, when the traditional roadside gallows at Boughton was finally declared obsolete. By now the so-called 'new drop' method of execution, involving a raised platform and trapdoor, was in common use and a temporary structure had been erected especially for the occasion on the east side of the prison. As if to add an extra touch of theatricality to the action about to unfold on the makeshift 'stage', a curtain was draped around the scaffold, which was opened on cue as the trap fell away.

According to the two rival Chester newspapers, the *Chronicle* and *Courant*, Thomas Done protested his innocence to the bitter end.

The *Courant's* execution report of 8 May began, 'On Wednesday last, about 2 o'clock, this unfortunate young man suffered the sentence of the law, which requires the execution of a murderer within forty-eight hours after condemnation.' It went on to state, 'He admitted that he had forced the young woman into the sack, when she was dead, and thrown her into the canal; that she died as a consequence of the liquor she had drunk on board his flat; and that he had thus disposed of her, under an apprehension, that if found dead in his vessel, he would have been accused of murdering her.'

The *Chronicle* of 4 May concluded its report, 'He…acknowledged himself guilty of almost every other crime, but the sin of murder he strenuously denied.'

A short note added to the official death warrant, preserved in the Cheshire Record Office, confirmed Done's 'not guilty' pleas and revealed that, following the execution, his body was delivered to Chester surgeon Griffith Rowlands and was subsequently 'dissected and anatomised in the Exchequer or Quarter Sessions room' at Chester Castle. The following day, in accordance with the then current practice, it was subjected to further medical analysis in a public display of the anatomist's art.

Before his remains were returned to his family for burial, Thomas Done had, therefore, been able to add a little to the store of knowledge about the hidden secrets of human life. But, as to the death of Betty Eckersley – who had been laid to rest with somewhat less ceremony in Lymm Churchyard on 5 September 1809 – it seems the inside story of that particular mystery was never fully exposed.

The jury appears to have been in no doubt that Done, having punched and kicked her, killed Betty with a single neck-snapping blow after a fight aboard the *Six Brothers*. But what could have provoked such an outburst of anger? What happened in the dingy, claustrophobic atmosphere of the young canal man's cabin to start the row which ended in Betty Eckersley's violent death?

Remembering her mother's comment about her once expressed concern that Done had married someone else, perhaps she had begged him to make an honest woman of her; and he made it clear he had no intention of being tied down. Or maybe Betty, her resistance blunted by alcohol the previous evening, decided in the sober light of dawn to heed her sister's warning and disentangle herself at the earliest possible opportunity; and it was Done, keen to have her share his company as well as his bunk on the trip ahead, who did the pestering.

Possibly, the old arguments about her having 'kept company with another man' were re-kindled, and this time Done's burning jealousy drove him beyond mere threats. Or was there a more mundane cause of the flare-up – like a sulky squabble over the captain's missing rum, for instance?

Whatever the reason, it seems probable that Done did not intend to kill Betty; but that by attempting to conceal the result of his moment of violence he compounded one fatal mistake with another, finally tossing overboard any hope of an accident or manslaughter verdict along with his bundled-up victim.

Today, with only the contracted, and contradictory, evidence of the depositions to go on, however, the truth behind the Body in the Bridgewater Canal Murder is, like the turbid depths of the once great waterway itself, as impenetrable as ever.

8

'Seduced by the Devil'

> The poor wretches were at length...delivered up, stript stark naked by the mob, their thumbs tied to their toes, then dragged two miles, and thrown into a muddy stream; after much ducking and ill usage, the old woman was thrown quite naked on the bank, almost choked with mud, and expired in a few minutes, being kick'd and beat with sticks, even after she was dead; and the man lies dangerously ill of his bruises; to add to the barbarity, they put the dead witch (as they called her) in bed with her husband, and tied them together...

The Gentleman's Magazine, 22 April 1751

I T HAD been 15 years since Parliament at last decreed that, in the eyes of the law at least, witches no longer existed; in practice, no one had been brought before the courts for dabbling in the black arts for over 30 years. And the devouring flame of persecution that once scorched through the land had last blazed almost a century before.

But in the remoter areas of the countryside old suspicions linger, the old ways die hard. And in a tiny hamlet in Hertfordshire a harmless old woman of 70 suffered a humiliating death at the hands of a hysterical mob after being 'put to the test'. The great fire of witch-hunting, fanned for 200 years by religious bigotry, superstition, irrational fear and ignorance, went out, not so much with a flicker, as a conscience-searing roar.

The 'ordeal by water' of Ruth Osborne – and, perhaps more significantly, the subsequent execution for murder of the mob's ring-leader – finally brought the nation to its senses, it seems. The dreadful delusion that at intervals had induced a sort of mass paranoia would never again excite such popular passion...the collective demon of witchcraft had been cast out once and for all.

The infamous incident at Long Marston, near Tring, in 1751 was the last recorded case of witch-baiting in England and the last time, in effect, that an alleged witch was put to death, though on this occasion without the sanction of the law. It was a turning point in judicial history, however. For the trial and condemnation of Ruth Osborne's murderer was a forceful demonstration that the legislature, which for two centuries had encouraged intolerance and prejudice, was now as much on the side of so-called witches as any other victims of injustice.

Ruth Osborne, whose unedifying end served as a warning against the kind of lynch-mob fervour with which so many innocent women had been hounded to their deaths in earlier times, died in far more excruciating circumstances than anyone ever suffered as a result of witchcraft. The allegations against her, as in the case of countless other loose-tongued, quick-tempered crones before her, arose out of a run-in she had had with one of her neighbours.

According to *The Gentleman's Magazine*, in an article dated 2 May 1751, 'a little before the defeat of the Scotch in the late rebellion' [i.e. the routing of the Young Pretender, Bonnie Prince Charlie, and his Jacobite army at the Battle of Culloden, 12 January 1746], the poor Mother Osborne called on a man named Butterfield, who kept a dairy at Gubblecote, and begged for some buttermilk. 'But,' the magazine recorded, 'Butterfield told her with great brutality that he had not enough for his hogs; this provoked the old woman, who went away, telling him, that the Pretender would have him and his hogs too.'

Some time afterwards several of Butterfield's calves went down with distemper and some of his friends, recalling the incident of the buttermilk, suggested the old woman had bewitched the animals out of revenge.

A few years later Butterfield, by now the landlord of a public house in Gubblecote, began to have fits, and once again he was persuaded that old Mother Osborne was the cause of his troubles. The doctors told him they could do nothing for him so, as a last resort, he consulted a 'wise woman' in Northamptonshire 'famous for curing diseases that were produced by witchcraft'.

The Gentleman's Magazine went on, 'This sagacious person...confirmed the ridiculous opinion that had been propagated of Butterfield's disorder, and ordered six men to watch his house day and night with staves, pitchforks, and other weapons, at the same time hanging something about their necks, which, she said, was a charm that would secure them from being bewitched themselves.'

When this ludicrous charade failed to have any effect, Butterfield and some of his cronies decided to take the law into their own hands. Through the criers of several neighbouring towns, they had it announced that both Osbornes, husband as well as wife (John Osborne was accused of being a 'wizard', though exactly why was never made clear) were to be put to the traditional witch test of 'swimming' at Tring on 22 April 1751.

'Swimming', in which the victim was usually immersed in the water with each thumb tied to the big toe of the opposite foot, was not so much a trial as a virtual death sentence. If the accused witch floated she was taken to be guilty and promptly despatched to the gallows; if she sank, and was therefore adjudged innocent, she was clearly in very serious danger of drowning.

When the parish officers heard of the threat, they had the couple admitted to the workhouse for their own safety; then on the night of the 21st they were removed to the sanctuary of the parish church. But the mob, led by one Thomas Colley and 'upwards of

A mid-17th-century engraving of four witches being hanged together. Key: A, Hangman; B, Bellman; C, Two sergeants; D, Witchfinder, taking his money. In Cheshire there were two occasions when three witches were hanged at the same time.

A depiction of the 'swimming' test for witches. The accused was usually immersed in the water with each thumb tied to the big toe of the opposite foot. If she floated she was taken to be guilty and promptly despatched to the gallows; if she sank, though adjudged innocent, there was every chance she would die from drowning.

5,000' strong, according to one 18th century account, demolished a wall at the workhouse and broke windows and fencing in their fury and threatened to burn the building down and fire the whole town if the workhouse master did not hand the Osbornes over. Their victims thus secured, the mob carried the helpless old couple more than three miles to Marston Mere.

The ensuing events were recounted at Hertford Assizes on 31 July 1751, when Thomas Colley was tried for Ruth Osborne's murder. Again *The Gentleman's Magazine* supplies the details, 'Having wrapped the deceased and her husband in sheets…the most active of the mob dragged the deceased into the water by a cord which they had put round her body, and she not sinking, the prisoner Colley went into the pond, and turned her over several times with a stick; after a considerable time she was hawl'd to shore, and the old man was dragged into the pond in the same manner; and this they repeated to each three times. The deceased after she was dragg'd in the third time, being pushed about by the prisoner, slipt out of the sheet, and her body was exposed naked; notwithstanding which the prisoner continued to push her on the breast with his stick, which she with her left hand endeavoured to catch hold of, but was prevented by his snatching it away. After using her in this manner till she was motionless, they dragg'd her to shore, and laid her on the ground where she expired; and then the prisoner went afterwards among the spectators, and collected money for the pains he had taken in shewing them sport. The old man afterwards recovered...'

Colley, a chimney sweep, was found guilty and was executed at Gubblecote Cross, about half a mile from the scene of the crime, on Saturday 24 August 1751. He was later hung in chains on the same gallows, the people living around Marston Mere having successfully petitioned against him being gibbeted near their homes, as would have been the more customary choice of site.

It was reported that 'the infatuation of the greatest part of the country people was so great that they would not be spectators of his death (perhaps from a consciousness of being present at the murder as well as he); yet many thousands stood at a distance to see him go, grumbling and muttering that it was a hard case to hang a man for destroying an old wicked woman that had done so much mischief by her witchcraft'.

Colley himself, in a signed declaration read by the minister just before he was turned off, admitted being instrumental in the 'horrid and barbarous' murder, however, and exhorted his listeners not to be 'deluded into so absurd and wicked a deceit, as to believe that there are any such beings as witches'.

As absurd and wicked as it undoubtedly was, the deceit of witchcraft deluded men of far superior status and intellect than Thomas Colley in its time: scholars and statesmen, lawyers and clergy, generals and even kings...all fell under its infectious spell once the witch plague took hold.

Witchcraft itself was rooted in the primitive beliefs and pagan rituals of 'the Old Religion', the simple faith in, and awe of, the forces of nature (fertility and the regenerative power of 'Mother Earth', the changing seasons, the weather and so on), which survived well into the Christian period. In the more inaccessible parts of the countryside, where the Church's redeeming light was slower to penetrate, the remnants of this ancient nature religion could still be discerned in the late Middle Ages in the presence in villages of the 'wise woman' or 'cunning man' who, as well as having the local franchise in knowledge and experience, dispensed potions and herbal remedies for a multitude of (as then) unidentified ills, supplied charms and other mystical preparations to order and who, when the occasion demanded, could be called upon to attempt more advanced forms of magic.

But the source of the contagion that caused the deadly outbreaks of witch-mania throughout Europe can be traced to the great religious upheavals of the Middle Ages. First there was the fanatical crusade of the Roman Catholic Church against the many-headed monster of heresy, a process of elimination whose most feared instrument of terror and destruction was the Inquisition, with its systematic torturing and burning of suspects.

Then, in the aftermath of the Reformation, both Catholics and Protestants alike waged campaigns to purge their imagined enemies.

In Scotland, where persecution was considerably more intense than in the rest of Britain, witches were also routinely tortured before being put to death; whereas in England, slower to react to the infection than her European neighbours, the use of torture was never legally applied. Contrary to popular conception, too, witches were hanged not burned to death, and the number of executions was not as high as was once believed. The now widely accepted estimate, first advanced by C. L'Estrange-Ewen in *Witch Hunting and Witch Trials*, published in 1929, is that in England between 1542–1736 the total was 'less than 1,000'.

The first witchcraft statute in this country, making it a capital offence to 'use devise practise or exercise, or cause to be used devysed practised or exercised, any Invocacons or conjuracons of Sprites wichecraftes enchauntments or sorceries', was passed in 1542. It was repealed five years later, but in 1563 it was replaced by a new Act which reinstated the death penalty for using, practising or exercising 'any Witchecrafte Enchantment Charme or Sorcerie, whereby any person shall happen to bee killed or destroyed'.

The English witch-hunting disease spread rapidly under the influence of Elizabethan law; but it reached new heights in the reign of James I (1603–1625).

James himself was a keen student of the phenomenon and came to be a firm believer in the power of witchcraft. In the year of his accession he authorised tougher new legislation ('An Acte against Conjuration Witchcrafte and dealinge with evill and wicked Spirits'), which now also made it a capital offence to 'consult covenant with entertaine employ feede rewarde any evill and wicked Spirit to or for any intent or purpose' and to disinter dead bodies for witchcraft purposes; while merely to injure a person or his property by witchcraft or even intend to do so was to risk the same fatal consequences.

And if that particular piece of law-making was the altar on which the unfortunate victims of the great period of English anti-witch zeal were to be sacrificed, and the Old Testament precept that 'Thou shalt not suffer a witch to live' (Exodus 22, verse 18) the scriptural rallying call, it was King James's book *Daemonologie* that became the witch-hunters' Bible. A powerful affirmation of the extent to which the 'works of Satan' were being practised and the devilish threat posed by witchcraft, it was a clear response to Kentish squire Reginald Scot's *Discoverie of Witches* (1584), a commendable attempt to take an objective look at the subject and counter the current hysteria.

Scot, a Protestant, concluded that most of those accused of witchcraft were 'old, lame, blearie-eied, pale, fowle and full of wrinkles; poore, sullen, superstitious and papists; or such as know no religion; in whose drousie minds the divell hath gotten a fine seat'.

James's experience, on the other hand, was quite different. And he had good reason to feel threatened. For in 1590, the future King of England (then James VI of Scotland) and his Queen were the alleged murder targets of a coven of witches in North Berwick who, it was said, had been prepared to resort to more conventional means (i.e. poison) if their spells failed to have the desired effect.

These were no old and ignorant dupes, either: of the four ring-leaders who were tried for their parts in the murder plot (three of them were subsequently executed), one was the daughter of a lord and one a former schoolmaster, while both the others were also educated people from good families. It was this uncomfortably close encounter with witchcraft that inspired James to write his famous treatise, which was published in 1597.

Nowadays it is almost impossible to comprehend how normal people could believe so implicitly in the destructive power of witchcraft or how the fear of, and hostility towards, its apparent practitioners could become a national obsession. To better understand, one has to appreciate the omnipresent influence the Church exerted over community life in the 16th and 17th centuries. Everything revolved around the parish; and when it is considered that the authority of the Church itself was based in part on fear – divine retribution for earthly transgressors was the dire warning underlining much of the Christian message at that time – it is easier to see how eccentric, non-conforming behaviour could be conceived as a threat to the moral majority. Furthermore, belief in the supernatural was widespread: was not the Christian faith founded on the tenets of mystic power, of resurrection and life after death, and of the Holy Ghost? And for anyone tempted to doubt that witches were a real menace to society, the Bible's 'death-to-them-all' decree was surely argument enough.

Mix these various stimuli together in a cauldron of ignorance and here was a witches' brew potent enough to befuddle the strongest heads into detecting sorcery in the odd doings of an ageing widow living alone with only a cat to talk to; in the senseless ramblings of some decrepit soul who today would be diagnosed as suffering from senile dementia; in the seemingly miraculous cures affected by self-appointed 'consultants' in herbal medicine...or even in the malicious ranting of a common scold.

Public attitude towards the latter, in fact, said a lot about the climate of intolerance wherein witch persecution flourished. Scolds, by common consent female, constituted a distinct class of offenders and could be hauled before the local sessions simply for uttering insulting words in the street (there was no equivalent offence for men).

The punishment for a convicted scold was usually some form of public humiliation, most frequently in the ducking-stool. But in many parts she could expect to be led through the town in a 'scold's bridle' or 'brank'. This was a metal cage completely enclosing the woman's head, with a bar protruding inwards to clamp the tongue (it was sometimes spiked to increase the agony).

The earliest known use of the brank was in 1623 in Macclesfield. And another 17th-century reference indicates that in Congleton a husband harangued by his wife could summon the town's gaoler to bring the instrument to his home, where the woman was duly caged and chained to a hook beside the fireplace until she promised to mend her ways. The Congleton brank is said to have been in use as late as 1824.

Against such a background, the notion of witch-hunting becomes less difficult to fathom. And while most people believed witches really were in league with the devil and should be dealt with in the same way as other capital offenders, others, contemptuous of the witches' powers, nevertheless felt that they should be condemned for intending to do harm. As with the 'swimming' test, the accused was a loser either way.

It is equally true that many women, with no threat of torture, actually confessed to such fiendish witch practices as indulging in sexual acts with Lucifer himself and giving suck to 'familiars', their own pet imps who materialised in animal form (another dangerous imagining was that a wart or some other minor skin growth found on a suspect witch was the special teat from which her little devil drew sustenance). They also claimed they could kill people by sticking pins into clay effigies and had the ability to fly, blight crops, raise storms and transform themselves into various creatures.

False confessions, however, are not unusual: even in modern times there has never been any shortage of people prepared to 'own up' to crimes they did not commit. And the bigger and more sensational the crime the greater the collection of odd-ball characters willing to admit their guilt (the man who sent the taunting tape-recorded message to police hunting the so-called 'Yorkshire Ripper' is one of the more notable recent examples of this).

That women did confess to being witches out of some perverse desire to achieve notoriety, or because of some mental disorder, is unquestionable. But there were those who really did believe they were mistresses of the magic arts.

As Gillian Tindall observes in *A Handbook On Witches* (Mayflower edition, 1972), '[Witches] were not entirely the hapless victims which some nineteenth- and twentieth-century commentators have painted them…it is fairly certain that a large number of the witches throughout history were anything but nice people…witches commonly attempted a little quiet murder or, at the least, some devious "doing down" of neighbours by blighting crops or cattle or by provoking diseases. Moreover, the operative word is "attempted": whether or not many witches succeeded in doing mischief, it is indisputable that at least some of them intended to do so and believed themselves capable of doing so…'

Life, she points out, was then almost unimaginably narrow and brutal by modern English standards; religion warned of hellfire and doom and, in condemning sin, made no distinction between magic murder and, say, fornication or skipping Mass on Sundays. 'In other words, if most of mankind was damned in any case, you might as well be hung for a sheep as a lamb, and gain a little power or fun on this earth in the process…'

The principle actresses in the North West's two most celebrated witch trials certainly believed they had magical powers. Elizabeth Southern, known as 'Old Demdike', and Anne Whittle, nicknamed 'Old Chattox', both in their 80s, were the heads of two families living in the Pendle Forest area of Lancashire. At first they were all one big happy coven, apparently; but at some stage there was a falling-out and a feud developed between the two rival 'gangs'. Consequently, when Old Demdike, now blind and said to have been a witch for 50 years, was arrested on suspicion of witchcraft, members of the two families made accusations against each other. The result was one of the most infamous episodes in criminal history.

At Lancaster Assizes on 17 August 1612, a dozen people, including friends of the families, were tried for various witchcraft offences, including the murder by sorcery of no fewer than 16 people. In a separate trial, eight others, six women and two men, from nearby Samlesbury were also accused of witchcraft.

Of this total of 20 defendants, 10 were eventually convicted and sentenced to death. Old Demdike had died in gaol awaiting the trial, but the nearly-blind Old Chattox (both women had confessed to having met the devil in various guises) and her daughter were among those executed. They also included Elizabeth Southern's married daughter Elizabeth Device and her grandchildren Alison and James Device.

Because it relied entirely on circumstantial evidence to secure a conviction (by its very nature it was an 'invisible' activity, unseen and, therefore, unprovable), witchcraft had a unique place in the legal code. Accordingly, the normally rigid court procedures went by the board. Suspicion and hearsay evidence were often the only bases for prosecution; the testimony of a single witness, even a known enemy of the defendant, could be enough to establish guilt. And children under 14, the then statutory minimum age, were frequently allowed to give evidence.

In the case of the Lancashire witches, in fact, hearsay evidence stretching over a period of 20 years was admitted…and the words of a nine-year-old girl, Old Demdike's granddaughter Jennet Device, helped send her mother, a brother and one of her sisters to the gallows.

In 1634 the tables were turned on Jennet Device. Then aged 30, she was herself convicted of witchcraft offences after a young boy had given evidence against her. This second Pendle affair led to a total of 17 suspected witches receiving the death sentence; but the judge cast doubts on the boy's testimony and the executions were postponed. Three of the condemned died in Lancaster Castle gaol; the rest were reprieved by Charles I following an official inquiry conducted by the Bishop of Chester.

The first Lancashire witch trial achieved widespread fame because the clerk of the court Thomas Potts, on the instructions of the judges, wrote and published a detailed account of the case in a pamphlet entitled *The Wonderful Discovery of Witches in the County of Lancashire*.

But possibly the most fascinating story of witchcraft in the region is the one I was able to piece together from documents in the Cheshire Record Office in Chester and at the National Archives in London. As far as I am aware the details have only ever appeared in print once before, in the original edition of this book.

It started, not with a public trial at the assizes (though the drama did move to that stage in due course, as we shall see), but with a hearing in the cloistered confines of Chester Cathedral and, more precisely, in the Consistory Court of the Diocese of Chester.

The court, also known as the Bishop's Court, was held in a room set aside especially for the purpose at the south-east corner of the Cathedral. The 'judge', the Chancellor of the Diocese, sat on a raised dais underneath a carved wood canopy embellished with heraldic devices. Below him the business of the court was transacted around a large square table completely enclosed by panel-backed benches. In a corner opposite was the curious high chair of the 'Apparitor', the official whose duty it was to see the orders of the court were carried out.

This type of ecclesiastical court was abolished as recently as 1963, but the courtroom, the only one surviving intact in England, is preserved today almost exactly as was in the 1660s when the central figure in our narrative, one Mary Briscoe, appeared there as the plaintiff in a defamation suit. The defendant, Anne Wright, was accused of slander by declaring in front of witnesses that Mary Briscoe had killed two of her children by witchcraft.

The two women were near neighbours in the old south Cheshire town of Nantwich, at that time the most important of the county's three salt-producing 'wiches' but well known, too, for the quality of its cheese and shoe-making. And, as in so many of these episodes, there was a history of bad blood between them.

The original cause of the animosity is unclear; but towards the end of 1657, a time when the great conflict dividing the nation's loyalties was still almost three years away from settlement, there were allegations that Mary Briscoe had used threats to try to gain possession of the house in which Anne Wright, then the widow Field, lived. Two of her neighbours would later testify to the Consistory Court that it was around this time that the widow Field's six-year-old son Hugh was struck down by a mystery illness and that when he died three months later she suspected that Briscoe had bewitched him to death.

When widow Field gave birth to an illegitimate child in late 1660, the year the country was finally delivered from the traumas of civil war, Mary Briscoe seems to have derived spiteful pleasure from broadcasting the fact around Nantwich (next to Royalist Chester the second major town in the county and a Parliamentary garrison during the war). Later Anne Field insinuated that Mary Briscoe had behaved immorally by 'keeping another woman's husband in her house four or five nights together' when her own husband was working away from home.

The ensuing row came to the attention of local magistrate Sir Thomas Mainwaring and Field was ordered to make a public apology for her 'scandalous and reproachfull words and speeches'. But she refused. Matters finally came to a head in December 1661, when Anne Field's 12-year-old daughter, also called Anne, died after a long illness.

Judging by the various depositions in the splendidly intact case file preserved at the CRO (though it must be remembered that official documents, even court records, were by no means as accurate during this period as one might expect), the suit appears to have been started at the beginning of 1662 and dragged on for two years. Altogether, 10 witnesses made statements and appeared at different times before John Wainwright, Doctor of Law, then Chancellor of the Diocese.

The case for the plaintiff (Briscoe) was directed towards impugning the character and reputation of the defendant (the recurrence of certain prescribed phrases to describe the behaviour of both women is another indication of society's attitude towards unruly females at this time). Much of the evidence centred on the earlier troubles between the two adversaries.

Sir Thomas Mainwaring confirmed that he had investigated a complaint lodged by Mary Briscoe that Anne Wright, then the widow Field, had injured her by saying she had harboured another woman's husband. Anne Field had admitted the wrong and he had issued a 'warrant of good behaviour' against her. The order obliged her to apologise in front of the local minister (Reverend Richard Jackson) and other witnesses. But, Mr Jackson's deposition revealed, she had declined to do so. And there the matter had been left, it seems.

Margery Echells, aged about 40 and the wife of George Echells, husbandman, said Anne Wright was 'a very contentious, troublesome and ill-tongued woman and often scoulding with her neighbours without cause many times'. And violent, too. 'She hath beaten this deponent twice or thrice upon very slight occasion given her', the witness claimed.

Of the allegation that Mary Briscoe had murdered the defendant's daughter by witchcraft, Margery Echells's deposition stated, 'This deponent and the defendant were neighbours five or six years before her daughter died and she never knew her but a very infirm and diseased child and much troubled with the King's Evil, which she believes was the cause of all her other distempers.'

'King's Evil', so called because it was formerly believed to be curable by the King's touch, was scrofula, the type of tuberculosis which affects the lymphatic glands in the neck.

In young Anne Field, said Margery Echells, the disease 'ranne and shifted into severall parts of her body insomuch that her mother was forced to take her away from her trade of knitting, which she had put her to, and sometimes she was not able to go without crouches [crutches]'.

Mary Briscoe, the witness testified, was 'a very civill and good neighbour and of good credit and account among her neighbours and acquaintances'.

Midwife Elizabeth Wright, 31, and married to Arthur Wright, button-maker (and presumably no relation to the defendant), said she had delivered Anne Field of a bastard child 'about the later end of the year after his Majesty came into England' (1660, the year of the Restoration of Charles II). When she asked who the father was, the defendant had 'cursed herselfe that she did not know'. She had never heard that Anne Field had done penance for it, either.

Witness also referred to Anne Field's recalcitrance in the matter of her earlier slander, 'She said she would rot in prison before she would acknowledge that she had done her [Mary Briscoe] wrong.' And she maintained that Anne Field's daughter had had the King's Evil 'for at least seven or eight years before her death'.

Arthur Wright's statement affirmed, 'For these dozen years last past, Mary Briscoe hath lived and behaved herself very civilly and orderly amongst her neighbours.' And another witness, widow Margery Wishall, 48, agreed that Briscoe was 'commonly accounted a very good neighbour, of good credit and behaviour' and that she 'never heard anything to the contrary'.

According to Anne Wright and her friends, however, nothing could be further from the truth; and such was the extraordinary nature of their allegations that, at times, it must have seemed as if Mary Briscoe herself was on trial (that experience was still to come). The story they told was quite remarkable.

Key witnesses for the defence were Elizabeth Jenkins, 56, and Anne Ridgway, her 20-year-old daughter by a previous marriage. These two seemed doubly determined to have their say for, as well as their individual depositions, mother and daughter also put their marks to a particularly damning joint statement.

Of the bitterness between Wright/Field and Briscoe, these two witnesses claimed that there had been 'fallings out and severall contentions betwixt the two' over the defendant's house, which Mary Briscoe 'had a greate mind of'.

Taking advantage of Anne's 'poverty and innocency', the joint statement said, Briscoe 'threatened her with several evil and bitter words and expressions that it were better for her to let her have it [the house], whereupon Hugh Field, son of Anne, suddenly fell sick at his heart and continued in a strange manner for a quarter of a year and dyed, the said Mary Briscoe supposed and suspected to bee the cause of the child's distemper and languishment'.

That was in February 1658. Then about September 1661, the two women clashed once more over the widow Field's house; again the defendant made it clear that Briscoe would not get possession of the property 'by threats or otherwise'.

The following Sunday, 12-year-old Anne Field was playing outside her house with other children when she suddenly ran indoors. She was 'very much affrighted' and said that Mary Briscoe had approached her and fixed her with 'the saddest looke…that ever she saw.'

The statement went on, '[Mary Briscoe] candled the eyes on her like a catt, all kind of colours. And suddenly the child fell downe in a fitt of great extremity and for thirteen weeks afterwards continued languishing in a very sad and dolefull manner. Her body swelled and her eyes hanged over her cheekes and sometimes would play on her forehead and sometimes up and downe on her face like two bladders, a very hideous and lamentable spectacle, and soe dyed; all alonge…in her extremity complayneing that Mary Briscoe pricked her to her heart with pinnes and needles, and noe body had done her any harm but shee (the said Mary Briscoe). And often desired that God would bring it to the light of the world for noe one knew what shee endured but God and shee.'

As if that wasn't sensational enough, there were more amazing allegations to come. For the statement also claimed that Mary Briscoe had attempted to bribe Elizabeth Jenkins, a poor woman, into testifying on her behalf with offers of 'moneys and victuals'; that she had 'deprived' Elizabeth Jenkins of two husbands, 'one she had driven out of town and the other she had taken his life'…and that the mother of Mary Briscoe had been *executed for witchcraft* (author's italics).

After the last revelation, the deposition added, 'Mary Briscoe is very much suspected by that evill and diabolical arte to have done harme to the defendant's children, and soe her husband and others have reported, and it is the common fame of her neighbours that she would come to the same end her mother did.'

We shall return later to the intriguing topic of Mary Briscoe's mother; on the subject of the deprived Elizabeth Jenkins and her two recently departed husbands, meantime, there were no further clues to that particular mystery in the Consistory Court file. A search through the registers of Nantwich Parish Church, however, turned up three relevant entries.

The first showed that before she married Maurice Jenkins, a husbandman, in July 1660, Elizabeth Jenkins had been the widow Clowes; the second referred to the marriage in November 1649, of John Clowes and a certain Elizabeth Wridgway (*sic*). Remembering that the court papers had given the surname of her unmarried daughter as 'Ridgway', it looked safe to assume that one of Elizabeth Jenkins's former husbands was John Clowes. That being so, the most interesting entry in the church registers was contained in the list of burials. Following page after page of curtly-inscribed memorials to the town's former inhabitants, it stood out as one of the few deaths that had apparently warranted more than a passing reference. Against the date, 9 September 1649, was the name 'John Clowes' and the cryptic two-word epitaph 'dyed suddenly'.

In an age when the poorer classes in their mean, unhygienic hovels were being struck down by all manner of unaccountable diseases (it was this lack of understanding of the causes of illness that had allowed the whole concept of witchcraft to command belief in the first place), why was this particular event singled out for comment? Had the demise of John Clowes resulted from something other than natural causes? Was there even then a suspicion that Mary Briscoe 'took the life' of the deceased?

The answers to those questions would emerge later when Elizabeth Jenkins was called upon to repeat her amazing story in another place...and Mary Briscoe found herself fighting for her life.

But to return to the cathedral atmosphere of the Consistory Court hearing. Corroboration of the Jenkins woman's evidence was given by two other defence witnesses – though what conclusion the court would draw from the remarkable similarity between their statements and the Jenkins/Ridgway joint testimony we can only surmise.

Cecily Wynne, aged about 50 and wife of Robert Wynne, also a husbandman, described Briscoe as 'a very wilfull, high spirited woman'. And she confirmed the strange happenings the day the child Anne Field had fallen ill.

She deposed, '...a daughter of Anne Wright being very well and playing at the door with some of this deponent's children and being on a sudden affrighted, runne into the house and said that Mary Briscoe had candled her eyes upon her like a catt as big as two saucers, and presently fell into a very sad fitt and lay a long time in a trance and soe long as she lived after had many strange fitts and was very sadly and lamentably handled with such violent fitts and passions, and when she went into them would catch and fight with any thing was neare her, and both in her fitts and when she was anything sensible and came out of them, would say that Mary Briscoe was the cause of it and tormented her and pricked her at the heart with pinns and needles and nails and the like, and soe continued till her death very sadly afflicted, her eyes many times tumbling out of her head and rowling on her face like two full bladders. And Mary Briscoe was suspected by many neighbours to be the cause both of the afflictions and likewise of a brother of hers which was sadly afflicted before that and dyed in a strange manner.'

Cecily Wynne went on, 'Before the child dyed, Mary Briscoe's husband, Thomas Briscoe, having heard something of it, came to this deponent and asked her whether the said childe had said any such things by his wife, as was reported; to whom this deponent replied "Yes"… Thomas Briscoe replied that he was very much troubled at it, but he would not rale her, and he was much afraid that she would come to the same end that her mother did, or to that purpose, for her mother began just in that manner and then left off a while and afterwards fell to it till it brought her to her end.'

Witness explained, 'Mary Briscoe's mother was some years ago arraigned and hanged at Chester for a witch.'

Finally, Elizabeth Whitlow, a widow aged 40, also testified on behalf of defendant Anne Wright. After giving her opinion that Mary Briscoe was 'a very troublesome, wrangling woman', she first enlarged on the bribery allegation.

She deposed, 'One day after this suit was begun and before Elizabeth Jenkins was produced as a witness in it, this deponent was with Anne Wright (then widow Field) at her house in Namptwich [sic], and the said Elizabeth Jenkins came into them and told her that Mary Briscoe would give her bread worth 8d in money and a cantell [cantle, a broken-off portion] of cheese if she would come and depose against Anne Wright.'

It must have been a tempting offer; in a town where more than a quarter of the near-3,000 population was officially classified as 'poor', food was a valuable currency.

Whitlow also trotted out the by now familiar story of young Anne Field's sudden illness, of her fits, the many times her eyes would 'hang upon her cheeks and rowle up and downe like two full bladders' and how the child would say that Mary Briscoe had 'pricked her to the heart with pinns and needles'.

Anne Wright herself had little to add to all this; she affirmed that the evidence relating to the deaths of her two children, as given in the various defence statements, was 'true as it is laid down…to her great grief and misery'. She hoped she had 'proved her demeanour and carr[i]age amongst her neighbours to be civill and peaceable', while on the other hand, she said, Mary Briscoe had been 'very bitter and invecting [sic] against her and her children and against others'.

A curious feature of the case file was the number of tantalisingly vague references scattered about the witnesses' statements to certain extraneous events of seemingly weightier consequence than the matter at hand: the apparent execution of Mary Briscoe's mother and the mysterious death of Elizabeth Jenkins's former husband, in particular. Now, as her parting shot, Anne Wright tossed another tasty morsel into the melting pot.

She said she was especially aggrieved because now, to add to her troubles, she was being 'vexatiously and maliciously persecuted' by Briscoe because she had appeared as a prosecution witness in the recent trial of Briscoe's husband, who had been charged with 'speaking treasonse against the Kinge'.

It meant another diversion…and a new line of inquiry, this one leading to the old Public Record Office in London and the records of the Chester Palatinate Court of Great Sessions.

As a county palatine, Cheshire had in medieval times been a virtually independent state, separate from the rest of England, with its own parliament, its own tax system, institutions and legal machinery. After 1542 only the judicial distinction remained; the 'Great Sessions' were the equivalent of the county assizes. And, though by the 18th century they had come to be popularly known as 'the assizes', Cheshire was not officially integrated into the more familiar circuit court framework until 1830.

Thomas Briscoe, described as a 'collar-maker' (that is, a maker of horse collars), was indicted for uttering 'seditious and treasonable words'. He was one of a number of Cheshire people opposed to the newly-restored monarchy who were dealt with at the county sessions between 1661–1663.

Nantwich had been obstinately pro-Parliamentarian in the Civil War and Briscoe had voiced his republican sympathies by declaring that 'Harreson and Cooke were good men or there were none', adding that he 'saw nothing that was good since the King came in but popery and…did believe that those times would come again to the same end that the other had done and that there would be a war again'.

'Harreson' was Major-General Thomas Harrison, the Cromwellian commander who had been responsible for seeing that the deposed King Charles was safely delivered to his trial at Westminster Hall on 20 January 1649; and he it was who first dubbed the king 'that man of blood'. Harrison, the son of a Nantwich butcher, had grown up in the town. The 'Cooke' Briscoe had referred to was John Cook (*sic*) who, as Solicitor for the Commonwealth, framed the prosecution's case and formally impeached the king as 'a Tyrant, Traitor and Murderer, and a public and implacable Enemy to the Commonwealth of England'.

Both men were among the 59 signatories to Charles's official death warrant (the king was beheaded outside Whitehall on 30 January 1649) and, in the inevitable act of post-Restoration vengeance, were themselves executed as regicides in October 1660. The first name on the royal death warrant had been that of John Bradshaw of Congleton, judge of the Sheriff's Court in London and Cheshire's Chief Justice, the lawyer appointed to preside over the historic tribunal (after several others had, for fairly obvious reasons, declined the invitation) and the man who had the unique responsibility for sending his sovereign to his death.

The outcome of Thomas Briscoe's trial on Monday 28 July 1661, was somewhat less epoch-making, though it was attended by a certain degree of public shame. He was ordered to 'stand' for half an hour in Nantwich town centre between 11am and 1pm 'at the hight [*sic*] of the market'.

'Stand', in this case, presumably meant 'stand in the pillory', the sentence imposed on other similar Cheshire offenders during the uneasy post-war period. Culprits thus subjected also had to have a notice pinned to their chests stating the nature of their crimes.

The Nantwich pillory was at this time in High Town; it was moved into Pillory Street in the early 19th century (the apparatus that can be seen there today is a modern replica).

Though Anne Wright insisted she had been 'by the law compelled' to give evidence against Briscoe and therefore had no choice in the matter, the trial was yet one more source of the discontent between her and Mary Briscoe that was so vividly ventilated at the Consistory Court hearing.

The former Consistory Courtroom in Chester Cathedral, largely unchanged since 1662 when Mary Briscoe was first accused of murder by witchcraft. Photograph: John Cocks, by permission of the Dean and Chapter.

When Briscoe finally had her say in the affair, she lambasted Wright, declaring her to be 'a very troublesome, contentious ill-tongued woman' who had 'fallen out [with] and scolded' many of her neighbours. In her statement to the court, the last remaining deposition in the CRO file, she said that 'no credit [should be] given to the sayinges and deposicons of Elizabeth Whitlow'. And she claimed Cecily Wynne was 'a common tatler, a tale-bearer and a common lyer'.

The charge that she had bewitched Anne Wright's daughter to death, she said, was 'most false and untrue'. The child, she argued, 'was and has been for many years before weake and sickly and lame and had the King's Evill or some other distemper and infirmity and the affliction she had was by reason thereof'.

And of her own character, Briscoe said, '...before, at and since the beginning of this suite [sic] she came to live in Nantwich, hath been and is a civil woman and (saving the unjust scandall in this suite lay'd upon her) of good repute and credit amongst her neighbours, and hath given...[none] of them justly occasion to revile or fall out with her.'

Despite defence witnesses' lurid accounts of the apparently terrifying effect that Mary Briscoe's evil eye had had on young Anne Field, the court eventually found for the plaintiff. When the hearing ended on 26 February 1664, Anne Wright was ordered to pay costs amounting to a then swingeing sum of £10 3s 6d (more than £1,000 by today's standards) and to do penance at Nantwich Parish Church on Tuesday 5 April. There, between 10am and noon, she was to stand up and state publicly that the court's decision had been just, to ask Mary Briscoe's forgiveness for the wrong she had done her and to promise 'not to offend in the like hereafter'.

Penitents were usually required to appear in a white sheet and carry a white wand. But whether that was the stipulation attached to the sentence in this case is academic; Anne

Wright resolutely refused to comply. The result, confirmed in an order dated 15 April, was that she was excommunicated. It was the court's ultimate sanction and a measure which cut her off from the Church and all its ceremonies, including the right to Christian burial, and effectively made her a social outcast as well.

In those days of superstition and the belief in eternal damnation, it was a terrible punishment…and one for which Anne Wright was soon seeking revenge.

Three months later, on 25 July, Mary Briscoe did find herself in a court of law on charges of witchcraft. The Chester 'assize' records in what is now the National Archives reveal that among those who testified against her were Cecily Wynne, Elizabeth Jenkins and Elizabeth Whitlow. But clearly identified as the instigator of the prosecution was…Anne Wright.

The retaliatory move appears to have been provoked when another of her children, a boy called Richard she had by William Wright and with whom she was pregnant during the latter part of the Consistory Court hearing, fell victim to a mystery illness at the age of about three months. Mary Briscoe was charged first with 'lately practising or exersising witchcraft upon Richard Wright…by reason whereof the said Richard Wright did pine away' (and eventually died, we must assume).

The second charge was that Briscoe caused the death of Anne Field by witchcraft. And indictment No. 3, which confirmed that John Clowes was the husband whom Elizabeth Jenkins claimed Briscoe had 'taken the life of', charged that the prisoner had killed him 'by diabolical arts'.

Unfortunately, there is no surviving record of the evidence presented to the court; all that is now known is that Briscoe pleaded not guilty and was acquitted on all three counts. She was not discharged unconditionally, however; instead the judge bailed her to appear at the next sessions, at which he repeated the process.

In all, Mary Briscoe was made to answer to her bail at four subsequent sittings of the court, a means by which she was effectively bound over to be of good behaviour for a period of two years. She was eventually 'exonerated' and discharged from bail on her sixth appearance before the court on 6 August 1666.

The Consistory Court files revealed one further notable incident: Anne Wright's illegitimate baby episode, as exposed during the defamation suit, did eventually catch up with her. In 1667 she was charged with bearing 'spurious offspring' by 'perpetrating the nefarious crime of adultery, fornication or incontinence'. She was once again ordered to do public penance at Nantwich Parish Church, though whether she accepted her punishment on this occasion is not recorded.

But the most unexpected, and puzzling, sequel to the whole affair lies behind a bald two-line entry in the Nantwich Church burial registers. It contains the date, 22 July 1678, the name Mary Briscoe and, in brackets, the short legend 'poysoned herselfe'. In another, only slightly more informative note in one of the Chester Crown Books (in which the business of the assizes, including inquests, was abbreviated), we read that 'Maria, wife of Thomas Briscoe, coller-maker of Namptwich' committed suicide 'by eating poison'. But

as the coroner's detailed findings have been lost, those are now the only facts on which to form a judgment on the mysterious death of Mary Briscoe.

An old engraving of Nantwich Parish Church, whose registers reveal that Mary Briscoe was buried there (though possibly in unconsecrated ground) on 22 July 1678 after she had 'poysoned herselfe'.

What, one wonders, was the private demon that drove this enigmatic woman to take her own life? Did she continue to be persecuted as a witch after her trial? And did the accusations and intimidation become too much to bear? Or did she come to believe that she did possess magical powers, and didn't want to end up swinging from a rope like her mother apparently did? We will never know.

And what of her mother? Here again we are left with an intractable mystery. She was said to have been hanged 'some years ago' at Chester; but any attempt at establishing a family connection with a previous conviction for witchcraft is seriously hampered by the absence of Mary Briscoe's maiden name, and therefore her mother's surname.

A lengthy survey of Cheshire's extensive marriage and birth registers failed to yield a single lead; the only possible clue to emerge from my researches was a reference to the issuing on 15 April 1625, of a special certificate authorising the marriage between one Thomas Biscoe (*sic*) and Mary Wickstead at Marbury, near Nantwich. But, while I was able to track down the names of seven alleged witches who were sent to the gallows by the Chester Court of Great Sessions between 1630-1663, none of them was a Wickstead.

The statement that the mother was hanged 'at Chester' is more likely to have meant at Boughton, where persons condemned at the county sessions were traditionally executed. But the trial could have been conducted in one of the local courts granted by ancient charter to Chester's own borough authorities; both the Crownmote and the Quarter Sessions had the power to try cases of felony and, therefore, to impose the death penalty, though by the beginning of the 17th century capital offences had generally become the province of the assizes. Unfortunately, the records for the period are missing from the city archives (the disruption of civil war and the Interregnum caused many such gaps in official documentation in the 1640s and 1650s).

We are left, therefore, to ponder whether Mary Briscoe was the daughter of one of the women known to have been condemned for witchcraft at the Cheshire sessions during the period which, in 1662 or thereabouts, might reasonably be covered by the unhelpful description of 'a few years ago'. Of the seven I managed to locate, it would seem prudent to eliminate the mother and daughter who were executed together, for if Mary Briscoe's accusers knew about her mother they would surely have known that her sister had also been 'hanged for a witch' at the same time; one was a spinster (by no means a certain disqualification, of course), while, by 17th-century standards, the death of a fourth, in 1631, occurred a lifetime ago and people trying to pinpoint the event 30 years later would, one feels sure, have used a more substantial expression: 'many years ago' or 'before the (civil) war', say. Of the remaining three, the only positive conclusion I could reach was that any one of them could have been Mary Briscoe's mother.

In the tradition of Macbeth, the most recent cases seemed to support the notion that, where witches were concerned, trouble did come in threes. After being sentenced at the Michaelmas sessions on 6 October 1656, Anne Thornton of Eaton, near Chester, and Ellen Beech and Anne Osboston, both of Rainow, near Macclesfield, were hanged together at Boughton on 15 October.

The charge against Thornton, a widow, was that on 9 February 1656, she did 'exercise and practise certayne divellish and wicked actes and Incantacons called Witchcrafts, Inchauntments, Charmes and Sorceries in and upon one Daniell Finchett, sonne of Ralph Finchett, of Eccleston [near Chester], yoman, beinge an infant of the age of three days'. The boy had died suddenly on 11 February.

In separate trials, Anne Osboston, wife of James Osboston, husbandman, was charged that between 1651 and 1655 she bewitched to death four people: three fellow villagers, John Pott, yeoman, his wife Barbara and John Ste(v)enson, husbandman, and also Anthony Booth, husbandman, of Macclesfield. Beech was accused of causing the death of Elizabeth Cowper of Rainow, spinster, by witchcraft on 20 September 1651, after she had 'consulted and covenanted with, entertayned, imployed, ffed and rewarded certayne evill and wicked spirits'.

All three cases were held before John Bradshaw, the regicide, who had been made Cheshire's Chief Justice some 10 years earlier. The son of Henry Bradshaw of Marple, he is most closely associated with Congleton, where he trained and subsequently practised as a lawyer and where, in 1637, he was elected Mayor.

The relevant Plea Roll in the National Archives records that all three pleaded not guilty to the 'murthers aforesaid' but that the jurors decided otherwise. An entry in the registers of the parish church of St Mary-on-the-Hill, which still stands at the north-east corner of Chester Castle (though it is no longer a place of worship), recorded that the 'Three witches hanged at Michaelmas assizes buried in the corner by the Castle Ditch in Churchyard.'

Almost exactly three years earlier, in October 1653, the gallows at Boughton had groaned under the weight of another similar multiple execution. The trio of hanged witches this time comprised Ellen Stubbs, wife of William Stubbs, labourer, of Great Warford, near Alderley Edge, her daughter Elizabeth, spinster, of Mobberley, and Anne Stanley, wife of John Stanley, labourer, of Withington. They had been sentenced at the county sessions on 9 October after being convicted of bewitching to death Elizabeth Furnivall, wife of Ralph Furnivall, Gentleman, of Nether Alderley. She had died on 16 June 1653, after being ill for nearly two weeks.

A second charge against the three, of the magical murder of Anne Lowe of Chelford seven years before, had been thrown out by the jury. And a further indictment, charging them with bewitching to death a black cow owned by Thomas Grastie of Great Warford, does not appear to have been proceeded with.

Before that there seems to have been an interval of more than 20 years to the next previous witchcraft conviction, though the impression, it has to be said, is based on evidence from a single source, the court's far-from-comprehensive Crown Books, and takes no account of the dislocation of administrative routine which occurred during the civil war.

This was a case in which Sybil Marcer (Mercer?), widow, of Acton, near Nantwich, was charged with murdering Hugh Basnett by 'wickedly and diabolically [practising] various wicked arts, enchantments and charms'. He died on 20 January 1631, at Acton. The woman was tried at the county sessions on Monday 18 April and was executed exactly one week later at 8 o'clock in the morning. And that was as close as I could get to tracking down Mary Briscoe's mysterious mother.

Dr J.A. Sharpe, while researching his book *Crime in Early Modern England, 1550-1750* (Longman, 1984), noted 11 executions for witchcraft-related offences in Cheshire between 1580–1709, though he was also working solely from Crown Book evidence, a source he concedes was only a 'rough guide'. He has generously shared some of the results of his studies with me, including references to several witchcraft cases he turned up in the period immediately prior to 1660. But none of them, unfortunately, yielded anything of further significance.

Both our investigations did confirm one thing, however, and that was that Cheshire was never a focus of the kind of witch-hunting zeal that broke out intermittently in some other areas, such as in Essex and other parts of the Eastern Counties (where notorious witch-finders Matthew Hopkins and John Stearne are said to have sent around 200 'witches' to the gallows in little more than a year between 1645–46), or in neighbouring Lancashire.

As we discovered, too, a charge of witchcraft was by no means an automatic death sentence. During the Interregnum and the 'reign' of Puritanism, a period regarded as a busy time for the witch hunters, for every one of the seven executions I could extract from the Cheshire Crown Books, there were two other accused witches who were acquitted, a two-thirds majority in favour of justice and commonsense. Dr Sharpe's findings over a longer time-span (11 executions out of 34 indictments between 1580–1709) suggests a similar acquittal rate.

It does not appear that Cheshire juries were particularly lenient, either; for during the 1620s, for instance, executions for all offences in the county averaged 17 a year (though by the end of the 1650s the average had dropped to three a year).

Immediately after the Restoration there was another short flourish of witch-hunting in England, but once again the Cheshire experience was that a conviction was the exception rather than the rule.

At Chester Assizes in October 1662, for instance, Margaret Percival, a widow, of Pickmere, near Northwich, was cleared on three counts of witchcraft. It was alleged that she 'did…bewitch, kill and murder' two of her neighbours in the parish of Great Budworth: Dorothy Key, wife of John Key, and Ann Peacock, a spinster. Their deaths had occurred four years earlier, but if Percival was believed at that time to have been responsible, the suspicions only seem to have been actively pursued after a further incident in October 1661.

This time the alleged victim was…a pig. A white pig, apparently, worth 40 shillings. It had belonged to one Ezekiel Lawrenson, husbandman, of Pickmere, and the indictment charged that Margaret Percival 'cursed [it] with many things'. Hogwash, said the jury, and threw the case out.

The 1670s and 1680s saw a gradual decline in witchcraft prosecutions, as JPs and judges began to demonstrate an increasing reluctance to accept the malicious claims of gossips and scandalmongers and the uncorroborated testimony of children and began to expose them for the fantasies and falsehoods they invariably were.

The new mood of judicial scepticism was perhaps best illustrated in the case of Jane Wenham of Walkerne in Hertfordshire, thought to have been the last person to be convicted of witchcraft in this country (she was later reprieved). At one point in her trial, at Hertford in 1712, it was alleged that the woman was able to fly. To which a scornful judge, Sir John Powell, retorted, 'You may – there is no law against flying!'

The last person to be 'hanged for a witch' in Cheshire appears to have been Mary Baguley, a widow of Wildboarclough, near Macclesfield. She was sentenced at the county sessions on 26 April 1675, after being accused of the magical murder of Robert Hall of nearby Wincle on 9 October 1674.

But it was with the execution of Alice Molland at Exeter in 1684 that the state-sponsored slaughter of the innocents finally ended. Before they were repealed in 1736, the witchcraft laws had been virtually redundant for 20 years. So firmly entrenched in popular attitudes had superstition and prejudice become, however, that incidents of witch persecution continued to flare up sporadically during this period and beyond.

It took the death of a harmless old woman and the shameful events at Long Marston in 1751 to break the spell completely.

The Abominable Midnight Ruffians

> On Sunday the mother of the deceased went to the grave, and at that time all was safe. On Monday morning all was still undisturbed. But on Tuesday morning it was discovered that the grave had been robbed, the coffin broken open, and the body taken away: the place was left in such a state as showed either that the parties had been disturbed, or that they were perfectly reckless of shame and decency...two of the defendants...were seen late on Tuesday night to go to the premises of Dr Albert Moss...and introduce a large hamper...

Liverpool Advertiser, 18 March 1828

CORPSES were spirited away from lonely churchyards in the middle of the night with startling regularity in the first three decades of the 19th century. They provided the grisly stock-in-trade of a thriving black market in human flesh which, in the manner of under-the-counter operations involving less macabre lines of merchandise, developed out of a demand that could not be met by lawful means.

In an age in which the quest for medical knowledge was intense, and private schools of anatomy and surgery were springing up all over the country, the only legal source of cadavers with which to practise dissection and study human anatomy – qualifications required of surgeons by law – was the gallows.

In 1540 Henry VIII had granted the United Company of Barbers and Surgeons the exclusive right to four bodies of 'condemned persons' a year for 'anatomies'. From 1752 Parliament directed that the bodies of all executed murderers should be handed over to the local surgeons for dissecting. But with executions apparently averaging 75 a year during the period 1800–20, it was not nearly enough to satisfy the rising generation of medical repair men eager to sharpen their skills on the dead for the ultimate benefit of the living.

Aspiring surgeons and physicians of a more determined nature at first took matters into their own hands, either by bribing grave-diggers and sextons to provide them with the bodies...or by going out and robbing the graves themselves. It is said that some of the most eminent surgeons of the first half of the 19th century were involved in body-snatching in their student days.

But it was the emergence of the professional body-snatchers, the so-called Resurrectionists, Resurrection Men and Sack-'em-up Men, that put the practice on a regular business footing. Evincing the kind of opportunism associated with more orthodox areas of private enterprise, they moved in to exploit the commercial potential of the situation… and ensured no ambitious surgeon need ever be without a fresh (though, in some cases, not so fresh) supply of 'subjects' on which to work.

In the end, too, it was their activities – and, in particular, the way in which the likes of Burke and Hare in Scotland and Bishop, Williams and May in London added a murderous new dimension to the ghoulish trade of the body-snatcher – that prodded the law-makers into providing a more acceptable remedy to this chronic medical dilemma.

However, in the 30 years preceding the 1832 Anatomy Act – which finally regularised the provision of bodies for dissection and buried the resurrectionists for ever – the sack-'em-up men bagged themselves a steady income from their nightly takings. With bodies fetching anything up to £15 a time, few burial grounds – not least those close to the main centres of anatomical learning such as London, Edinburgh, Glasgow, Manchester, Liverpool and Leeds – escaped the attentions of this grim new breed of underworld entrepreneur.

During this time untold numbers of dearly departed made a speedy come-back from the grave and a quick profit for the resurrection men. And so expert did the robbers become, that many a bereaved relative would return to the grave of a loved one shortly after the funeral to grieve unsuspectingly over an empty tomb.

The 'season' for body-snatching was October–May, when the anatomical schools were open. It was carried out at night and, where such a surveillance system operated, between watches. At first it was a crude business, the robbers' only thought being to get at the body as quickly as possible and make their get-away before they were discovered. But the mess they left behind to attest to their visit meant a more attentive watch would be kept on the cemetery in future, and a new source of supply would have to be found. So the resurrection men became more adept at covering their tracks…and this way they were able to return to the same graveyard time and time again.

The tactics of the more organised teams of body-snatchers began with careful reconnaissance earlier in the day, possibly disguised as mourners or workmen. Then, before getting down to business, they would note the positions of flowers and wreaths and any pebbles, twigs, shells or other markers placed there by cautious relatives as a means of checking whether the grave had been disturbed. They usually wore smocks and their standard equipment included a lantern, ropes, hooks, a ladder, a large tarpaulin and short, dagger-shaped wooden spades which would cope easily, and comparatively noiselessly, with the loose earth of the freshly dug grave. Then, in the muffled light of the lantern, sometimes with armed sentries posted to warn of the arrival of any unwanted observer, they were ready to begin.

After the removal of any obvious markers, the normal method was to dig down to expose the head-and-shoulders portion of the coffin only, each spadeful of soil being transferred, with practised care, on to the tarpaulin spread out alongside the hole. On reaching the coffin, hooks or a crowbar were used to snap the lid, sacking deadening the sound of the splintering wood. The body was then yanked out, more often than not with a rope tied around the deceased's head, and bundled into a sack. The earth was shovelled off the canvas sheet back into the hole, the flowers and markers replaced…and to all but the most minute inspection the grave looked exactly as it had done before. Depending on the number of people involved, the whole process could be completed within an hour.

An essential precaution, too, was to take away the corpse only. In itself the act of stealing a body was not regarded as serious; in law it was classified as a misdemeanour, punishable by a fine or short term of imprisonment. But if the robbers also made off with the shroud, some other article buried with the body – or the coffin – then the offence amounted to felony and the offenders risked tougher jail sentences or even transportation.

In the absence of an effective legal deterrent, therefore, it was left to the local community, the owners and keepers of the private cemeteries and individuals to arrange their own preventive measures. Some were elaborate, like constructing watch-houses and look-out towers and organising vigilante patrols. Others were downright dangerous: in extreme cases graves were booby-trapped with spring-guns and trip wires. But the majority – devices such as iron-grilled mortsafes, table-tombs, iron coffins and sealed vaults – were either too costly or impracticable.

With such patchy safeguards, it was no wonder the resurrectionists prospered. Unless they were nabbed red-handed, they were virtually immune from prosecution, too. Often the grave-diggers and sextons, if not themselves the culprits, were in the pay of the body-snatchers. And, as far as the surgeon-customers were concerned, the desire to protect their supply of subjects from interruption was an equal guarantee of silence. The strictly-cash-no-questions-asked terms of the deals suited them particularly well, in fact. For the arrangement meant the surgeons could always claim they had no certain knowledge of the way in which the bodies were procured (corpses could be obtained legally from a number of overseas countries) and allowed them to distance themselves from their despised confederates, whom they regarded as necessary evils.

The law did have its occasional successes, however. And the harrowing details of the activities of the grave-robbers came to the public's attention through the reports of some celebrated court cases. The North West's annals also contain revealing glimpses of the way in which the body-snatchers worked…and of the nature of the men at opposite ends of the supply line.

Probably the most infamous affair in the history of the North West resurrectionists centred on the discovery of what became known as 'The Hope Street Cellar of Horror' in Liverpool in the Autumn of 1826. Perhaps surprisingly, it was the only time that the existence of a systematic trade in bodies came to light in this teeming seaport which, in those pioneering days of sail, handled many a rare cargo.

As the *Liverpool Mercury* reported on 13 October, 'Instances of the disinterment of one or two human bodies, for the purpose of dissection, have occasionally come within our knowledge, in this town, as well as in others; but it would seem…that there has existed an organised company of resurrectionists in Liverpool, for the purpose of supplying the medical students of Edinburgh with subjects for dissection on a large scale.'

The 'extraordinary circumstances', the paper said, had 'produced a strong excitement of feeling, and an unpleasant sensation amongst all classes of the community'.

It all began on Monday 9 October, with an event that would have been repeated dozens of times in Liverpool's bustling dockland that day. As dusk began to settle on the waterfront – its basins bristling with the masts of some of the world's great sailing ships, its wharves a frenzy of activity as vessels made ready to catch the evening tide – a horse-drawn cart lurched to a halt on the cobbled quayside of George's Dock Passage opposite where the smack *Latona* was taking on goods bound for Leith. The cart contained three large Newfoundland oil casks which, according to the delivery note carter George Leech clutched in his hand, were being shipped aboard the *Latona* by the Carron Company 'from Mr Brown, Agent, Liverpool, to Mr G. H. Ironson, Edinburgh'.

Both the note, signed 'J. Brown', and the markings on the outsides of the wooden barrels, identified their contents as 'Bitter Salts'. It was a label that turned out to be incomplete in some particularly distasteful details…though it fairly accurately described those unfortunate members of the crew who were present when it was learned what the casks stowed away in the ship's hold really did contain.

It was the following morning, as they went about their duties, that the men first became aware of the offensive smell coming from the area in which the casks had been stored. The ship's master, Captain Walker, was called to investigate. And when he removed a 'wisp of hay' stopping up a hole in the side of one of the barrels, 'the stench became almost intolerable', recounted the *Mercury* four days later. The captain at once ordered one of the bungs to be started and, inserting his hand into the hole, he was horrified to feel the unmistakable form of a human body.

In fact, when the police were summoned and all three casks were transferred to the city 'dead house' in Chapel Street, they were found to conceal no fewer than 11 bodies, six men and five women, packed in salt.

Police officer Robert Boughey, in charge of the investigation, got to work immediately. And later the same day his inquiries took him to the Hope Street address that was to produce an even greater sensation. For in a cellar underneath the private school run by the Reverend James Macgowan at No. 8, Hope Street was what the *Mercury* described as 'a wholesale charnel-house'. In three further casks and three sacks reposed the lifeless remains of another 22 bodies – nine men, five women, five boys and three girls.

The sight (and stink) of that vault of horrors can only be imagined; several of the bodies had lain there for up to a week and were in an advanced state of decomposition. Yet, that this was the regular place of work for a highly organised firm of grave-robbers, there could be no doubt: a number of dirty canvas smocks hung on the wall – 'supposed to have been worn by the miscreants in their nightly employment', the *Mercury* not unreasonably concluded – and a large brass syringe, similar to the type used by embalmers, rested on a table nearby.

All the bodies were 'entirely naked' and bore no marks of violence or any other indication that death had not occurred naturally. And if confirmation were needed that they had, indeed, been disinterred, it was provided by police surgeon Dr Thomas William Davies. At the mortuary, to where all 33 cadavers were eventually moved, Dr Davies noticed a piece of thread that had apparently been tied around the big toes of one of the young women, which practice, the *Mercury* explained, was 'used in some families to keep the feet of deceased persons together' preparatory to burial.

From the various materials found in the cellar, it was conjectured that the bodies were first immersed in a strong solution of brine and, when thoroughly 'pickled', packed in the casks with dry salt. Some were also injected with a preservative liquid.

The basement 'warehouse' had now been closed down; but where – and who – were the busy body-snatchers who had kept it so well stocked? By that time, officer Boughey had already interviewed two vital witnesses. He had succeeded pretty quickly in tracking down the carter Leech and he had also spoken to a dumbfounded Revd Macgowan. Both provided him with important clues as to the suspects' identities.

It was Leech who had led police to the Hope Street premises from where, he said, he collected the casks he delivered to the *Latona*. He had become involved in the drama as he plied for hire at the dry dock.

Between 3 and 4 o'clock on that Monday afternoon, he was to testify later, he was approached by 'a tall, stout man, with black whiskers and a Scotch accent'. The stranger had a job for him. And, after agreeing a charge of two shillings, the two men went together to No. 8, Hope Street (long demolished, the property stood at the north end of the street opposite what is now the Everyman Theatre). When they arrived two other men were in the process of lifting a cask out of the cellar, and Leech helped them load this and two more on to the cart. For his trouble he received an extra sixpence from the big bewhiskered Scotsman, and a warning to 'be careful in putting the casks down on the quay'. After telling of his subsequent trip to George's Dock Passage, the carter then gave Boughey descriptions of the three mystery men.

Macgowan supplied sketchy details of a fourth suspect who, it soon became clear, was the leader of the grave-robbing gang. He said that in October 1825 he had agreed to rent the cellar, for the sum of £15 per annum, to a man calling himself John Henderson. His new tenant told Macgowan he came originally from Greenock and was a cooper by trade, though he had added, with unrecognised candour, that he also dealt in 'any goods he could make a profit by'.

The clergyman-schoolmaster said both he and his pupils had detected an unpleasant smell coming from the cellar for some weeks before the gruesome discoveries. But when he complained, one of the men employed by Henderson said it was fish oil that was being stored there. Macgowan recalled, too, that he had frequently seen casks brought to the cellar in hand-carts and taken away later on horse-drawn vehicles.

His tenant Henderson, named later in court as 'the main agent in the business', was never brought to trial. Statements given to police by various witnesses make it probable that one of his accomplices also slipped through the net. Three other members of the gang, however, did not escape justice.

The trio – James Donaldson, John Ross and Peter McGregor – had lodged together at the house of William Gillespie in Caroline Court, Kitchen Street, Liverpool. Gillespie, who was himself taken into custody early in the investigation but later released, told police the men were 'frequently out at nights'.

Donaldson, also a Scot, aged 25, was arrested first, during the evening of Saturday 14 October. He was recognised by a group of women as having been employed in the Hope Street cellar; and, with details of the previous Tuesday's revelations still vivid in their minds, they lost no time in informing the police.

Donaldson appeared at Liverpool Quarter Sessions on 27 October. The indictment charged that he 'conspired, with divers other persons, lately at Liverpool, and unlawfully, wilfully and indecently dug open certain graves there', and had 'disinterred, taken and carried away divers dead bodies'.

The case had attracted a great deal of publicity and the Press had referred in some detail to its more sensational aspects. But the trial still managed to produce a shock or two – particularly when it came to the evidence of those who were present at the time police first opened up that foul-smelling den of corruption in Hope Street. And one testimony caused more than just gasps around the courtroom.

It came from a witness who had taken part in the search of the cellar. Among the casks was one that would normally have held provisions. It was open at the top and appeared to be filled with brine. But, said the witness, when the liquid was poured off, the barrel was found to contain 'the bodies of some babies'.

The statement had a stunning, and dramatic, effect. The *Liverpool Mercury*, in its report of the trial published on 3 November, said, 'An audible shudder ran through the court on the mention of this last circumstance: the foreman of the jury was taken suddenly ill, and obliged to retire from the court for a short time.'

Earlier, Mr Raincock, prosecuting, had revealed that Donaldson, when he was captured, had on him two shipping notes similar to the one that accompanied the casks delivered by Leech to the *Latona*. This time, though, the dockets specified 'chymical salts' (sic) and 'dyeing colours' as the cargoes.

The court also heard, from an officer of the local workhouse, that a number of bodies had recently been removed from the parish cemetery in Mount Pleasant, just around the corner from Hope Street.

Mr Rotch, defending, contended that the evidence had not proved the charge of conspiracy. But the jury took only 20 minutes to reach a guilty verdict. Mr James Clarke, the Recorder, sentenced Donaldson to 12 months in the Kirkdale House of Correction and fined him £50.

On 6 November, 10 days after Donaldson began his sentence, police arrested Peter McGregor. And, two days later, John Ross was also in custody. Undeterred by his erstwhile conspirator's fate, McGregor was in the process of resuming the shipment of bodies to Scotland (albeit by a different route now) when he was detained.

The bizarre events leading to his capture began on Sunday 5 November, when a box was left at the White Horse coach-office in Dale Street, Liverpool, addressed to 'Captain Woodsdale, R.N., Mitchell's Lodgings, 12, Castle Street, Edinburgh.' Some time later the book-keeper noticed the crate was giving off a particularly disgusting odour and, on opening it, he discovered the body of a young woman. It was immediately despatched to the nearby police office.

Then, during the evening of the following day, a man arrived at the Golden Lion Inn, also in Dale Street, with another suspicious package, bearing the same forwarding instructions. The book-keeper was able to detain the man, who turned out to be McGregor, and broke open the box. Inside was the body of another woman.

McGregor had in his possession a key which, it was found, fitted the lock of the vault at the parish cemetery, to where both the dead women had been taken for burial. Another body had also recently gone missing from a coffin left overnight in the vault. McGregor was seen loitering with two other men near the cemetery during the funeral of the second woman and was further identified by a female neighbour who had often seen him working in the basement in Hope Street.

Ross was captured on the Wednesday evening, 8 November. He was spotted in Redcross Street by George Leech and recognised as the man who had hired him to take the casks of 'Bitter Salts' to the *Latona* and handed him the falsified shipping note. Ross fled, but Leech and a companion, a fellow carter named James Hughes, gave chase and eventually cornered him in a privy in the pig market in Chapel Street. In his pocket were other similar shipping notes and a rather interesting letter.

It was addressed to 'John Mack, Gamekeeper, to be left at the Post Office, Liverpool.' Dated Edinburgh, 6 November, it read, 'My dear Sir – Accept my best thanks for your kind attention to me. I am sorry you did not say by what conveyance you have sent the parcel; I hope, however, it has been sent by heavy coach, and that it will arrive safe. I am surprised you can do anything there now! Send as many as you can procure in good condition, and let them be packed in a plain fir box, covered with canvas, well sewed up…You will see plenty such packages going daily out of Liverpool. But, be sure always to write me at same time, and by what coach, &c. At the office, let it be booked, Mr Kerr, 33, York Place, Edinboro': or, put a card with Capt. Burns, R.N., care of Mr Steventon, Royal Mail Coach-office, Edinboro'. Be so good as write me, by return of post, by what conveyance you have sent the last, in case of miscarriage, or anything else. Our friend Smellie is settled at Hull. With best wishes for your prosperity and success, and many thanks for your exertions, believe me.'

It was signed 'Most faithfully your's, John…' (the rest of the name had been torn off) and at the bottom had been added, 'N.B. The moment anything arrives, I shall write you, enclosing the needful, J.L.'

The letter, written on the day of McGregor's arrest, possibly by the now absconded 'Henderson', was obvious confirmation that, even though the gang had been exposed, the Scottish end of the operation was anxious that it should be 'business as usual'.

The trial of McGregor and Ross for disinterring dead bodies took place at the Quarter Sessions on 20 January 1827. By then the excitement caused by the bodies-in-the-cellar episode had, apparently, cooled. And, with so much of the evidence already public knowledge, the *Mercury* paid scant attention to the court proceedings.

Mr Rotch represented the prisoners and, said the newspaper, 'made an able defence'. But 'after a short consultation', the jury pronounced them both guilty. And with a few admonitory words about the 'heinousness' of their crime, the Recorder handed out sentences similar to that given to Donaldson: a year in the Kirkdale House of Correction plus fines of £25 apiece.

There was, however, one further revealing item mentioned in the *Mercury* report. It was an affidavit submitted to the magistrate prior to sentencing, in which the defendants admitted their parts in the grave-robbing racket and sought to mitigate their guilt. In the statement, said the *Mercury*, McGregor and Ross claimed that they were 'poor and destitute' and that they had been 'hired by the anatomical students at various universities, who offered them very large rewards; and that it was their necessities, and not their will, that led them to traffic in dead bodies'.

In Liverpool at this time, there were, apparently, two private anatomical schools, one in Seel Street and one in Pomona Street. From the large number of bodies stockpiled in their basement lair, it would seem reasonable to conclude that the elusive Henderson and his gang catered for this local demand, too. But, with anatomists in Scotland prepared to pay between £10 and £15 for a body, trade north of the border was clearly a much more lucrative proposition.

Apart from the fact that institutions like Edinburgh University were in the forefront of anatomy teaching, the problem of providing the mushrooming medical faculties with sufficient subjects for study was made more acute by the stricter precautions taken in Scottish graveyards to guard against the invasions of the body-snatchers. So agents –men, presumably, like Henderson – were sent to England, where supplies were, in general, more readily obtainable.

A significant postscript to the discovery of the Hope Street Cellar of Horror was added by the Liverpool city fathers in November 1826 when, in response to the observations of the grand jury at the October sessions, the corporation sent a copy of the evidence in the trial of James Donaldson to the Home Secretary, Sir Robert Peel. With it went the hope that 'some legislative enactment might shortly put a stop to so great an outrage to public feeling as the present practice, by legalising that supply of subjects which was admitted on all hands to be necessary to the advancement of anatomical science'.

It was to be another six years before such legislation appeared on the statute book, however. In the meantime, the 'present practice' went on…and public feeling continued to be outraged.

In Manchester in 1827, other influential voices were raised against the 'nefarious and revolting proceedings' of the resurrection men, following a strange little case involving the sexton of a private burial ground in the city. The sexton, John Eaton, was charged not with grave-robbing but with what was regarded as the more serious offence of stealing a coffin. But there was strong evidence to suggest that he was involved in supplying dead bodies to the local medical fraternity.

Rear view of St George's Chapel and graveyard in Manchester, whose Sexton, John Eaton, was strongly suspected of supplying dead bodies to the local medical fraternity. Key: 1. The Chapel; 2, Eaton's house; 3, The necessary (where a coffin containing a dead child was discovered).

And the private publishers of a pamphlet, ostensibly about the trial, used this latest incident to cite recent examples of the 'shocking delinquency' occasioned by the shortage of subjects for dissection and to argue the case for establishing a means of remedying the deficiency that was 'not so disgraceful as those used at present'.

The anonymous author, seemingly more concerned with the moral, rather than medico-legal, position and clearly well-connected, declared, 'That anatomical science cannot be cultivated with success without dissection, every reasonable man must acknowledge; but it may be questioned whether the advantages obtained by the present method of procuring subjects for this purpose, counterbalance the dreadful mental agonies which are inflicted on the living. This science in itself so beneficial to mankind, has certainly been promoted by favourable opportunities for prosecuting its principle operation, dissection; but it is only during the present age that it has become a source of regret and disgust.'

The pamphlet listed some of the more practical suggestions for resolving the problem, including the right of properly qualified surgeons to receive, on payment of an appropriate fee, the unclaimed bodies of people dying in 'hospitals, infirmaries, work-houses, poor-houses, foundling-houses, houses of correction and prison' for the purpose of anatomical study. The fees paid would also cover the cost of burial later. This system, the broad principle of which was eventually embraced in the 1832 Anatomy Act, was then said to be operating successfully in Paris. And, observed the pamphleteers, 'If means like this were adopted in this country, perhaps we might not have occasion to lament or execrate the spoliation of the grave.'

But, they insisted, 'every obstacle should be thrown in the way of the abominable midnight thief, who fearlessly violates the sepulchre'. And 'the best and probably the most certain means' of putting a stop to grave-robbing, they contended, was a simple three-point plan that involved enclosing and securing burial grounds; rendering all parties to the offence liable to the charge of felony, and appointing only men of 'probity and character' as sextons. The soundness of the latter requirement, it was claimed, was ably demonstrated by the facts of the John Eaton case.

Before proceeding to the trial, however, the writers also took a swipe at the editors of the Manchester papers for suppressing the story of Eaton's examination. They had done so, it was supposed, to avoid distressing the families of the dead children named at the hearing.

But the pamphlet argued, 'Whatever may be their feelings as to the importance of the present case, they will not venture to deny that improper proceedings have existed; and with very little trouble, if they had felt so disposed, they might have found, that this place has long been suspected in that neighbourhood as furnishing the anatomists with subjects. But they ought to recollect, that prompt exposure might prevent such abominations in future…every exposure excites popular indignation, and every burst of that feeling is one step towards a legislative measure, which will prevent the men of science from being the employer and companion of the midnight ruffian.'

That John Eaton was a 'midnight ruffian', the magistrates and the jury at his trial at Manchester's New Bailey Quarter Sessions on 11 May 1827, appeared satisfied, though that was not the point at issue in the case.

Eaton was sexton of St George's Chapel, a place of worship belonging to the Swedenborgian sect, just off Oldham Road. Attached to it, on open land to the rear, was a private cemetery used mainly by the poor. Towards midnight on Tuesday 24 April 1827, a Mr Thomas Holme overheard a coachman asking the way to a chapel-yard where lived a man who 'clipped game cocks'. When the coachman was directed to St George's Chapel, Mr Holme became suspicious and, summoning the assistance of a local watchman and another man, he went after the hackney. Outside the chapel the coachman was challenged and he admitted that he had come to collect a body 'for the gentleman in the coach'. But before the mysterious occupant could be questioned, the coach was driven off.

Mr Holme, a warden of the similarly named but unconnected St George's Church nearby, roused the sexton from his quarters in the adjoining lodge and he and his companions searched the premises. In a cellar which opened on to the graveyard (though the door was missing) they found 15 coffins, nine of which contained the bodies of infants. The other six were empty. In Eaton's house were a further four coffins containing dead children; one of them rested on a ledge in the 'necessary' (lavatory). Some of the corpses were in a highly putrid condition. One of the coffins in the cellar appeared new and bore a plate inscribed 'John Buckley, aged three years, 1827'. The body was missing.

The child's mother testified that her son had been buried in the chapel-yard at the beginning of February. After the funeral, she and her husband had left the sexton standing at the open grave, apparently ready to fill it in. The following day she returned to find the grave closed up.

Eaton, who pleaded not guilty, explained that he used the cellar – in part of which he also kept poultry and pigs – as 'a regular vault' for the temporary storage of still-born babies.

Funeral ceremonies were not usually performed in such cases, and it was his practice, he said, to wait until he had a large number before burying them in a mass grave. Of the Buckley boy's casket, he said he had 'done his duty' and buried it, but a few days later had found it empty in the chapel-yard.

The court heard that, in the process of interring the dead children, a grave was disturbed which contained a coffin that had been broken open and the body of a 56-year-old woman removed.

Eaton admitted he knew that bodies were 'continually stolen out of the yard', but claimed he had been unable to prevent it. He had informed the owners of the cemetery of the situation, he said.

The jury had no hesitation in finding Eaton guilty of stealing the coffin. And the chairman of the magistrates, in sentencing him to six months hard labour, voiced the wider suspicions of the court. He told the prisoner, 'It appears from the evidence…that you have taken the body and the coffin along with it, and we therefore must consider, that availing yourself of your situation, you have taken the opportunity to steal this body and coffin to make money of them.'

The hackney driver was cleared of complicity after coming forward and volunteering a statement, though he was unable (or unwilling) to identify the man in the coach who, it appeared, had been in the market for a body.

There was no shortage of suspects; for there were in Manchester at that time two major schools of anatomy. Joseph Jordan, hailed as 'the father of provincial medical education', had started the city's first anatomy school at his home in Bridge Street, off Deansgate, in 1814. A year later he opened dissecting rooms which, by 1827, were located in premises at the corner of Mount Street and Albert Square. There was also Thomas Turner's Royal School of Medicine and Surgery in Pine Street, behind the Piccadilly Infirmary. The first complete medical school in the provinces (it would in 1834 absorb Jordan's students as well), it was founded in 1824.

That was the year in which Manchester witnessed its first real public outcry over the depredations of the resurrection men. It came after reports of some odd goings-on at a stable in a yard between Tib Lane and Back King Street. For several months, the stable had been occupied by a number of men engaged in some private business – and obviously intent on keeping it that way. They were frequently heard leaving the place late at night and returning in the early hours with a gig. Then on the morning of Saturday 14 February 1824, following another nocturnal excursion, the men seemed unusually busy and three packing cases were carried into the stable. Now fully convinced that the newcomers were a gang of thieves preparing to pack up and take off with their booty, a group of neighbours took their suspicions to the authorities.

So, at about 3 o'clock on that Saturday afternoon, a Mr Lavender (possibly the Borough Reeve, whose job it was to supervise the work of the city's 'police' officers), accompanied by two beadles, swooped on the back-street hide-away and found two men about to fasten down the lid of one of the packing cases. The other two, already nailed shut, stood on the floor nearby. The boxes looked innocuous enough: all identical, they each measured only about 2ft by 2ft by 13in. Yet, to their astonishment, when the unexpected visitors took a look into the still open one they saw, jammed tightly together inside, two adult bodies. And both the other cases contained similar consignments, all destined for different addresses in London.

The two men, William James Johnson and William Harrison, were arrested and Mr Lavender set about identifying the six crated corpses.

The *Manchester Guardian*, in a report on 21 February, explained, 'Advertisements were immediately issued, and the bodies…were exposed to view in one of the rooms of the George Inn, which is now unoccupied. During the whole of Tuesday, crowds of persons, who had recently lost relatives or friends, applied at the Police Office for tickets of admission, to inspect the bodies; but it was not until Tuesday evening, that any of them were identified.'

All the bodies – two men, two women and two children, their ages ranging from six to 74 – had been taken from the new Catholic Chapel in Granby Row, a mile or so from the Tib Lane stable. They were buried between 25 January and 13 February in a communal grave not yet completely filled and, consequently, left only with a covering of boards. The defect was to make the task of the body-snatchers comparatively simple and, consequently, life difficult for the man in charge of the graveyard.

Said the *Guardian*, 'The crowd assembled at the re-interment were inclined to maltreat the sexton, whom they suspected of some complicity in the transaction; and Mr Lavender had some difficulty in protecting him from them.'

The two resurrectionists eventually appeared before the Salford Easter Sessions on Wednesday 12 May 1824, charged on three counts of stealing bodies. They were both sentenced to 15 months in Lancaster Castle Gaol. Johnson, aged 33, from London, was said by the *Manchester Mercury* to be of 'very respectable appearance', while Harrison (42), from Liverpool, was described as 'a mean-looking fellow'.

According to the *Guardian* account, Johnson, married with four children (the latest of whom had been born since his arrest) had 'recently failed in business'. Harrison, said the *Guardian*, was 'a pauper belonging to this town' whose only child was now in the workhouse.

It was not just the professional dealers in human flesh, rogues and criminals mostly, who risked the censure of the law, of course. Their customers, often men of reputation and influence in society, and the enthusiastic 'amateur' body-stealers – usually students seeking to add a bit of excitement to their academic lives – made periodic appearances in the dock, too.

At Kirkdale Quarter Sessions on 8 February 1828, Dr William Hill, who ran the Seel Street School of Anatomy in Liverpool was accused of grave-robbing. He was cleared of that charge but fined £30 for receiving the body of a young woman stolen from Walton Churchyard, for the purpose of dissection, knowing it to have been unlawfully disinterred.

The previous year, also at Kirkdale sessions, a case first came to court that produced one of the best documented accounts of a trial involving allegations of body-snatching. It also perfectly illustrated the conflict, not to say ambivalence, created by the increasingly unsatisfactory provision for dissection that then existed and the mounting pressure for legal reform.

The body in question was that of Jane Fairclough, aged 24, who in life had been 'a young woman of very fine personal appearance'. A farmer's daughter from Burtonwood, near Warrington, she had died on Tuesday 25 September 1827, and been interred three days later in the burial ground attached to the Hill Cliffe Baptist Church across the River Mersey in Appleton, Cheshire. The following Tuesday 2 October, the grave was found vandalised and the body stolen. Judging by the havoc they had left behind, the robbers were either ham-fisted novices or they had been disturbed in their illicit work.

The old burial ground attached to Hill Cliffe Baptist Church in Appleton, which in October 1827 was the target for grave-robbers. The body of Jane Fairclough was stolen and sold to a young medical student, John Davies, for the purpose of practising dissection.

Late that same day, two young men, John Davies and William Blundell, called at the home of Dr Albert Parry Moss, physician, in Sankey Street, Warrington. And, some time afterwards, three men were seen heaving a large hamper through a trapdoor in the rear wall of the property.

Acting on this information, Mr Peter Nicholson, attorney and clerk to the local magistrates, went the following evening with Mr Samuel Fairclough, the deceased's brother, to Dr Moss's house. The hamper was in the back garden. Inside was Miss Fairclough's body 'in a state of perfect nakedness'.

Davies, a 23-year-old student at Warrington Dispensary who went on to become a leading doctor in the town, and his friend Blundell, aged 17, an apprentice stationer whose elder brother was also a student at the dispensary, were sent for trial on various counts of conspiring to rob graves, of unlawfully disinterring the body of Jane Fairclough and of receiving the body for dissection knowing it to have been unlawfully disinterred. Charged with them were Edward Hall, a recently qualified surgeon, of Sankey Street, Warrington; Richard Box, a Warrington livery stable keeper, and Thomas Ashton, a solicitor's clerk, also of Warrington. They all pleaded not guilty.

The former Warrington Dispensary in Buttermarket Street, in which building John Davies was studying when he was charged with various offences relating to the disinterment of a dead body. From an original illustration in the archives of Warrington Library.

The case was due to be heard at Kirkdale Quarter Sessions on 5 November 1827. But, because of the hostility it had engendered locally, it was switched to Lancaster Assizes, where it was heard on Friday 14 March 1828. Details of the trial were widely circulated in a transcript published at the time by the printers of the *Liverpool Mercury* – for the particular benefit of the medical profession, they announced – and received extensive Press coverage.

Dr Moss, physician to the Warrington Dispensary – it was founded in 1810 in rented accommodation in the old Corn Market but by this time it had moved into purpose-built premises at No. 80, Buttermarket Street – said that in the early evening of Tuesday 2 October 1827, Davies had called to ask if he could use one of his outbuildings for 'opening a young subject' which 'someone had promised to bring'. He agreed, and at about half-past midnight, as he was returning from an engagement, he met Davies and Blundell at his gate. They told him they had brought the body. The three of them then went into an outbuilding at the bottom of the garden, where the body of a young woman was taken from a sack and placed on a table.

Cross-examined by Henry Brougham, the distinguished lawyer and statesman who was defending Davies and Hall, Dr Moss explained that 'the usual way for medical men to obtain bodies is from unknown persons, and in the night'.

Henry Brougham, the distinguished lawyer and statesman who, in defending John Davies, made a typically eloquent speech in which he argued the need for medical men to be allowed to dissect 'subjects' in order to acquire anatomical knowledge and surgical skills.

In this particular night-time transaction, however, there was a middle-man: the surgeon Edward Hall. Hall was not called to the witness stand; instead, the judge, Mr Baron Hullock, allowed a statement – which he had made voluntarily to a local magistrate when Davies and Blundell were examined – to be read out. He ruled, however, that the names of any other persons mentioned in the statement should be withheld.

Hall revealed that he had purchased the body from a man 'who had been several times in Warrington before', though he said he did not know who he was. He claimed he had been acting for another person (obviously Davies), who had authorised him to pay four guineas for a subject. He had made the arrangements when he saw the shady Mr X on Friday 28 September, the day of Jane Fairclough's funeral. And, at around 5am on the following Tuesday, the man delivered the body to the cellar of an empty property in Sankey Street, from where it was later moved to Dr Moss's. Witness stated he merely helped carry the corpse out of the cellar.

The case was notable for a typically eloquent closing speech by Henry Brougham, the man who, in 1820, had so famously defended Queen Caroline in the adultery proceedings instituted by her husband, King George IV. The engagement of the eminent (and expensive) barrister – who in two years time would become both the first Baron Brougham and Vaux and Lord Chancellor – to represent the junior surgeon and the apprentice may have been a measure of the importance attached to the case by the men of medicine in Warrington and, indeed, further afield. His fee, probably, would have been beyond the means of the two defendants, Davies especially, without help from somewhere. And, certainly, Brougham's final submission was as much a plea on behalf of the medical profession as for the two obscure young practitioners in the dock.

Mr Sergeant Jones, prosecuting, had described the events as 'an outrage on public decency and private feeling'. And he had argued that the necessity for surgeons to have bodies to study was a question with which members of the jury should not concern themselves.

Mr Brougham considered otherwise, however. He went so far as to submit that the issue they had to decide was 'neither more nor less than whether a surgeon should ever, henceforth, be allowed to dissect a subject, or whether surgical science should be acquired'.

There was, he contended, 'not a tittle' of evidence to tie in any of the defendants with the theft of the body. That left the second part of the indictment, the allegation of receiving the body knowing it to have been unlawfully disinterred.

Dissection, he said, was not only necessary for the continuance of anatomical and surgical study, but was 'positively encouraged by law'. And it could not be carried out without a supply of bodies. The court had heard that a surgeon most commonly obtained a body from a resurrection man 'without knowing anything of the manner in which it was got'. That, said Mr Brougham, was exactly what had happened on this occasion. For all the defendants knew, he added, the body could have been imported from Ireland, as a great many were, or from France, where surgeons had the right to dissect bodies of persons who died in certain circumstances.

And he declared, 'If the jury should go as far as to say, under the second charge, that if he took a body into his possession, and dissected upon it, without knowing anything of the manner in which it was obtained, he was therefore guilty of an offence, let their verdict plainly say so, and let all the frightful consequences follow.'

Hall, Box and Ashton were acquitted on all charges. The extent of the evidence against Box had been that he helped carry the hamper from the cellar to Dr Moss's outhouse. Ashton's only link with the offences was that he had a key to the vacant cellar.

Davies and Blundell were also cleared of conspiracy; but the jury decided that these two knew more about the affair than they had admitted. They were convicted on the receiving charge.

Sentence was postponed until 17 May, when it was announced in the Court of King's Bench by Mr Justice Bayley. He told the pair, 'You are both very young, and have borne generally a good character; but there is no doubt that this is a very serious offence of which you have been found guilty, and it is one which is calculated in a very high degree to distress the feelings of the relatives and friends of any departed persons whose bodies are thus indecently disinterred and indecently and unlawfully dissected. The court should take great care lest it should do anything from which it might be inferred that they consider this a slight offence. But the court does look at the circumstances of the case.

'You, Davies, it appears, were led into temptation by a stranger, who offered you a subject for dissection at a stated price, and though it was a great offence in you to make any such contract, you were led into it by a man more criminal than yourself.

'The case of Blundell stands on rather a different footing as he was not in any way concerned in the matter till after the disinterment, when he thoughtlessly lent his assistance to a friend in the manner that has been stated. Blundell, it appears, is in a very bad state of health.

'We have considered all these circumstances in your favour and we hope the mildness of the sentence will not have the effect of giving encouragement to offences of this description.'

He fined Davies £20 and Blundell £5 – an encouragement, no doubt to both of them (not to mention the highly distressed relatives and friends of the departed Miss Fairclough) to consider they had got off lightly. The fines, noted the *Manchester Gazette*, were paid immediately.

The outcome left no blemish on Davies's academic record, either. He remained at the Warrington Dispensary – the impressive Georgian listed building in which it was latterly housed can still be found in the shadow of the town's St Mary's Roman Catholic Church, fully restored though now sporting a somewhat unsympathetic white-painted façade – until 1830. When he left to continue his studies, first in Paris then Edinburgh, the management committee's minute book acknowledged his 'good conduct during the whole of his apprentice [*sic*]'. And as Doctor Davies, he returned to the town about four years later; was in 1838 appointed an honorary physician to the by then expanded 'Dispensary and Infirmary' (in succession, incidentally, to the late Dr Moss) and, during a 40-year career in general practice, performed all-round sterling service to the community.

He died after intermittent illness on 3 June 1876, at his home at Holly House in Sankey Street, aged 71. In an obituary, the *Warrington Guardian* said of him, 'He attended his patients up to the last; and even during his confinement to his house he has prescribed for a number of them who were loathe to forsake him…[He] had a very successful practice in the town and was highly respected by all who knew him.'

In this era of the resurrectionist not all disturbed graves were down to foul play. In many instances, following a reported visit by the abominable midnight thieves, the graveyard would next day be besieged by anxious relatives fearful that the robbers had made off with their late loved ones. And, often, the only way to pacify them was to open up the graves and check the coffins.

As a youngster, William Chadwick, a former Chief Constable of Stalybridge, witnessed painful grave-side scenes after one such alarum in Ashton-under-Lyne towards the end of the 1820s. In his *Reminiscences of Mottram*, first published in the 1860s, he gave this graphic recollection of the proceedings, 'The grave was emptied to the coffin, and at a given time the friends of the deceased, to the number of 20, assembled round the grave while the sexton descended, and in their presence opened the coffin. He was muffled up round the mouth and nose with a cloth, and primed with a glass or two of spirits. It was often a sickening sight to the friends to view the remains, but they endured it to set their minds at rest that the body was safe. Of course empty coffins were found, and at last the authorities were compelled to put a stop to the re-opening of graves.'

By now, too, moves to put a stop to the whole vexatious situation were gathering momentum nationally. On 22 April 1828, Henry Warburton, among other notables, formally petitioned Parliament over the difficulties of obtaining bodies for dissection. Warburton, radical MP for Bridport in Dorset, was subsequently appointed chairman of a select committee charged with inquiring into the practice of anatomy in the UK and recommending the best method of providing sufficient subjects for study. It met for the first time on 28 April…and was still sitting when sensational developments in the story of the resurrectionists were occurring that would produce an even more compelling reason for action.

The evil exploits of William Burke and William Hare, which exploded on to the public stage as the year drew to a close, are now a familiar part of British legal history. Between December 1827 and October 1828, these two depraved monsters operated a murderous new variation on the 'legitimate' trade in dead bodies. In their two-year rampage they killed at least 16 people in the populous West Port area of Edinburgh to create a supply of 'man-made' products with which to furnish the dissecting tables of Dr Robert Knox and his fellow anatomists in Surgeons Square.

Burke was condemned to death on Christmas Day 1828 (Hare had been granted immunity from prosecution after turning King's evidence) and was executed on 28 January 1829, in Edinburgh's Lawnmarket, watched by a crowd estimated at between 20,000 and 25,000. Ironically, under the terms of the 1752 Murder Act, Burke's body was handed over to a university professor of anatomy to be put to the same scientific use as all his victims.

Two months later Warburton's first Anatomy Bill, 'for preventing the unlawful disinterment of human bodies and for regulating Schools of Anatomy', was placed before Parliament. But it had been hastily drawn up; even the Royal College of Surgeons opposed it. After a stormy passage through the House of Commons, the bill was blocked in the Lords and was withdrawn.

Final agreement on the change of law took a further two years…and another murder.

It followed the case of a London gang of resurrectionists-turned 'burkers' led by John Bishop, a carter who claimed to have raised up to 1,000 bodies during his 12-year 'career'. Bishop, together with his brother-in-law Thomas Williams and John May, a butcher's assistant, were convicted at the Old Bailey on 2 December 1831, of murdering a 14-year-old Italian boy, whose body they planned to sell to anatomists. May was reprieved after being exonerated in the confessions of the other two, but he collapsed in his cell on being told the news and died a few months later. Bishop and Williams were hanged outside Newgate Gaol on 5 December…and once again the surgeons' suppliers ended up under the knife.

It was the final jab Parliament needed. Later that month Warburton tabled his revised bill; it sailed through both houses and became law on 1 August 1832. In its preamble, the act referred to the 'divers grievous Crimes, and lately Murder' that had been committed in order to obtain subjects for the anatomists. Among the steps it proposed to prevent such atrocities in the future was to permit a body to be dissected at the behest of the deceased or with the appropriate permission of relatives, executors or 'other party having lawful possession'.

This last clause was included specifically to allow the unclaimed bodies of people dying in workhouses and other similar institutions to be used for the benefit of medical science. The act required individual licences to practice anatomy and the routine inspection of all places where dissections were performed. It also put an end to the dissecting of executed murderers – though, interestingly, it re-affirmed the right of courts to order their bodies to be hung in chains.

Most significantly, however, it meant the twilight days of anatomical research were over; for the pioneers of surgery a clear new dawn of discovery beckoned. Time was up for the midnight ruffians.

10
Murdered by a Favoured Customer

The town of Warrington has in the last few days been thrown into great excitement by the murder of a female of the name of Minshull, the daughter of Mr Thomas Higginson of the Legh Arms...who was found lying dead in the privy on the morning of the 8th instant. The case was investigated by the coroner, but no clue arising to excite suspicion against any individual, a verdict was given that the deceased came by her death by violent means but under what circumstances was unknown. On Saturday, however, something transpired which excited the attention of the police...

Manchester Chronicle, 16 December 1837

THE SOUNDS of celebration had died away for another year, and the dark streets were almost deserted. It had been the last night of the fair and now only a few of the sturdier revellers could still be seen drifting slowly homewards. Suddenly, what had been good humoured merry-making turned to violence among one group of stragglers. Fuelled by drink, a fight broke out.

Alice Thomas, licensee of the Barley Mow, became aware of the disturbance outside as she made her routine security check on locks, window-catches and fire-guards before retiring to bed. That was why, she would explain later, she was too frightened to leave the house to investigate when, shortly afterwards, the screaming started.

Next door, at the Legh Arms, the festivities had gone on until past midnight; but they ended abruptly after a row flared between two of the young men who had spent the evening drinking in the taproom. When the landlord's daughter ordered them to leave, all but one of the remaining company followed to watch the quarrelsome pair scuffling drunkenly in the market square outside. That was how matronly Betty Minshull came to be left alone with her killer.

After bolting the front door on the trouble-makers, Betty and her solitary guest returned to the bar for a nightcap. When they had drained the remnants of a jug of ale, she took a lighted candle and led the way through the side door and down the narrow entry that ran between the pub and the adjoining property. Reaching the bottom of the entry, she paused to let the man out of the back gate, her only concern then, it seemed, was to lock up as quickly as possible and head for the beckoning arms of sleep. That was when Betty Minshull's nightmare began.

As she went to open the big yard gate she was grabbed and dragged into the pub's crude lean-to lavatory at the end of the passageway. At that point it was not murder her attacker was bent on. But when Betty resisted his clumsy sexual advances and began to call out for help – cries that went unheeded, if not unheard – he panicked. And in his frantic efforts to stifle the woman's screams, he ended up throttling her.

Betty, aged 52 and possessing the kind of ample proportions her friends would describe good-naturedly as 'bonny' rather than fat, had kicked and clawed desperately at her assailant but she was no match for the strong, stockily-built man. She was raped as she fought for her life in the blackness of that stinking out-house. Then, after she had lost consciousness – indeed, she may already have been dead by then, it was suggested later – her body was violated again as it lay crumpled up on the rough stone floor.

Betty Minshull was murdered at around 1am on Friday 8 December 1837. Her body was discovered shortly after 5 o'clock the same morning by Mary Pritchard, a live-in servant at the Legh Arms. It was stretched out on its back with the head propped up against the privy wall and the feet touching the door.

Despite the fact that the dead woman's long flowing skirts were up around her knees, that the yard gate was unfastened and the padlock and key were lying beside the body, along with a candlestick, no one at first suspected foul play. When Mary woke her master, Thomas Higginson, with the news, he appears to have been satisfied his daughter had died as a result of one of the fainting fits to which she was periodically subject. And he began making preparations for the funeral.

It was only when a conscientious local lawman called at the pub to investigate later in the day, after hearing of the circumstances in which the woman was found, that the expanding industrial town of Warrington learned it had a murder in its midst for the first time in living memory. And more than that: one which had been doubly aggravated by the attendant crimes of rape and robbery. For as the final deed in his barbaric act, Betty Minshull's killer had also emptied the contents of his victim's pockets and stolen cash, a snuff-box and a penknife.

The man whose persistence prevented a murderer going scot-free was James Jones, Deputy Constable of Warrington and one of four constables at that time appointed by the local Manor Court. Though they were even then being referred to as 'the police', they had not as yet, apparently, acquired the power of interrogation – as Jones himself was to be shortly, and sharply, reminded – and Warrington does not seem to have had a recognised police force until after its incorporation in 1847. It was, nevertheless, established ahead of the nationwide police network which, imposed by an Act of 1856, owed its inspiration to the success of the pioneering Metropolitan Constabulary founded in 1829 by Sir Robert Peel.

When he inspected the body, Jones found a number of telltale marks on the dead woman's face and neck. And, after informing Higginson of his suspicions, he insisted on calling in the coroner. To begin with, Higginson was hostile to the idea of an inquest; and he remained sceptical about Jones's theory until the preliminary post mortem examination had been completed. Then he had to acknowledge that the Deputy Constable was right: his daughter had been strangled.

The inquest duly opened on Monday 11 December. After hearing the medical evidence and Alice Thomas's testimony about the screams in the night, the jury returned their verdict that Betty Minshull had met her death by violent means, though at that time they were not in a position to say how.

As police inquiries progressed, however, it became apparent that there was one man who might be able to answer that question. His name was William Hill, a 27-year-old cotton weaver who had been among those celebrating at the Legh Arms on the night of the murder. As witnesses told how the party had broken up in angry disarray, it was revealed that Hill had hung back when Mrs Minshull called time on the taproom rowdies. One of them alleged, too, that, earlier in the evening, bachelor Hill had made some salacious boast about his intentions towards the woman.

Despite the *Manchester Chronicle*'s reference to something having 'excited the attention of the police' on the Saturday, it was four days after the murder that William Hill was arrested. He immediately denied the charges, though he did admit to having stayed behind drinking with Mrs Minshull for a short while after everyone else had left the pub. Next day, when magistrates remanded him in custody pending further investigations, the police still did not have any strong evidence against him. It was not until they visited the mill in which the prisoner worked that they nosed out their first real clue…the old snuff-box that had been lifted off the abused body of Betty Minshull. It was found exactly where William Hill was said to have told one of his supervisors he had disposed of it.

The recovered item, though having the appearance of silver, was probably not the genuine article; it was certainly not thought to be worth much. But the stolen snuff-box, and the witness's statement that led police to it, were to be of immeasurable value to the prosecution's case.

William Hill was tried on the single count of murder on Thursday 29 March 1838, at Liverpool Assizes which, since their institution three years earlier, had been held in the massively grand, neo-classical surroundings of St George's Hall. The proceedings took place before Mr Justice (Sir John) Patteson, with Dr Brown and Mr Boileau appearing for the prosecution and Mr Brandt and Mr Hulton counsel for the defence.

The opening scene was set in a pamphlet about the trial printed by John Haddock of Market Gate, Warrington, who, according to a contemporary trade directory, was also a bookseller, stationer and proprietor of a 'subscription and circulating library and news-room' as well as an agent for the Royal Exchange Fire and Life Office. It was published in collaboration with two other leading Warrington printers, Thomas Hurst of Sankey Street and J. and W. Booth of Horsemarket Street. It recorded, 'The prisoner is a delicate and (though not handsome) a rather interesting looking young man, of light complexion. On the usual question being put to him, the prisoner said, in a melancholy tone, "Not guilty".'

If Hill's features were 'delicate', the rest of him clearly was not: newspaper reports described his physique variously as 'stout', 'well-built' and 'broad-shouldered'. The *Liverpool Mercury* of 30 March said there was 'nothing unprepossessing about him, excepting about the lower part of his face' which, the report continued mysteriously, 'indicates strong animal propensities'. And the correspondent added, 'He was better dressed than the generality of persons of his situation in life.'

The trial began at 9.30am. After pleading, Hill, about 5ft 7in tall with light-brown hair, sat down in the dock in front of a prison officer and gazed across the courtroom with grey expressionless eyes as Dr Brown rose to open the case for the Crown. As he outlined the events of 7–8 December, the prosecutor traced the movements of the principles involved on a large model of the pub and the surrounding buildings.

Echoing the sentiment of Dr Brown's opening remarks, and by way of a public warning of the unpleasant revelations to come, the preamble to the Haddock pamphlet stated, 'It is seldom that a Court of Justice is called upon to discharge the painful duty of investigating into the particulars of such horrible and revolting crimes as are the subject of the present enquiry. Murder, rape and robbery from the person form a climax of offences which fortunately are not often charged to have been committed by a single individual, and it is difficult in recapitulating a short statement of the evidence to refrain from an expression of those feelings of horror and disgust which must affect the mind of every person engaged in the prosecution.'

Dr Brown explained that the murdered woman had been the wife of Samuel Minshull, a reed-maker of Manchester. But for the previous 18 months she had kept house for her widowed father and helped him run the pub. The Legh Arms, built originally in 1651 and long since demolished, stood then on the north side of Market Place and to the right of the Barley Mow when viewed from the market square. The latter pub, which dates back to 1561, is still there, marvellously restored as part of the town's Golden Square central shopping area re-development.

An engraving of Warrington Market Place, 1843, by T. Dixon. The Legh Arms pub, misspelled with an 'i', can be seen on the extreme right of the picture. From an original illustration in the archives of Warrington Library.

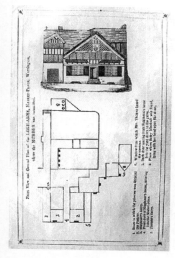

Sketch and ground plan of the Legh Arms in a contemporary pamphlet recounting the murder of Betty Minshull in 1837. From an original illustration in the archives of Warrington Library.

On the night of Betty's death, Warrington's eight-day winter fair which traditionally began on the eve of St Andrew's Day (30 November), was coming to an end. And the Legh Arms, in common with most of the town centre pubs, was packed with people having a final fling. It was a time when, as noted local historian William Beamont wrote in his book *Walks About Warrington*, published in 1887, the town was invaded with 'orse dealers and 'orse jockey lads, and such like swaggering chaps'.

But at the Legh Arms, as the evening wore on and the ale went down, there was much jockeying and swaggering among the local chaps, too. And, some time after 12.30am, what had started as a bit of drunken banter between two of the young men who shortly before had been laughing and singing in the taproom, began to develop into a more serious confrontation.

It was at this point that Mrs Minshull, sensing trouble, stepped in and ordered them out. And, mindful of the time – in the 1830s the permissive licensing laws gave almost total freedom to publicans to determine their own opening hours – she decided it was an opportune moment for the rest of the company to clear off home, too. As the pub began to empty, a crowd gathered outside to jeer and taunt the two combatants who were now squaring up for a fight. But whereas there had been six other men in the taproom when the argument broke out, only five of them were among the spectators when the punch-up finally began. And for Betty Minshull, doubtless relieved to be shot of a potentially unpleasant situation, the real violence was yet to come.

It started soon after 12.55am, according to the evidence of landlady Alice Thomas. That was the time, she told the court, that she had gone into the front room of the Barley Mow to make sure the fire was safe and the doors and windows were secure before going upstairs to bed. She said, 'I heard a loud noise as if persons were fighting in the Market Place and making a disturbance.' Mrs Thomas then went to her bedroom and 'in a short time' she heard a woman's screams coming from the back of the Legh Arms.

Her bedroom overlooked the little alley that served as a rear access to both pubs and which led from their back gates into the town's mug market. She opened her bedroom window but could see nothing; though only 25 yards away, her view of the Legh Arms privy was obscured by the pub's gable. So, she said, 'I called out as loudly as I could.'

Mrs Thomas went on, 'From the screaming it appeared as if someone was abusing a female. The screaming continued for some minutes, then the voice began to falter and grow weak, and at length it ceased altogether.'

Although her daughter and servant were with her at the time and also heard the screams, no one went to find out what was going on. Mrs Thomas explained, 'I was afraid of going out of my house on account of the noise in the Market Place.' She closed her window and went to bed.

Meanwhile, next door, Mary Pritchard was already sleeping soundly. Thomas Higginson's servant had gone to bed shortly after her master, between 11 and 12 o'clock, leaving Betty Minshull in the bar with William Hill and seven or eight of his friends. They had arrived at the pub around 8pm, Mary said. Mrs Minshull treated them to half a gallon of ale and Mr Higginson gave them another quart. Later, when the men started a sing-song, Mrs Minshull joined them in the taproom for a time. She seemed particularly pleased with Hill's singing, said Mary.

Betty, with whom she shared a room, eventually told her to go on up and that she would be along presently. When Mary awoke around 5am and realised her mistress was not in bed, however, she said she 'became alarmed'. Lighting a candle, her fears grew as she searched the house in vain for the missing Mrs Minshull. Then she discovered that the kitchen door leading into the backyard was open.

Mary Pritchard stated, 'I took a candle and went straight down to the petty at the bottom of the yard and there I found the deceased lying on the floor. Her clothes were up to her knees and I pulled them down. I examined her and found that she was dead.' A bunch of keys, a candlestick, a hang-lock and the key to the yard door were lying beside the body, she added.

Mary roused Betty's father and with the help of two lodgers, labourer Nicholas Murphy and a soldier named William Dansmore, a private in the 69th Regiment of Foot, they carried the body into the pub. A search revealed Betty's pockets were empty; but though she habitually carried around with her a silver-look snuff-box and a penknife with a buck-horn haft – and it was normal for her to have some cash from the night's takings on her at closing time – the discovery, along with the other unusual circumstances, provoked no immediate misgivings, it seems.

Asked about her initial thoughts on the possible cause of Betty's death, Mary Pritchard said in cross-examination, 'Mrs Minshull was a lusty woman and was subject to fainting fits when put out of the way [sic].'

And Thomas Higginson, when he, too, was questioned by the defence about it, replied, 'My daughter was subject to fainting fits at intervals and, at first, I thought she might have died in one.'

The truth was to emerge when James Jones turned up at the pub later in the day. The Warrington Deputy Constable testified that as he examined Betty Minshull's body he noticed two marks, which looked like they had been caused by finger-nails, under the dead woman's chin. There were marks, too, on her throat which, he said, 'appeared as if they had been produced by pressure'. On the right side of the nose was a further nail-mark.

But for Jones's timely intervention, Betty Minshull's murder may well have gone undetected; and his 'indefatigable exertions' in the days following had also earned him the gratitude of the whole town, the Haddock preface acknowledged. Yet, bizarrely, when the hero policeman left the assize court it was with the sounds of condemnation, not commendation, ringing in his ears. For while he was giving his evidence, the judge interrupted to give him a wigging for being over-zealous.

The amazing interlude began when Jones revealed that, on the Tuesday night after the murder, he had questioned Hill while he was locked up in the town's bridewell (which was also the officer's home) in Dial Street. He said he asked the prisoner whether he had been at the Legh Arms the previous Thursday evening, 7 December. Hill replied that he had been in the pub that night and agreed that he had remained alone with Mrs Minshull after his friends had left. But he said he could not remember how long he stayed behind drinking with her.

By interrogating Hill in this manner, Jones had apparently over-stepped his authority. And, after cross-examining on the point, Mr Brandt, for the defence, asked the judge to rule that this part of the witness's evidence was inadmissible.

According to the *Liverpool Mercury*, reporting the case in some detail in its issue of 30 March 1838, Mr Justice Patteson interjected, 'It is a very wrong thing. Leave off that practice immediately, Mr Jones, and don't pretend to ask questions of persons in your custody which you have no right whatever to put.' To take down, and seek explanations for, statements given by prisoners voluntarily was one thing; but to question them otherwise was contrary to his duty, rapped his Lordship.

Jones insisted he had simply been trying to ascertain whether Hill could account for his movements on the night of the murder and that he had 'no idea at the time of giving the conversation in evidence against the prisoner'.

But Judge Patteson warned him, 'If you persist in doing that sort of thing, I shall strongly recommend that you be turned out of the police directly.' He went on, 'I don't at all suppose that, in putting these questions, you intended to do anything wrong. But I speak as strongly as I can do, in order to put an end to such a bad practice. Don't do it again!'

After Jones's cursory examination of the dead woman, and his subsequent report to the coroner, a post mortem was carried out by Dr John Davies, physician and surgeon (see Chapter Nine). In court the doctor detailed the results, which had confirmed Deputy Constable Jones's provisional murder analysis.

The body of Betty Minshull, he said, was 'remarkably fat'. There were two bruises on the right side of the neck and a mark on the right side of the nose. Both sides of the neck were swollen and the muscles 'much bruised'. The woman's forearms were also bruised, particularly about the elbows and wrists. And, on opening up the chest, Dr Davies found the lungs 'gorged with blood'.

He said, 'I am convinced that sufficient violence must have been used to cause death, and I have no doubt that death must have been caused by strangulation, caused by external pressure.'

Dr Davies had carried out his examination on Monday 11 December. The next day William Hill was arrested and the murder inquiry began in earnest as police set about interviewing the prisoner's drinking companions on the fateful Thursday night out. Among them were several of his workmates at the Warrington factory of Hadfield and Frost, cotton spinners and weavers, in Cockhedge Lane.

It was one of a number of mills that had sprung up in the town during the early 19th century rise of the South Lancashire cotton trade, giving new impetus to a local weaving tradition that had established its place in history by supplying much of the sail-cloth for Nelson's victorious fleet. And William Hill was one of the comparatively new class of workers – the factory hands and mill girls – who had been the human products of the revolution in the textile industry, brought about in general by the increasing mechanisation of manufacturing methods and, in particular, the advent of steam power.

Hill himself operated a power-loom, the invention, first used commercially in a Manchester mill, that released weaving from the solitary confinement of the home and into the crowded captivity of the factory, where long hours, hard work and autocratic employers were the tough new disciplines. There, in a noisy, dangerous and all-round unhealthy environment, the mill workers toiled for 12–15 hours a day (even children as young as nine were employed for up to nine hours a day). And in the developing northern industrial towns, where housing expansion tended to follow closely behind the mushrooming factories, the quality of their domestic lives could be almost as harsh.

They lived, invariably, in cramped, unsanitary houses in densely-packed streets, with raw sewage flowing in open drains down the middle of the roadway. It was little wonder, therefore, that so many mill hands sought escape from such squalid reality in the open-all-hours distractions of the ale-houses – which were only required by law to close during divine service on Sundays and on Good Friday and Christmas Day – and the beer-shops.

Hill came from just that kind of background. He lived quite close to his place of work, in Cockhedge Lane itself. Today this part of Warrington is the site of another major town centre retail re-development project; in the late 18th century, as Arthur Bennett wrote in *The Dream of a Warringtonian* (1900), it was a quiet, little used and 'sweetly shaded' lane. But, by 1837, he lamented, it had become 'a nest of reeking slums'.

It was from here, at about 7.45pm on 7 December, that Hill set out to walk the quarter of a mile to the Legh Arms. He got there at around 8 o'clock and, within an hour, there were nine young men and at least one young woman drinking together in the taproom. Among them were three of his workmates, Ralph Kerfoot, James Holbrook and Holbrook's sister Eliza.

Kerfoot said in evidence that during the early part of the evening, Mrs Minshull came into the taproom and sat with Hill for about an hour. Between midnight and 1am, with the party now down to eight, a quarrel broke out between Edward Cox and Joseph Yates; a few minutes later they went into the Market Place to settle their differences there. All but Hill followed them out, said Kerfoot. He added, 'Cox and Yates then began to fight in the Market Place opposite the house. They fought a few rounds, then we all left…Hill was not with us.'

What had happened to the prisoner was revealed by James Holbrook, also a weaver. Up to the time of the row, he confirmed, the evening had gone well. 'There was a good deal of singing,' he stated. 'We were all merry, laughing and joking.' He also recalled a conversation he had had with Hill while Betty Minshull was out fetching them a fresh supply of ale. In it, Holbrook alleged, the accused passed some indecent remark about what he intended to do to 'that old b–––––' (referring to the woman) before he went home.

When Cox and Yates began arguing, Holbrook said, Mrs Minshull ordered them out as 'she did not like any disturbance in the house'. He went on, 'We all went out, except Hill, at the door looking out into the corn market. I saw the prisoner and Betty Minshull together near the door, and the door was closed as soon as we got to the bottom of the steps. Betty Minshull closed the door and the prisoner was then inside.'

Both Holbrook and his sister also testified to seeing Hill when they arrived at work at 6 o'clock the next morning and noticing scratches on his face that had not been there the night before. Said Holbrook, 'There were four marks on his left cheek, which appeared like finger-nail marks.' He said nothing to Hill at that time but later in the morning he asked him where he had got to the previous night. 'He told me he had stayed about 20 minutes after we left,' Holbrook stated.

Eliza Holbrook asked Hill how he had come by the scratches, and he claimed he had got them attempting to intervene in the fight at the pub. Eliza had left the Legh Arms around 9 o'clock so she was unaware that the prisoner had, in fact, taken no part whatsoever in the fracas. She learned of Mrs Minshull's death at lunchtime on the same Friday and said to Hill, 'Why, Will, that woman's dead.' She said he replied, 'Ay, by God, is hoo [she]?' He also told her he had remained drinking with Mrs Minshull for a quarter of an hour.

The time he did leave the Legh Arms was pinpointed by Isaac Bellas, a plasterer who lodged in a house at the bottom of the mug market. The house faced the end of the passageway that led to Higginson's yard gate. Though he was not to know it at the time, Bellas saw the prisoner within minutes of the murder taking place.

He told the court he had been out late that night and returned to his lodgings to find his landlord, James Longshaw, already in bed and the house locked up. It was while he was hammering on the front door to rouse Longshaw that he spotted Hill coming down the passage towards him. It was a moonlit night and as the prisoner got within a few feet of him he said he called out, 'Bill is that thee?' But the other man made no reply and hurried on in the direction of Horsemarket Street.

If the case against Hill was built on circumstantial evidence, the one concrete piece in its construction was Betty Minshull's stolen snuff-box, its strongest buttress the testimony of Richard Lyon. The latter was acknowledged as such by the defence, though Hill's counsel argued that it was too unbelievable a story to be true. As well he might…for what Lyon had to tell was a weird tale indeed.

Richard Lyon was an 'overlooker' and Hill's immediate superior at the Cockhedge mill. He said that a few minutes before 3am on Friday 8 December, he was awoken by a knock on the front door of his house in Stoney Lane. On getting up to go to his bedroom window, he saw the defendant standing in the street below. He went down to let him in and Hill proceeded to relate how he had been at the fair and had had 'the best lark he had ever had in his life'. In somewhat more lurid language, he boasted of having had sex 'with a landlady'.

Less than two hours after committing rape and murder – where he had been in the meantime was never explained at the trial – Hill was apparently knocking up a workmate to admit having just been with the dead woman.

Next, said Lyon, Hill produced a small clasp-knife with a buck-horn handle and asked his supervisor to keep it 'for a memorandum' (*sic*). He then suggested he might stay the night there; for, although his own house was quite close by, he 'thought he should not be up in time enough for work in the morning' if he did not get to bed soon.

Lyon said he persuaded his unexpected late-night caller to return to Cockhedge Lane, however, after promising to call for him to make sure he got to work on time. The two did walk to work together as arranged on the Friday and the day passed uneventfully.

The next incident of significance occurred at work on the Saturday morning when, said Lyon, Hill asked to borrow a knife, an essential tool of the weaving trade. Lyon reminded him of the clasp knife he was holding for him and returned it to Hill. Also, said Lyon, 'before the workmen were paid', Hill handed him a half-sovereign and six shillings in silver for him to keep until Christmas time, when the two were planning to visit a friend in Bolton. The inference, clearly, was that this was money Hill had taken off Betty Minshull.

Hill's seemingly suicidal behaviour continued on the following Monday, according to Lyon. He said that, while at work, the prisoner 'appeared very uneasy' and brought up the subject of the murder at the Legh Arms, by now the main talking point among the mill workers. The ensuing conversation, the *Liverpool Mercury* informed its readers gravely, was 'unfit for publication'.

The Haddock text was less circumspect, however. Its account of this part of Lyon's evidence stated, 'He told me that on the night of Thursday, after the other company left, he drank two glasses of ale with her, which was left in the jug…The woman, he said, then went out with him to the back door, to light him out; that the back door was left open; and when they got to the bottom of the yard, he laid hold of her, and put her in the necessary. She screamed and scratched his face.'

In parentheses, Haddock reported, 'The witness added further statements of the prisoner, which left no doubt that he had…committed one capital offence. One of these statements conveyed an intimation of so revolting a nature, that a murmur of horror and indignation ran through the court.'

The pamphlet had already revealed the substance of the statement, however, in its initial resumé of the case. Describing Betty Minshull's violent struggle and Hill's successful attempts to silence her, Haddock said the prisoner had 'by this means affected his purpose… twice; once as the prisoner said to Lyon…after the unfortunate woman was *fallen asleep* (his italics), which must have been when she was dead'.

Lyon then came to the crucial evidence linking Hill with the theft of Mrs Minshull's snuff-box. Referring again to his Monday morning chat with the prisoner, he stated, 'During this conversation, he showed me a snuff-box which he said he had taken from Betty Minshull. It had the appearance of silver. It was moulded at the opening and ribbed, and the ribs were broader in the middle than at the edge, and it had the mark "No.66" inside. He told me he had thrown the knife into the reservoir on the Saturday and that he would throw the box into the reservoir also. He afterwards told me he had done so.'

The reservoir in question adjoined the cotton mill at which Hill and Lyon worked. On Saturday 23 December, Deputy Constable Jones and Assistant Constable Thomas Joynson were present when part of the reservoir, indicated by Lyon, was dammed up and a team of 10 workmen began emptying it to try to find the important piece of evidence. With the job almost completed, however, the dam began to give way and the men had to hurriedly search the bottom of the reservoir with their hands before all the water poured back in on them. It was then that labourer John Thomason's fingers closed around a small, familiar object in the mud below. After cleaning it off he handed it to Joynson. It was later identified by Richard Lyon as the snuff-box Hill had shown him at work on the Monday after the murder. Mary Pritchard confirmed it had belonged to the deceased.

The case for the prosecution closed with the formal submission of the statements the defendant made, first to the examining magistrate (to which the illiterate Hill had put his customary mark) and then during the committal proceedings. In them, Hill admitted being alone with the woman for a short while after closing time, but maintained that she had been alive when he left in the early hours of the morning.

Opening for the defence, Mr Brandt said the first question for the jury to decide was whether the deceased had come by her death by violence; secondly, whether that violence had been committed by the prisoner 'under circumstances that amounted to the crime of murder'. Neither, he said, had been proved.

Mr Brandt then dealt at length with the evidence of Richard Lyon. Counsel said he did not believe that 'in human nature there could be such a monster of barbarity' as Hill would have had to be to have acted in the manner alleged by his overlooker...'or such a beast in intellect, so void even of the animal instinct of self-preservation as he must have been if, with the consciousness of having occasioned the death of a fellow creature, he went straight away, at 3 o'clock in the morning, to boast of what he had done, and furnished then and subsequently, the only evidence that could convict him – his guilt, if he were guilty, being then known to himself alone'.

Mr Brandt said he conceded that if a man, in committing or attempting to commit a felony, caused someone's death, the offence was murder; even though the offender had no intention to kill. Consequently, if the prisoner had, in raping or attempting to rape Betty Minshull, occasioned her death, it was the duty of the jury to find him guilty. But, he argued, this had not been made out in evidence; on the contrary, said Mr Brandt, there was 'a strong presumption' that the deceased had died 'in one of those fainting fits to which she was subject' and which they had heard were 'liable to be produced by any excitement'.

In his summing up, Mr Justice Patteson re-affirmed the defence's reading of the law regarding a violent death caused in the commission of a felony. He told the jury, 'If you are of opinion that the prisoner at the bar, in attempting to have connection with the deceased against her will, and by force – that is, in attempting to commit a rape – occasioned her death, it is immaterial whether he intended to kill her or not; the offence was murder.'

It was 3.50pm when the jurors retired to consider their verdict. An hour and 10 minutes later they returned to declare William Hill guilty as charged. The judge said he was 'not at all surprised' at their conclusion; everyone who had heard the case, he said, 'must be convinced that he is in truth guilty of the offence imputed to him'.

His Lordship told the prisoner in the dock, 'I by no means mean to say – nor do I think that any of the jury mean to say – that, when you went out at the back of the house with the unfortunate deceased, you intended to murder her, or had any such notion passing in your mind. But I do believe that you were determined at that time to have connection with her, either with or without her consent – in other words to commit a rape upon her – that she resisted as much as she could, and that in the attempt to stifle her screams you strangled her.'

The prisoner had, in fact, been guilty of murder, rape and robbery. And, said the judge, the case had been such an aggravated one that he could not 'hold out the slightest hope of mercy'.

William Hill may have become a murderer by accident, but the law's purpose was now quite unequivocal: as the traditional black cap was placed on the judge's head, in ritual preparation for the passing of the death sentence, the condemned man braced himself for the inevitable grim recital.

Haddock recounted, 'During the passing of the sentence, the prisoner closed his eyes and became apparently faint and nearly insensible, but he uttered not a word, nor exhibited any violent emotion. At its conclusion, he walked from the bar accompanied by an officer, but scarcely availing himself of the support which the officer attended to afford.' The court, Haddock noted, was 'crowded almost to suffocation' throughout the five-and-a-half hour trial.

Despite the judge's crushing comment about the prospects of clemency, efforts to obtain a reprieve for Hill began immediately upon his return to Kirkdale Gaol in Liverpool. It was to be an excruciatingly long wait; but, as the days turned into weeks and there was still no word about the date for his execution, the prisoner was doubtless encouraged by the delay. On Thursday 19 April, however, came the official announcement that the court's decision had, after all, been upheld.

In a letter read to Hill that evening, Sir John Patteson stated that he saw nothing in the case to alter his opinion that the accused had caused Betty Minshull's death in the course of a felonious act. He said he had considered carefully the petition on Hill's behalf and had submitted it, together with his own notes on the trial, to other eminent legal experts, who had all concurred with his view.

Hill was said to have borne the news with 'great resignation' – though, as we shall see presently, his hopes of a change of heart were raised literally at the last minute. The most graphic description of the execution, and of the dramatic incident in which the prisoner's life looked to have been saved even as the noose was being tightened around his neck, was published in the *Liverpool Albion*. The report is reproduced at some length as it also provides a sharp illustration of the attitude towards public executions that still prevailed, at least among a certain section of the populace, even towards the middle of the 19th century.

William Hill was hanged outside the walls of Kirkdale Gaol at 8 o'clock on the morning of Easter Saturday 21 April 1838. Formerly the local 'house of correction', the building had opened in 1819. The prison was demolished in the 1890s and the site was turned into a recreation ground. The *Albion* report stated,

It was very generally believed that the execution would take place at noon, as on former occasions. The appointment of an earlier hour, therefore, must have been the cause of bitter disappointment to many who had promised themselves the pleasure of witnessing the ignominious and violent death of a fellow being. Notwithstanding the alteration, however, not less than four or five hundred people had assembled. This, however, was but a mere handful to the vast assemblages that have poured to the spot from all quarters to witness former executions [later ones were equally well attended and the developing railway companies reacted to the demand by laying on extra trains].

From half-past seven to eight o'clock, numbers of people, principally, but not all, of the humbler classes, were seen wending their way, with delighted eagerness, along the various avenues leading to the gaol. Amongst these were many females and children; some of the former attended by young men, while many of the latter were accompanied by their parents. All parties seemed to be stimulated by extreme curiosity, and it was with hurried footsteps and smiling faces that the majority of them pressed forward to the spot from whence a view of the gallows could be best obtained. As the spectator neared the walls of the gaol, it was easy to see that many people were not unmindful either of their pleasure or their appetites.

A marquee had been erected at the south-west corner of the gaol. Here some determined dealer had removed a barrel or two of beer, and the extensive array of white mugs, of all dimensions, showed that he expected to drive a thriving trade. One or two fellows, regardless of the early hour, were already whetting their whistles, while numbers of others were jumping and frolicking about in the area or field opposite.

Beneath the black scaffold, which was erected near the top of the prison wall, at the north-west corner, the crowd had compacted themselves into a solid mass.

There they stood, with the self-satisfied and determined air of people who, having by their early attendance secured good places, are determined not to give them up. There was a little occasional pushing and hustling amongst the people, but, generally speaking, this portion of the crowd stood steady enough, the majority being either afraid of the police or of losing their places…Had it not been for the admirable regulations made, and for the rigour with which the officers kept the people within the prescribed bounds, we have no doubt great damage would have been done to the property adjacent, as scores of the worst characters from the town were on the ground.

Referring to Hill's time in prison, the *Albion* revealed that he 'did not make any decided confession'. He had 'acknowledged, at different times, that he was the cause of the death of the unfortunate woman…but he never entered into any particulars from which the true nature of the crime could be inferred'. The newspaper had it from a reliable source, however, that Hill continued to insist he was 'entirely ignorant' of the injury he had done to Mrs Minshull and that 'when he left her, he had not the least idea of her being dead'.

Hill's aged mother and brother had visited him last on Good Friday. The meeting, said the *Albion*, was 'a melancholy one, and marked by much painful emotion'. Then, returning to the execution preliminaries, the report continued,

Shortly before eight o'clock [Hill] was led through several passages to the area beneath the scaffold ante-room. Here Mr Amos, the Governor, delivered him into the charge of the Under-Sheriff. When the Under-Sheriff addressed the prisoner, the latter took off his hat, which, however, he resumed again as he ascended the steps.

On his arrival at the ante-room, he was placed in a chair, where the executioner… pinioned his hands and arms and placed the rope about his neck. As the operation last named was performed, the prisoner showed the first symptom of emotion. His countenance became pallid and his breast heaved convulsively. The feeling, however, seemed to be but transient and, when he arose from his seat, he exhibited the same firmness of demeanour as had before characterised him…He was then taken hold of by the executioner, who led him to the scaffold, whither he walked with a firm step. He was placed under the drop and the rope was adjusted.

Then, just as the chaplain began reading the valedictory prayers, the proceedings were brought to a sensational halt. The *Albion* reported,

At this painful moment, when the unhappy creature was suspended, as it were, between life and death, a most distressing incident occurred. A messenger approached the passage leading to the scaffold, in breathless haste, holding in his hand a letter addressed to the Reverend Mr Horner. There was a general and simultaneous shout of 'Stop!' and the letter was put into the hands of the chaplain. It bore the superscription 'To be delivered instantly - affecting life and death'. The awful ceremony was, for an instant, suspended, and the minister left the scaffold to open the letter. To the surprise and indignation of all present, it was an anonymous production, written by some well-meaning but very ignorant person, imploring the execution to be stayed on account of the supposed innocence of Hill.

This was a truly painful occurrence, for the general impression seemed to be that the communication was the harbinger of the unhappy man's deliverance from that grave on the brink of which he then stood. The worthy chaplain was deeply affected at this annoying, and at the moment, most harrowing event.

The cruel hiatus over, however, the proceedings were swiftly resumed and the executioner concluded his deadly business. As the *Albion* put it, 'The bolt was drawn and William Hill bade adieu to this world of suffering.' Then, with a touch of grim finality, 'He struggled momentarily.'

The last public gesture of William Hill, however, was made not from the rude wooden platform of a prison gallows, but from the more inspirational stage of a church pulpit. It came in the shape of a letter composed by the convicted weaver while in Kirkdale Gaol and which, the following day, Easter Sunday, became the unusual centre-piece of a sermon preached at Warrington Parish Church by the Rector, the Hon. and Revd Horace Powys.

It was the prisoner's dying wish, it seems, that the ending of his young life should be cited as a warning to others tempted to follow his ungodly ways. The eloquent Mr Powys, in fact, used the events of what he described as 'this mournful tale' to launch into a blistering pro-Temperance tirade, attacking the evil of alcohol in all its manifestations: from the laxity of the licensing laws to the loose morals of the drinking classes, from the ill-gotten profits of the liquor trade to the unscrupulousness of all those employed in it. And, to get his message across to a wider audience, the crusading cleric later had the transcript of his sermon, including the contents of the Hill letter, published in pamphlet form.

It would appear that Messrs Haddock, Hurst and Booth, the consortium behind the Hill trial and execution pamphlet, had approached Mr Powys for permission to quote from the condemned man's final words (dictated to Revd Horner) and also from the covering letter in which they were conveyed by the Kirkdale prison chaplain to the Warrington rector. But, in an introductory note, Powys explained that he had chosen to have the documents published – the pamphlet was printed, incidentally, by the rival firm of Thomas Hope of Buttermarket Street – as an integral part of the sermon in hopes that 'they may be so turned to a better purpose than the mere gratification of idle curiosity'.

He wrote, 'I have no time, if I had the disposition, to revise or qualify any of the expressions used from the pulpit. The occasion, to my mind, called for an earnest appeal; and warrants the strong terms I used, with regard to the daily increasing evils of ill-regulated public-houses and beer-shops. The latter being, I believe, the greatest curse that ever was inflicted by the legislature on the people of England.'

Revd Horner's note concluded, 'William Hill was once a member of the Warrington Temperance Association but broke his pledge; a sufficient proof that human pledges without religious principles are not sufficient as a radical cure for drunkenness…In all conversations which I had with the unhappy convict in Kirkdale, Sabbath breaking was the first, and drinking the second, cause to which he always reverted as the foundation of his offences against God and Man.'

As the text of his sermon, Revd Powys took the second book of Kings, chapter eight, verse 13: 'And Hazael said, "But what, is thy Servant a Dog, that he should do this great thing?"' It was a quotation from the story of how God wreaked vengeance on the Israelites for turning their backs on Him. He chose as his earthly tool Hazael, a man of high rank who was close to the ailing ruler Benhadad. When Hazael murdered Benhadad by suffocating him with a damp cloth as he lay on his sick-bed, and proclaimed himself the new King of Syria, there began a bloody reign of terror that had been foretold to Hazael by the prophet Elijah.

The latter had confided, 'I know the evil thou wilt do unto the children of Israel; their strong-holds wilt thou set on fire, and their young men wilt thou slay with the sword, and wilt dash their children, and rip up their women with child.'

The Powys text was Hazael's immediate 'what-sort-of-a-person-do-you-take-me-for?' reaction to the prophecy. And in a further emotional outburst that suggests Hill's trial lawyer had been inspired by the same passage from the Scriptures, the Syrian chief proclaimed, 'Am I so fierce, barbarous, and inhuman a being that I should be capable of committing such acts of wanton barbarity?'

Reaching the central theme of his dissertation, Rector Powys said there were 'many points of similarity' between the story of Hazael and the case of William Hill.

Powys clearly cast Hill in the Hazael role, punishing the purveyors of liquor (in the guise of Betty Minshull) for the wickedness he believed flowed from their ungodly trade. The rector insisted he did not want to be seen as 'passing an uncharitable judgment upon the character of one who has become the victim of another's guilt'. But he had this to say about the late Mrs Minshull, '…of *what class* of persons did this unhappy woman form a part? [She was] one of those by whom the vicious current of depraved vice is fed from day to day…But a few minutes before her awful death was she engaged, unknown to herself, in inflaming the passions of her murderer…For months and years had she…lived on the wages of unrighteousness, earned by pampering sinful passions…A *landlady* of a public house, maltreated, robbed, and murdered by a favoured customer' (his italics).

Like Hazael, Powys believed, William Hill had not planned the criminal results of his 'night's debauch'. And to anyone predicting such an outcome, Hill would no doubt have responded in much the same way as the Old Testament tyrant had in answering the prophet's warning.

The rector went on to tell his congregation that Hill had asked him to make his appeal so that others 'from his great fall may learn to watch and pray, lest they enter into temptation'.

Revd Horner, in his letter to the Warrington rector, had said he found Hill 'a man of few words', who would not speak of his conduct towards the dead woman. When pressed to do so, he would reply, 'They know too much of that already. I do not like that to be talked of.' But he did get a lot off his chest in a statement taken down by the prison chaplain. Powys read it verbatim to his by now thoroughly attentive flock. It ran,

'I wove at a hand-loom from the age of nine to 21 when I went to Mr Eskrigge's factory [Thomas Eskrigge, cotton-spinners of St James Street, Latchford, and Hope Mill, Warrington]. I left off going to church when about 14 or 15 years old and spent my Sundays in walking about with other young men, often spending my evenings in drinking...I began to drink hard when about 20 years old. I drank both ale and spirits...and led a sad, wild life. I...cannot say that my bad conduct was from anything but drink. Had I followed going to church, it would not have happened.

'About a year ago I was working at Bolton and lodged with James Kitchen, who advised me continually to go to church. I promised him I would, but never went. I spent my time in roving about and drinking but never joined any thieves nor was intimate with any I thought such...My mother was at me every day about drunkenness, till it brought me here.

'I hope all young men will take warning by my example, and avoid drink, loose company, and Sabbath-breaking. It may come to their lot to die suddenly, and they may not have even the same opportunity for repenting that I have had.'

Hill ended with a reference to the sexual assault that preceded Mrs Minshull's death and confirmed that the woman had in no way encouraged him.

Revd Powys, a well-loved Rector of Warrington who did much to improve the education of the poor and who achieved hero status for his ministrations when a plague of Asiatic cholera wiped out 169 of his parishioners in 1833, made a fervent plea to his congregation to heed Hill's warning. He exhorted, 'Oh flee from, and never again enter, those haunts of vice, where drunkards, fornicators, adulterers, blasphemers, thieves and Sabbath-breakers love to meet and carry on their vicious revels.'

Outside his congregation, however, his earnest entreaties seem to have fallen on stony ground; and the roll of Warrington 'students' seeking an education in the alcoholic arts showed no sign of reducing. On the contrary, such was the demand that by 1853 the number of inns in Warrington had increased from 84 (in 1824) to 103, serving a population of around 21,000.

And drunkenness continued to bedevil the town. On 25 June that year, the fledgling *Warrington Guardian* revealed that, in the 11 weeks since its first edition appeared, of 323 charges heard by the local magistrates, no fewer than 107 had involved drink. And a little more than a month later, in its issue of Friday 30 July, the *Guardian* carried the story of a liquor-crazed mob that had gone on the rampage in lower Buttermarket Street. 'For some time,' the newspaper reported, 'running fights went on between men and women in every stage of drunkenness.'

Quite what the Reverend Powys made of that particular affair is not recorded; but a year later he left Warrington for more peaceful pastures after being consecrated Bishop of Sodor and Man.

11

Bessie: Bride of Jack the Ripper?

> On Friday another addition was made to the series of horrible crimes that has created a panic in the East End of London...the unfortunate woman was found lying dead and frightfully mutilated...(in) a scene more terrible than any of the others...

The Illustrated Police News, 17 November 1888

> The exhumation of a body is so rare an occurrence that when one takes place it cannot fail to arouse the greatest interest...Not only did the exhumation at Lymm on Saturday attract much morbid curiosity, but the interest spread to London...

Warrington Guardian, 29 November 1902

IN ITS tree-shaded spot just inside the lych-gate, the solidly handsome headstone records, in 13 neatly etched lines, the passing of four members of the Taylor family. But there's a significant detail missing from the otherwise comprehensive inscription. It's the name of a murderer.

The last listed occupant of the grave is given simply as 'Bessie', daughter of Thomas and Betsy Taylor who, along with their daughter Mary Gertrude, also lie buried in the same plot in the pretty little hillside cemetery attached to the parish church at Lymm. However, closer examination of the weathered sandstone reveals evidence that part of the engraving has at some time been removed and re-done. The purpose: to erase the former Bessie Taylor's married name and, thus, all reference to the husband who was alleged to have been her killer.

Bessie's death, and the subsequent exhumation of her body, figured largely in a sensational murder trial in 1903. The case aroused national interest and attracted crowds of curiosity-seekers to the tiny Cheshire churchyard; and it was to deter this unwanted attention, apparently, that the Taylors' relatives, possibly at the suggestion of the Vicar, the Reverend Granville Thurston, agreed to have the memorial stone's inscription altered.

The obliterated surname was 'Chapman'. It belonged to George Chapman, otherwise Severin Antoniovich Klosowski, a Polish-born immigrant, philanderer and alleged triple murderer. More memorably, he was also the man some believe was...Jack the Ripper.

That Chapman, convicted of murder by poison, was also the fiend of Whitechapel, the blood-crazed knifeman who cut the throats and ripped open the bodies of a succession of London prostitutes in the Autumn of 1888, has been suggested, with varying degrees of confidence, by several self-styled experts on the case which, in keeping with its undisputed claim as the greatest criminal mystery of all time, has inspired as many theories as there have been books written on the subject.

From 'the highest in the land' to a humble slaughterman; from men of rank, their names named and reputations forever blackened, to a procession of faceless nonentities – all, in their turn, have been put in the dock by a seemingly unending procession of would-be prosecutors.

It has been claimed that Albert Victor Christian Edward (Prince 'Eddy'), Duke of Clarence, grandson of Queen Victoria and Heir Presumptive to the throne of England, no less, was Jack the Ripper. Sir William Gull, Physician in Ordinary to Queen Victoria, has also been accused; so, too, has Prince Eddy's close friend and tutor James Stephen, a lawyer/poet who was supposed to have killed 10 times, taking as his guiding text the reference to 'ten harlots of Jerusalem' in the bawdy ballad *Kaphoozelum*.

But in what is by far the most amazing, if ingeniously argued, disquisition to date, the enigmatic Jack is revealed not as one man but three, with Sir William Gull, the artist Walter Sickert and a hired coachmen called Netley the murdering triumvirate, launching their campaign of death and mutilation as part of a masonic conspiracy to safeguard the Monarchy by covering up the clandestine marriage and resulting offspring of Prince Eddy and a Roman Catholic commoner...all with the connivance of the Prime Minister (Lord Salisbury) and the Metropolitan Police Commissioner, Sir Charles Warren.

This entertaining saga of crime and corruption in high places, concocted by the late Stephen Knight in his book *Jack the Ripper: The Final Solution* (1976), has it that four of the five prostitute victims were silenced because they knew too much about the royal intrigue and the fifth was slain by mistake.

Like the fascinating game of Hunt-the-Ripper, more than 120 years old and showing no sign of losing its appeal, the list of suspects goes on...and on.

Among others identified have been: Montague Druitt, a cricket-playing barrister-turned-teacher who drowned himself in the River Thames after, it has been suggested, carrying out the murders on some kind of insane moral-reforming crusade (one of the more popular theories, this); poisoner Neil Cream, the Scottish doctor who was said to have confessed to being Jack the Ripper on several occasions before he was hanged in 1892, even, it was claimed, with his dying breath; a brilliant surgeon avenging the death of an only son who had contracted a fatal disease from a prostitute; a doctor dispensing his own extreme brand of medicine in an attempt to cure one of the more common social ills of the day; a mad Russian secret agent out to discredit the British police...and a collection of anonymous types, including a seaman off a Continental cattle-boat (a possibility raised by Queen Victoria herself, apparently), a Jewish ritual slaughterman and a midwife/

abortionist, the latter being the leading candidate commended by those favouring a 'Jill the Ripper' twist to the tale.

And then there is George Chapman...

Chapman, a former barber who latterly cut something of a dash as landlord of several London pubs, was hanged in April 1903, for the murder of Maud Marsh, one of three 'wives' (it is doubtful whether he was ever legally married to any of the women) who were all eventually found to have died from antimony poisoning. Bessie Taylor, daughter of a Cheshire farmer, whose death went unqueried for nearly two years before the truth was unearthed, was the second of his three alleged victims.

The possibility that Chapman was Jack the Ripper, and that England's most celebrated murderer once went a-courting down the leafy lanes of sleepy Lymm village in north Cheshire, is said to have occurred first to Detective Inspector Frederick Abberline, who led each of the Ripper murder investigations, though it does not seem to have become public knowledge until some time after Chapman's death. During the time Chapman was in custody, Abberline, by then a chief inspector, was reported to have tracked down the Polish woman with whom the prisoner was living at the time of the Ripper killings and quizzed her about his movements. The woman told him that Chapman, or Klosowski, as she knew him, was regularly out until 3 or 4 o'clock in the morning and would give no explanation for his absences.

Abberline, it has been claimed, never wavered in his belief that Chapman and the Ripper were one and the same person; there was the famous occasion when, on seeing Chapman brought in for questioning about Maud Marsh's murder, the police chief made a comment to the arresting officer on the lines of 'I see you have got the Ripper at last!' Other Ripperologists, however, have since insisted that the focus of Abberline's suspicions later switched to a Russian doctor who just happened to be Chapman's double.

And while agreeing that Chapman might have had the opportunity – he was working in the area throughout the period of the Ripper murders – and the capability (the prosecutor at his trial spoke of his 'history of unbridled, heartless and cruel lust'), most commentators have been unable to accept that such a sadistic and exhibitionistic sexual murderer, as the Ripper undoubtedly was, could have so changed *modus operandi* as to become a secret domestic poisoner and have, ultimately, dismissed the proposition as being too improbable to be worthy of serious consideration.

But is it any more fantastic, one is bound to ask, than the idea of an unholy trinity working for the greater good of the Throne, the Government and Freemasonry? Or of a titled surgeon, used to making house-calls to Royalty, suddenly going off the rails and stalking the stinking alleyways of lowlife London disembowelling whores? Or the notion of a Red spy at night overdoing it with the cloak-and-dagger stuff?

Unprecedented as it might be, the George the Ripper theory had two notable champions. In *Trial of George Chapman*, published in 1930, Hargrave L. Adam drew on court records, police files and other official documentation to compile a massively-detailed dossier on Chapman. And, while conceding that there was never any material proof of the connection, he nevertheless concluded, 'A reasonable case for supposing that Chapman was Jack-the-Ripper has, at least, been furnished.'

But the most positive identification of George Chapman as Jack the Ripper came from Arthur Fowler Neil, a retired detective superintendent who ended his police career as one of the top four CID officers at New Scotland Yard. He had worked on the Chapman case while he was a detective sergeant and in his autobiography, *Forty Years of Manhunting*, published in 1932, he stated that, although the police were never able to secure proof that Chapman was the Ripper, it was 'the most fitting and sensible solution to the possible identity of the murderer'.

As such a high-ranking officer, he would almost certainly have had access to even the most top-secret police intelligence on the case, and he hinted as much when he wrote, 'My statement is a theory, I admit, but it is backed up by facts that bear the cold searchlight of reason, that is, facts that have *evidence to support them*' (author's italics).

Of all the subsequent pronouncements on the possible identity of Jack the Ripper made either publicly or privately by police officers serving at or soon after the time of the murders, Neil's is arguably the most assured. Before putting the supporting evidence once more under the searchlight, however, it is necessary to re-state some of the less contentious facts about the Whitechapel mystery.

The story has been told many times before; the bare bones will be familiar to the countless thousands who have read the books, seen the films and plays or heard the arguments aired on television and the radio. But the subject has been exposed to so much dissection (no pun intended) and dissertation, the minutiae examined and re-examined and the various theories put up and picked off like the perpetually revolving targets in a fairground shooting gallery, that some of the more fundamental truths – the unimaginably squalid social conditions in which the murders took place, the almost inhuman savagery with which they were committed, the sheer unmitigated evil inherent in the crimes and the feelings of fear and revulsion they spread throughout the land – have lost much of their original impact, their power to shock drained by the surge of literary debate, the awfulness of their reality blurred by the soft-focus of popular drama.

Seeking to rationalise the irrational and solve a mystery that is probably beyond solution, recent authors have inevitably concentrated on analysing and revising previous judgments, dismantling old arguments or, more commendably, have undertaken new areas of research to produce fresh clues, even documentary 'proof' to support their own particular theories. But the atmosphere of terror-on-the-streets and the wider sense of outrage and anger over the ineffectualness of the forces of law that prevailed in Victorian England in that Autumn of 1888 were created, not by the primary school phraseology of police-coached witnesses' statements or the measured tones of long-suppressed official reports, but by the emotive language of the daily Press coverage.

Local as well as national newspapers reported the sensational events in ever gorier detail; and, although some of the more lurid revelations had little basis in reality, it was the fourth estate which provided the public's first source of information about the unbelievable horrors being perpetrated by this apparent phantom who, it seemed, had dubbed himself 'Jack the Ripper'. So, before returning to the Chapman case and the Cheshire connection, we shall first go back to those same public pages to get a flavour of the times when the shadowy figure who was seemingly 'down on whores' flitted, silent and deadly, through the mist-shrouded mean streets of London's East End.

The widely accepted view, confirmed by the re-discovered notes of Sir Melville Macnaghten, who was appointed Assistant Chief Constable at Scotland Yard in 1889, is that, despite the many postulated permutations, the Ripper struck five times only in his 10-week reign of terror. And, though collectively they have come to be known as the 'Whitechapel murders' (mainly because the first occurred there and several other similar killings in the district were originally thought to have been the work of the same hand), four of the five were committed in neighbouring Spitalfields.

In each case, however, the territory the mysterious assassin chose was the suffocating mesh of streets, passageways and courts that was at the foul heart of East End slumland – a seething mass of overcrowded tenements and dirty doss-houses – and his every victim a member of that street-wise sisterhood the Victorians referred to delicately as 'unfortunates' and who, along with the pimps and procurers, the thieves, muggers and drunkards, made up a sizable proportion of the area's population.

The first was Mary Ann ('Polly') Nichols, aged 42, a small, dowdy mother-of-five long since separated from her husband who, after being dismissed from her last job as a domestic servant for stealing from her employer, had degenerated into a life of alcoholism and prostitution. She was murdered between 2.30 and 3.15am on Friday 31 August in Bucks Row (now Durward Street), an ill-lit thoroughfare close to the busy Whitechapel Road. She was last seen staggering drunkenly into the night, swanking about her 'jolly' new hat and cheerfully confident she would soon find someone willing to buy her favours for the fourpence price of a bed in the Spitalfields common lodging-house from which she had just been evicted.

Her body was discovered by a Pickford's driver on his way to work. At first he mistook it for a tarpaulin strewn on the pavement; then, when he realised it was a woman lying there, he thought she had been 'outraged' and 'gone off in a swoon'. Polly Nichols's 'jolly' new hat had come off in the struggle and was on the ground nearby. Patrolling police constable John Neil, on arriving at the scene shortly afterwards, also jumped to the wrong conclusion.

The *Illustrated Police News*, the leading scandal-sheet of the day, reported in the following week's edition, '...in the dim light the constable at first thought that the woman had fallen down in a drunken stupor and was sleeping off the effects of a night's debauch.' But he quickly realised his error. 'With the aid of the light from his bullseye lantern, Neil at once perceived that the woman had been the victim of some horrible outrage,' the newspaper went on. 'Her livid face was stained with blood and her throat cut from ear to ear.'

It was not until the body was removed to the Whitechapel mortuary, however, that the full extent of the woman's terrible injuries was revealed. Needless to say, the *Illustrated Police News* described them in detail; but it was not only the racier sections of the Press who broadcast the pathologist's findings. The traditionally more temperate *Warrington Guardian*, for instance, did not mince words, either.

Its issue of Saturday 1 September declared, 'The brutality of the murder is beyond conception or description.' But it managed, 'Not only was the unfortunate woman's throat cut…but the knife was stabbed into the lower part of the abdomen and savagely drawn upwards twice, one cutting left of the groin and hip, the other slitting the abdomen as high as the breastbone.' The conclusion was obvious, but the paper stated it anyway, 'The brutality of the crime leads the police to believe that the perpetrator must be a ferocious maniac.'

The *(Manchester) Guardian* spread the shocking message to a wider regional audience. SHOCKING MURDER OF A WOMAN IN LONDON its headline blazoned on that same opening day of September. And in both its news-in-brief digest and its more comprehensive story on a later page, it spoke of 'a sensational crime', of the murder of a woman 'in barbarous fashion' and of her body being 'shockingly mutilated'. The deceased had been wearing 'a rough brown ulster with large buttons in front', said the paper, adding, 'Her clothes are torn and cut up in several places, bearing evidence of the ferocity with which the murder was committed.'

Though the terminology had not yet been introduced into the language – the sinister nickname that would guarantee the murderer a sort of anonymous immortality did not become common currency until after the next attack – Ripper-mania had taken root.

Victim No. 2 was Annie Chapman, whose bloody end eight days later was a carbon copy of the Polly Nichols murder. 'Dark Annie', as she was known on account of her dark, wavy hair, now streaked with grey, was 47. Like Polly Nichols, she was a once respectable woman, the widow (she said) of a Windsor veterinary surgeon and mother-of-two who had fallen on hard times and resorted to prostitution as a means of raising money for drink and her nightly doss. And on the night she died she, too, had been roaming the gloomy streets in search of business after being turned away penniless from her usual lodgings in Dorset Street, Spitalfields.

At around 6 o'clock on this Saturday morning, 8 September, she was discovered lying spreadeagled obscenely at the foot of the steps leading into the backyard of No. 29, Hanbury Street by a market porter, one of 17 people then living in the tenement's four floors of rented accommodation above a basement cat-meat shop. Her body had previously borne the marks of a recent fight with a fellow lodger, a black eye and a badly bruised chest which had required hospital treatment. Now it looked as if it had been operated on by a psychopathic surgeon…or a deranged butcher.

The *Guardian* reported on 10 September, 'When the police arrived they found the woman had been murdered in a terribly brutal fashion. Her clothes were disarranged, her throat cut and her body mutilated in a manner too horrible for description.'

Again, the local *Warrington Guardian* had no such inhibitions. In its 12 September edition, the paper revealed, '...her throat was cut from ear to ear and the body ripped open. Not only so, but the heart and liver were torn out and lying on the ground.'

In fact, the latter statement was untrue – though, if anything, the atrocities performed on Annie Chapman's body were even more horrible than that. Her head had been all but severed from her body, her entire abdomen had been laid open, the intestines detached and draped grotesquely across her shoulder and her womb and one of her kidneys removed.

Was it any wonder that the Warrington newspaper, in a powerful editorial, should remark with some feeling, 'Murder follows murder in the East End of London with apparently studied regularity, a fiendish ferocity and systemised cruelty which is nothing short of appalling. The annals of the lower forms of inhuman crime will be searched in vain for any parallel series of murders. The Whitechapel tragedies stand out alone in their ghastly singularity...'

And there was worse to come. Much worse.

During the early hours of 30 September, the Ripper struck twice within the space of an hour. Once again his hapless targets were middle-aged prostitutes whose miserable hand-to-mouth existence seemed to follow the same endless route, an eternal triangle between the doss-house, the pub and the dark doorways and back-alleys of their chosen 'beats'.

Elizabeth Stride, née Gustafsdotter, was a 45-year-old Swedish woman who, at five feet five inches, was by Victorian standards taller than most of her sex and, thus, had acquired the nickname of 'Long Liz'. Just before 1am on that particular Sunday, she seems to have found herself a client and gone with him into Dutfield's Yard, a narrow passageway leading to the rear of the International Workers' Educational Club in Berner Street. He was no ordinary punter, however; and, as the hour chimed, the Ripper's razor-sharp knife flashed again and Long Liz sank to the rain-dampened ground, a crimson flood pouring from a gaping throat wound beneath the check scarf with which her killer had probably overpowered her.

Just at that moment, however, it would appear that he was disturbed by a horse and cart turning into the yard and, for the first time, he was unable to round off his ghastly work with the usual flourish of *post mortem* mutilations. It had been Louis Diemschutz, the steward of the workers' educational club (a popular rendezvous for members of the large local Jewish community, particularly Russians and Poles), who had almost caught the Ripper red-handed.

The Illustrated Police News of 6 October revealed, 'On turning into the gateway he had some difficulty with his pony, the animal apparently determined to avoid the right-hand wall. For the moment Diemschutz...thought perhaps some mud or refuse was in the way. Failing to discern anything in the darkness, Diemschutz poked about with the handle of the whip and immediately discovered that some large obstacle was in his path. To jump down and strike a match was the work of a second, and then it became at once apparent that something serious had taken place.'

The front page of *The Penny Illustrated Paper* of 6 October 1888, recording the 'double event' of 30 September, in which Jack the Ripper struck in Berner Street and Mitre Square in Whitechapel within the space of an hour.

Alone, Diemschutz was clearly wary of examining the woman's body stretched out before him, so he rushed into the club for assistance, returning to the spot a few moments later with a fellow member. The two men then took a closer look at the corpse of Elizabeth Stride. *The Police News* reported, 'The body was still warm, and the clothes enveloping it were wet from the recent rain…and the stream of blood in the gutter terminating in a hideous pool near the club door showed but too plainly what had happened.'

It was what happened next, however, that was to provide the most revealing clue to the character, if not the identity, of Jack the Ripper, a man driven by a demonic rage to not merely murder his women victims but to hideously disfigure them as well. Frustrated in his designs on the body of Elizabeth Stride, he was consumed by an ungovernable urge to find another object (for, surely, that was how he saw these pathetic street women) on which to vent his destructive lust. He soon found one.

At about the same time, Catherine Eddowes, a small, slimly-built woman of 43, was being released from Bishopsgate police station after being found in a drunken stupor in the street and locked in the cells to sober up. With characteristic chirpiness she had bid the duty sergeant goodnight and swayed off in the direction of Aldgate, heading away from the safety of her lodgings in Church Street, Spitalfields…and into the arms of the fleeing Jack the Ripper.

Their paths crossed at about 1.45am and less than 15 minutes later, barely half a mile from the spot where Liz Stride had died, another East End pavement bore the terrifyingly familiar imprint of the killer's bloody trail. And, uninterrupted this time, he had hurled himself into his grisly task with even greater ferocity.

Catherine Eddowes's body was picked out by the beam of Police Constable Edward Watkins's lantern as he probed the darker recesses of Mitre Square on his regular city beat. The *Illustrated Police News* described what the officer saw in the south-east corner of the square, in front of a high-boarded fence and, curiously, opposite a house occupied by a city police colleague, 'The scene…disclosed was a most horrible one. The woman…was lying on her back quite dead, although the body was still quite warm…The throat was cut half-way round, revealing a dreadful wound, from which blood had flowed in great quantity, staining the pavement for some distance round. Across the right cheek to the nose was another gash, and a part of the right ear had been cut off. Following the plan in the Whitechapel murders the miscreant was not content with merely killing his victim. The poor woman's clothes had been pulled up over her chest, the abdomen ripped completely open, and part of the intestines laid on her neck.'

In addition, and as reported in later editions of the newspapers, the woman's left kidney and part of her womb had also been carved out and carried away and, as a bizarre and contrastingly delicate 'refinement', the lids of both her eyes had been lacerated in almost identical fashion.

Panic, bordering on hysteria, was now abroad. 'The Metropolis', announced The *Guardian*, had been 'thrown into a state of renewed consternation' by the latest murders. And it referred to the 'public indignation' at the police's inability to catch the culprit. But, while they didn't exactly come out of the affair covered in glory, the police were being pitched into a state of some confusion themselves at this point in the investigation.

Cranks, hoaxers and the public-spirited alike were hampering their inquiries with a stream of phoney confessions, false trails and doubtful clues. There was the gruesome business of the portion of a human left kidney sent in a package to the chairman of the newly-formed Whitechapel Vigilance Committee, which the correspondent, claiming to be the murderer, stated he had removed from the body of Catherine Eddowes; and there was the apparently cryptic accusation contained in the famous writing-on-the-wall ('The Juwes are The men That Will not be Blamed for nothing') discovered, along with a bloodstained fragment of Eddowes's apron, a short distance away from Mitre Square.

It was around this time, too, that the world first heard mention of 'Jack the Ripper', the name that would forever after cast its evil shadow across the pages of crime. It was appended, not so much a *nom de plume* as a *nom de couteau*, to a letter sent to the London-based Central News Agency three days before the murderous 'double event'. The letter was one of possibly only three items of correspondence from among the many thousands received by the police during the Ripper investigation that have ever been seriously considered as genuine, though the more recent consensus is that they were as bogus as all the rest.

It did not help the police, as well, that their expert medical advisers were divided as to whether the victims' injuries indicated a killer with surgical experience or simply the kind of crude skills that, say, a slaughterman might possess. With murder No. 5, it seemed there could be no argument…though, while the precise handiwork of the surgeon could definitely not be detected in this final Ripper outrage, 'butchery' hardly appeared an adequate description, either.

The body of Mary Jane Kelly, or Marie Jeanette Kelly, as she sometimes called herself, wasn't mutilated…it was shredded, comprehensively hacked to pieces and parts of it were strewn about the one-room hovel she called home. With the exception of Elizabeth Stride, when he was obviously prevented from finishing the job, the brutality of the

Ripper attacks had increased with each new victim; even so, no one could have been prepared for the orgy of blood-letting with which his campaign of horror was to end.

The official police photograph of Kelly, her mangled corpse scarcely recognisable as human as she lies on her blood-saturated bed, has been familiar to Ripperologists since 1972, when it was first published in Daniel Farson's book *Jack the Ripper*. Repeated study does nothing to lessen its impact. As Sir Melville Macnaghten wrote later, 'Without seeing [it] it is impossible to grasp the extent of the awful mutilation.'

The *Illustrated Police News* did its best, however, to convey a true picture of the revolting spectacle which greeted police when they broke into that seedy little ground-floor apartment in Miller's Court, off Dorset Street, Spitalfields, just after mid-day on Friday 9 November. The officers, summoned after Kelly's rentman had glimpsed the awful carnage through a broken window-pane, had waited until medical examiners arrived before entering the room which, apart from the bed, was furnished only with a food cupboard, a chair and a small bedside table. *The Police News* went on,

> When this had been done, a scene more terrible than any of the others that have preceded it was disclosed. Such a shocking state of things was there as has probably never been equalled in the annals of crime. The throat had been cut right across with a knife, nearly severing the head from the body. The abdomen had been ripped partially open, and both of the breasts had been cut from the body. The left arm, like the head, hung to the body by the skin only. The nose had been cut off, the forehead skinned, and the thighs, down to the feet, stripped of the flesh. The abdomen had been slashed with a knife across and downwards, and the liver and entrails wrenched away. The entrails and other portions of the frame were missing, but the liver, &c., it is said, were found placed between the feet of this poor victim. The flesh from the thighs and legs, together with the breasts and nose, had been placed by the murderer on the table, and one of the hands of the dead woman had been pushed into her stomach...'

This appalling climax differed in two other significant ways from the four previous murders: here the man who had hitherto always killed outside and at night-time, and carried out his extensive mutilations with amazing speed in little, if any, light, had moved indoors and was thus able to indulge his vile obsession at leisure into the early daylight hours. And, unlike the four other victims, Irish-born Mary Jane Kelly was young (25) and strikingly attractive. She was also three months pregnant at the time of her death.

The apparent change of tactics sent the public's growing sense of alarm spiralling to frightening new heights, too; but with the Miller's Court bloodbath, the Ripper's work was finally over.

The search for his identity, which led to the arrest of more than 150 suspects in the immediate aftermath of the murders, goes on to this day, however. And whenever the subject is debated, George Chapman is inevitably one of the candidates offered for consideration. So let us now examine his personal claims to the title of 'Jack the Ripper'.

Severin Antoniovich Klosowski, as he was born on 14 December 1865, appears to have come to England from his native Poland at the beginning of 1888. The son of a carpenter from the village of Nargornak, he was sent at the age of 15 to be apprenticed to a surgeon at Svolen, though he does not seem to have qualified for any more skilled a role than hospital assistant or 'barber-surgeon'. The latter, in Polish *feldscher*, would have involved him in performing minor operations like bleeding, cupping or removing warts and moles, for example; this kind of doctoring was also provided as a sideline in many hairdressing establishments in this country at the time. And it was his quasi-medical training that is one of the first pieces of evidence cited by the Chapman-the-Ripper supporters. Of even more significance, though, was his presence in the East End of London during the period of the Ripper murders.

His first known address after arriving in England was a hairdresser's shop in the basement of a public house in Whitechapel High Street – right in the heart of the Ripper's killing ground – where he started work as an assistant and eventually became the proprietor. He apparently remained there until 1889.

In that year Klosowski, as he then was, married Lucy Baderski, also a Pole, in Whitechapel and the couple lived in various parts of the district until 1890 when they emigrated to America. Early in 1891, however, Mrs Klosowski split with her husband because of his infidelities and returned to England alone. He followed a year or so later and there was a brief reconciliation, before his continuing unfaithfulness drove her away for good.

A man with a seemingly insatiable sexual appetite, Chapman did not remain without female companionship for long, however. Soon afterwards, he met and lived with a woman called Annie Chapman, an odd coincidence which, if Severin Klosowski was Jack the Ripper, was made even more bizarre by the fact that it was as a result of this relationship that he appears to have assumed the name George Chapman.

Chapman's treatment of women as mere objects for his personal gratification was already well-established; that he was also capable of destroying them in a callous and sadistic manner when they became an inconvenience to him, would become equally apparent from his actions during the series of affairs on which he now embarked. And here again, it is suggested, the characteristics he displayed invite comparison with the perceived psychological profile of Jack the Ripper.

His career as a serial murderer by poison began with the death of Mary Isabella Spink, the estranged wife of a railway porter with whom he became friendly while working as a 30-shillings-a-week barber's assistant in Leytonstone. Though neither was legally divorced – Mrs Spink's husband had left her on account of her drink problem, apparently – they claimed to have 'married' in October 1895, and two years later, from the £600 inheritance which had recently come the way of his new 'wife', they bought a hairdresser's shop in Hastings. There, with her blonde hair cut fashionably short, the bonny Mrs Chapman also lent practical support to the business, helping Chapman with the lathering and shaving and also entertaining the customers at the piano. This novelty double-act quickly proved a popular and profitable attraction and, after only six months, the couple were able to sell up and move into the licensed trade.

Returning to London, they took over the Prince of Wales tavern, just off the City Road in Bartholomew Square. And it was there, at Christmas-time 1897, that the first of Chapman's seemingly cruel sequence of personal tragedies occurred. Mary Isabella, a woman of remarkably good health considering her history of alcohol abuse, suddenly took to her bed after a bout of vomiting, complaining of intense stomach pains. The doctor was called but his prescribed medication proved ineffective. Mary grew progressively weaker and after hovering on the brink for several days, she died early on Christmas Day. She was 41. The doctor certified the cause of death as 'phthisis', a progressive wasting disease.

Though he opened up for business as usual later that same day, Chapman appeared grief-stricken by his loss. Within months, however, his regulars could not help noticing that he was taking a more than managerial interest in the new housekeeper-cum-barmaid he had hired to help him run the pub.

Elizabeth ('Bessie') Taylor had applied for the job around Easter 1898, in response to a newspaper advertisement. After leaving her family home in Lymm, Cheshire, in her early 20s, she had worked in the London area for about 10 years, first as a domestic servant but latterly as manageress of several restaurants, most recently in Peckham. When she first met Chapman she looked the archetypal farmer's daughter: rosy-cheeked and full-bodied, a picture of rude health, as could clearly be seen in the photograph police found among Chapman's possessions after his arrest. It had apparently been taken by Chapman, who seems to have been as handy with a camera as he was with a poison bottle. It showed the two of them posing rather stiffly between a pair of potted plants, with Chapman's collection of militaria, including a couple of tattered flags, a brace of pistols, a rifle and a sword, adorning the wall behind.

Was this man Jack the Ripper? Multiple poisoner George Chapman pictured with Cheshire farmer's daughter Bessie Taylor, one of his victims, in a photograph taken by the murderer himself.

After Bessie's rather hasty 'marriage' to Chapman – police were never able to find any official record of this union, either – her health began to fail, however.

First, she started to lose weight, though this may well have had something to do with the fact that, just before Christmas 1898, she had had to go into hospital for about a week with a nasty gum infection, which had caused her face to break out in lumps. By now the couple had left the Prince of Wales and were running The Grapes at Bishops Stortford. Immediately after her discharge from hospital, Chapman seems to have become increasingly unpleasant towards her. An old friend, Mrs Elizabeth Painter, who had once been 'in service' with Bessie, visited her at The Grapes and Bessie told her that Chapman had 'carried on' at her the minute she arrived home and that evening had 'frightened her with a revolver'.

The relationship continued to deteriorate, along with Bessie's health, when they later returned to London to take over the Monument Tavern in Union Street, Borough. And by December 1900 Mrs Painter had become so concerned about her friend's condition that she made a point of calling to see her every evening. She would say at Chapman's trial, 'She seemed to be fading very much. She complained of pains all over her, and her head was bad. She always felt sick, and it always came on after she had had anything to eat or drink.'

When Bessie's brother, William Taylor, a salesman, travelled from his home in Hornsey to see her, he, too, was in for a shock. 'She appeared to be very ill and shrunken; she had gone like a little old woman,' he described to police later. She had told him she had 'violent pains in her inside'.

Bessie's elderly mother came down from Cheshire to stay with her, and a nurse was also in daily attendance. But Chapman insisted on preparing some of Bessie's food himself. He also regularly gave her medicine prescribed by the doctor and was often observed to shake the bottle, hold it up to the light and peer closely at its emulsifying contents. And throughout this worrying time he displayed a particularly perverse attitude towards Elizabeth Painter.

On more than one occasion, when she popped into the pub to inquire about Bessie, Chapman told her, 'You're friend is dead.' And she had rushed upstairs to the bedroom to find Bessie still alive. Then, the day after Bessie really did die and Mrs Painter called unknowingly to see how she was, Chapman said she was 'much about the same'.

In February 1901 Bessie had rallied briefly. The doctor arrived one day to find her up and playing the piano, announced himself pleased with her improvement and sent the nurse home. But two days later, on 13 February, at about 1.30 in the morning, she died. She was 36.

Dr James Stoker, who had visited Bessie almost daily since 1 January, and who had sought not only a second opinion on the baffling case but a third and fourth as well, gave the cause of death as 'intestinal obstruction, vomiting and exhaustion'. Earlier, all four doctors, none of whom, it should be said, had treated the previous 'Mrs Chapman', Mary Spink, had each come up with a completely different conclusion about Bessie's illness. Dr Stoker's initial diagnosis had been constipation, while the other experts in turn suggested an infected womb, a severe form of hysteria and 'some cancerous disease of the stomach or intestines'.

Not one of them suspected poison; nor, despite the unusual degree of professional disagreement, did they consider that it might be prudent to carry out a post mortem before issuing the death certificate. Another innocent victim had to die before the medical profession got wise to Chapman's murdering ways.

Barmaid Maud Marsh booked herself a place among the headlines when she inserted an advertisement in the 'Situations Wanted' columns of the local newspapers. Chapman saw it, offered her a job at the Monument and in August 1901 the 19-year-old labourer's daughter from Croydon followed Mary Spink and Bessie Taylor behind the bar – and, in due course, between the sheets – of the poisonous publican.

From their first meeting with him, Maud's parents had been unconvinced that Chapman's intentions towards their daughter were entirely honourable; and, despite his smooth talk and oily manner, their dislike of him persisted even after their whirlwind courtship and eventual 'marriage' less than two months later – a course of events which culminated in Chapman's by now well-rehearsed charade of informing a few friends that he and his bride-to-be had planned a quiet wedding at a secret location and then disappearing for half a day before returning to the pub at night with his new 'wife'.

So, when Maud went down with the same symptoms twice within a short space of time – she had recovered from the first attack after spending three weeks at Guy's Hospital – it was only a matter of time before the Marshes' suspicions were aroused and they asked their own GP to investigate. Unhappily, their decision came too late to save the unfortunate Maud.

On agreeing to take the case, Dr Grapel had first consulted Maud's physician, the same Dr Stoker who had attended Bessie Chapman; then, on 21 October 1902, the two of them paid a visit to The Crown public house in the Borough High Street, where the Chapmans were now in business following a serious fire at the Monument. After examining the patient, to the obvious discomfort of Chapman, Dr Grapel journeyed back to West Croydon with the strengthening conviction that Maud Marsh was being poisoned. And, by the time he got home, he had come to the conclusion that the poison was arsenic.

He at once telegraphed Dr Stoker urging him to make the necessary tests to confirm his opinion. Before Dr Stoker could act, however, Chapman, alarmed by this threatening new development, gave Maud what turned out to be the final, and fatal, dose of poison. She died on 22 October 1902. As with Bessie Taylor and Mary Spink before her, it brought to an end what Solicitor General Sir Edward (later Lord) Carson later referred to as another 'miserable story of torture and suffering'.

Dr Grapel's intervention would not save Maud Marsh's life, but it did ensure this time that Dr Stoker insisted that there could be no question of issuing a death certificate until a post mortem had been carried out. It was the decisive, if somewhat overdue, deed that, to quote Sir Edward again, was to expose Chapman as the 'determined and malicious' killer that he was...and set the stage for his dramatic entrance as a candidate for the role of Jack the Ripper.

The autopsy on Maud Marsh revealed that it was not arsenic that had hastened her end, but antimony; colourless, odourless and practically tasteless, it is easily soluble in water and, of even greater appeal to the poisoner, produces symptoms almost indistinguishable from those of gastro-enteritis. As little as one-and-a-half grains has been known to kill; in Maud Marsh's case, her body was found to contain more than 20 grains. Another interesting property of this highly dangerous substance, as the police were about to discover to their advantage, is that it preserves the body in recognisable form long after death.

On 25 October, the day of Edward VII's coronation procession through London, police, armed with the post mortem results, arrested Chapman and began instituting proceedings to obtain the authorisation necessary to exhume the bodies of the two previous 'wives' who had died in similar circumstances.

Mary Spink had by this time been buried for almost five years and, consequently, barely four grains of antimony could still be detected in her surviving organs. But, as the prosecutor would say at Chapman's trial, Bessie Taylor's body, like that of Maud Marsh, was 'literally saturated with antimony'; Dr Thomas Stevenson, the Home Office analyst who supervised both disinterments, calculated the amount at a little under 30 grains.

As one would expect, the exhumation of Bessie Taylor aroused a great deal of interest in the little Cheshire village of Lymm. Although her family had in recent years resided at Hill Top Farm in nearby Preston Brook, Bessie had been born and grown up in Lymm, living first on a farm at Booths Hill and later at Heatley. Her father, a one-time member of the old Lymm Local Board, had been well-known in the greater Warrington area as a farmer and cattle dealer. He had died, less than 18 months after Bessie, in June 1902, of a blood clot following a freak farm accident in which he was run over by a manure cart after the horse had been startled and suddenly bolted. He was 69. Two months later, Mrs Taylor, aged 73, joined him and their two daughters in the family plot in Lymm Churchyard.

It was to here, on the occasion of Bessie Taylor's funeral, that George Chapman had come on his last visit to the village. He had been in Lymm several times before, when he was courting Bessie. He always stayed at the same local inn and once joined in a smoking concert and insisted on paying for three bottles of champagne.

In tracing Chapman's local connections, the *Warrington Guardian*, in a report published in its edition of 1 November 1902, also unwittingly provided interesting testimony on another important element in the case for George Chapman being Jack the Ripper.

Of all the countless number of witnesses interviewed in the hunt for the East End maniac, George Hutchinson, a friend of Mary Kelly, furnished police with what they felt at the time was the most likely description of the Ripper. It was of a man seen talking to Kelly at about two in the morning just around the corner from her home and possibly only minutes before she became the Ripper's fifth and final victim.

Hutchinson's detailed statement said of the man, 'Age about 34 or 35, height five feet six inches, complexion pale. Dark eyes and eyelashes. Slight moustache curled up each end and dark hair. Very surly looking. Dress, long dark coat, collar and cuffs trimmed astrakhan...button boots and gaiters with white buttons, wore a very thick gold chain with linen collar, black tie with horseshoe pin, respectable appearance...'

Apart from the age difference – he would have only been 22 at this time – Hutchinson might have been describing Chapman. The general size, the dark hair and curly moustache, even the surly looks – they all fitted perfectly. And the *Warrington Guardian* bore out his reputation as a snappy dresser. The paper said of him, 'He is remembered as being a bit of a "toff", stylishly dressed with numerous rings and a flashy heavy gold guard.'

The *Guardian's* correspondent was, of course, unaware of any possible link between Chapman and Jack the Ripper; his sole preoccupation was news of the move to dig up Bessie Taylor. It was not often that down-page Lymm featured in a big national story like this, and an eye-witness account of such an unusual event would make good copy. It was an opportunity not to be missed, and the reporter stuck to his task with characteristic tenacity.

On 29 November, under a three-deck headline that ran THE GRUESOME TALE OF LYMM CHURCHYARD. EXHUMATION OF MRS CHAPMAN THE SECOND. A REPORTER'S EXPERIENCE, he wrote, 'When the order for the exhumation was made known it became my duty to keep a watchful eye upon the churchyard. I haunted the village day and night for a fortnight, at the end of which time all my efforts seemed in vain. Try as I would I could not get any information as to the probable date and time that the exhumation would take place.'

His vigil was finally rewarded when, on Saturday 22 November, he returned to the churchyard to find police guarding the entrances and a screen of white sheets surrounding the Taylors' plot. His narrative resumed, 'I got into the good graces of the landlady of the Church Inn, who allowed me the use of her yard, from where I had a tolerably good view of what was taking place...Presently Mrs Chapman's coffin was placed on a bier covered with a white pall, and conveyed across the churchyard to the sexton's tool-house. There the coffin was unscrewed, and the parts needed for the analytical examination were taken away by the doctors.'

Bessie Taylor's remains which, though they had been in the ground for 21 months, were in a remarkably good state of preservation due to the presence of the antimony, were eventually re-interred and the grave sealed once more. 'The proceedings', noted the *Guardian* reporter, 'were very impressive indeed, and will long be remembered by those few who witnessed them. The officials had been successful in their efforts to keep the affair secret, for only a small knot of people assembled in the roadway, and they could see very little of what took place.' When he visited the grave on the following afternoon, however, he observed 'a large number of people looking with curious eyes upon it'.

The scientific investigation completed, the inquest into the death of the third Mrs Chapman and the protracted police court hearing began almost simultaneously. The proceedings dragged on well into the New Year, with the result that it was not until Monday 16 March 1903, that the trial of George Chapman finally opened at the Old Bailey.

The 36-year-old publican, already charged on the coroner's inquisition with the murder of Maud Marsh, was now also formally arraigned with the murders of Bessie Taylor and Mary Spink. He pleaded not guilty to all three indictments. In charging the jury to try the case of Maud Marsh only, the judge, Mr Justice Grantham, ruled, however, that evidence relating to the deaths of the other two women was admissible – much to the disgruntlement of the defence, whose counsel, Mr George Elliot KC, had argued strongly against any such latitude, with its potentially damaging implications for his client.

Though the trial took four days to complete, there seems to have been little doubt as to how it would end. The prosecution built up an overwhelming case against Chapman: the three women had all died from ingesting antimony; he had been the only person in all three cases to have had the opportunity to administer the poison; evidence was given that he had the means and, according to one witness, the intent, too.

A woman named Florence Rayner testified that in June 1902, while she was living-in and working as a barmaid at The Crown, Chapman began making advances towards her. He would often kiss her when Maud was not there and at one point he asked her to run off to America with him. When she pointed out that he was already married, Chapman, she alleged, replied, 'Oh, I could give her that' – snapping his fingers – 'and she would be no more Mrs Chapman.'

Chapman was also shown to have been less than clever in covering his murderous tracks. William Henry Davidson, who was in business as a chemist in Hastings at the time Chapman and Mary Spink were performing their barber-shop duets, produced his poisons' register book, bearing Chapman's signature, to prove that on 3 April 1897, the accused had purchased from him one ounce of tartar emetic for twopence. The principle ingredient of tartar emetic is antimony and one ounce would contain about 146 grains of the poison. Davidson, who had often enjoyed a 'musical shave' at the Chapmans' salon, stuck one of his special red-coloured poison labels on to the bottle of white powder and wrote on it, 'Dose, one-sixth grain to one-quarter grain: to be used with caution'.

So far as the contents were concerned, it was a warning that George Chapman obviously intended to disregard, to his own ultimate cost as well as that of his three victims. Less comprehensible, however, was his total lack of caution regarding the rest of his dangerous purchase. For the distinctive red label was later recovered by the police preserved inside one of several medical books Chapman had also bought off the Hastings chemist. And traces of antimony were found in a bottle (possibly the very one that had held the tartar-emetic), which detectives removed from Maud Marsh's bedroom at The Crown.

Other interesting items discovered by Inspector George Godley among Chapman's personal effects included an American revolver, fully loaded, a pharmacopoeia and, curiously, a copy of the autobiography of the former public hangman James Berry (see Chapters Twelve and Thirteen). It was Insp. Godley who arrested Chapman and he was the officer to whom Chief Insp. Frederick Abberline made his oft-quoted 'Jack the Ripper' comment.

Godley had himself worked on the Ripper investigation, while the other police officer previously mentioned as having a connection with both cases, Arthur Neil, made a brief appearance on the third day of Chapman's trial. The detective sergeant gave evidence of searching the local civil registers and failing to find any record of Chapman's supposed marriages to Bessie Taylor and Mary Spink.

Though the law had been changed some five years earlier to allow such an option, the defendant was not put on to the witness stand. The defence, in fact, called no evidence on his behalf; the only insight into his response to the murder charges, therefore, was that contained in the prosecution's case.

For example, Insp. Godley told how, when informed that he was to be arrested in connection with the death of Maud Marsh, Chapman commented, 'I know nothing about it. I do not know how she got the poison.' Later, after his request for bail had been refused and Godley had pointed out the seriousness of his situation, Chapman said, 'She did not die suddenly. If she had been poisoned she would have done.' When eventually charged with Maud Marsh's murder, he replied, 'I am innocent.'

Initially, Chapman had been 'booked' in his assumed name; but as a result of police inquiries, he was subsequently charged under his real name of Severin Klosowski (a fact ascertained from personal papers uncovered in the search of his private apartments at The Crown). His first reaction, said Godley, was to declare, 'I do not know the other fellow. I do not know anything about the other name.' And when charged with the two additional murders, he answered, 'By what means? Stabbing, shooting or what?'

Insp. Godley said he had also found a diary among Chapman's possessions. One entry, dated 13 February 1901, read, 'Bessie Taylor dead, at 1.30am, with great sorrow.'

Inspector William Kemp gave details of a conversation he had had with the accused in the charge room at Southwark Police Station after his arrest. Referring to Maud Marsh he was alleged to have said, 'I would not hurt her for the world.' And, closer to the truth, he added, 'I have had a lot of trouble with my barmaids, but I took a great fancy to this one.'

Mr Elliot, in addressing the jury, conceded the 'magnitude' of his task, though he claimed Chapman's position had not been helped by the prejudice which had surrounded the case, not least because his client was 'an alien' (foreigner). Mr Elliot could do little, however, to shake the prosecution case.

Chapman, he argued, had no motive for killing the three women: he had never been legally married to them and all he needed to do, if he wished to free himself of one to live with another, was to show her the door. Of the crucial evidence regarding Chapman's purchase of the tartar emetic from Davidson, Mr Elliot suggested, somewhat lamely one might think, that the chemist's memory was defective (along, presumably, with this poisons' register). And of the testimony of Dr Stevenson, which he admitted was 'overwhelming', defence counsel could only urge the jury not to condemn a man to death solely on scientific evidence 'without strong corroboration'.

The Solicitor General, in his closing speech, had only to reiterate the facts to demonstration that there was corroboration aplenty with which to condemn Chapman. And to many ears, the judge also leaned heavily towards the prosecution in delivering his summing-up. He was outspoken, too, in his observations on the succession of medical men who had failed to recognise the symptoms of Chapman's malignant hatred.

It was, he said, 'a sad reflection' on the profession, when a mere hairdresser could, if the evidence was correct, carry on such practices for five or six years without the slightest fear of the doctors being able to detect what was going on.

The jury took less than 10 minutes to find Chapman guilty of the murder of Maud Marsh.

Before sentencing him to death, Mr Justice Grantham made a point of calling the prisoner 'Severin Klosowski', saying that 'the only satisfactory feature' of the case was that he was able to address him as a foreigner and not as an Englishman. And, concurring with the jury's verdict, the judge told him, 'It is not necessary for me to go through the harrowing details of the case, nor to refer again to the frightful cruelty of which you have been guilty in murdering year by year the women on whose bodies you had gratified your vile lust.'

He was hanged at Wandsworth Gaol on Tuesday 7 April 1903. Right to the last he denied murdering the three women, each of whom, despite his saturnine looks, his inelegant manners and his strangely haphazard grasp of English, he had charmed into masquerading as his wife. In a letter he sent to friends from the condemned cell, he is reported to have written (in a style which displayed his peculiar 'command' of the language),

'Believe me, be careful in your life of dangers of other enimis who are unnow to you. As you see on your own expirence in my case how I was unjustly criticised and falsly Represented. Also you can see I am not Believed. Therefore you see where there is Justice.

'They can take my life, but they cannot kil my soul and take it from me. God is my Judge and I Pray to have Mercy on my soul, for my sins which I have dun durin my life.

'But as to crime I am innocent and I have clear conscious of it...'

He also maintained that he really was George Chapman, an American, and not Severin Klosowski. In another letter, in which he also made passing reference to the death of Bessie Taylor, he stated,

'One thing whod I wish is this to be Remembered as I am an American orphend of good family and I left my foster father, against his wish, and I took to erning my own living at age of ten.

'And since that time I worked the best I could get, and although I never been so unlucky since I lost that poor Bessie Taylor and therefore I regretted that day ever since I have stopped in this country...'

Thus, being of such un-sound mind, did Chapman/Klosowski (who, in his will, apparently left property to the value of £140 to Bessie Taylor's relatives in Cheshire) make his last testament of innocence. That he was, indeed, a vicious multiple-poisoner, however, is a judgment from which he alone seems to have dissented. Even in court his presence was menacing; Lord Carson is on record as describing him as 'looking like some evil beast', adding, 'I almost expected him to leap over the dock and attack me.'

But, despite Chief Insp. Abberline's reputed interest in his possible involvement in certain other outstanding matters, at no time does Chapman/Klosowski appear to have been confronted with the 'Jack the Ripper' accusation. So could 'the Borough poisoner' really have been the wicked whore-murdering monster of Whitechapel as well?

I have to say right away that to conceive of someone who murders with such explosive and bloody abandon suddenly dropping out of sight and then, after an interval of nine years, resurfacing metamorphosed into a sly and systematic poisoner, does require the agility of a mental contortionist. This psychological gulf, which has confounded almost everyone who has tried to link the two cases, appears wider, too, in the light of more recent research into the phenomenon of the serial murderer. And Hargrave Adam's contention that the Ripper's last crime was 'obviously perpetrated indoors to afford him greater security', and that 'if Chapman was actually Jack the Ripper, poisoning, as a much safer means of killing, might easily have suggested itself to him', falls well short of a convincing attempt at bridging the credibility gap.

My own personal view, for what it's worth, accords rather more closely with the conclusions reached by those two foremost Ripperologists, Colin Wilson and Robin Odell, in their collaboration *Jack the Ripper: Summing up and Verdict* (Bantam Press, 1987), a thorough and dispassionate appraisal of the many and varied theories about the killer's identity.

To assert that he was anything other than a sadistic maniac with a compelling sexual urge to mutilate women seems an obvious, though often unrecognised, absurdity; that his peculiar addiction to murder ended in suicide, or total mental breakdown and consequent committal to an asylum, is an equally irresistible explanation for the Ripper's mysterious disappearance. Like Wilson and Odell, I, too, favour a suspect who was an insignificant nobody rather than some familiar figure with an extreme case of split personality. And

to me the swift, brutal and concentrated way in which he wielded his knife indicates forcibly that Jack the Ripper's regular day-job was more likely to have been in an abattoir than an operating theatre. In that respect, I can't help feeling that he had more than one thing in common with Samuel Thorley, the mad pork butcher of Congleton, whose solitary act of human slaughter is documented earlier in this book (see Chapter Two).

Memorial marking the Taylor family plot in Lymm Churchyard. The less weathered lower section of the headstone shows where the inscription was re-done to remove the name of Bessie's murdering 'husband'.

Of one thing I am certain, however: that, like each of the murderous acts he committed, the true face of Jack the Ripper will forever remain hidden in the shadows. The case files at Scotland Yard and the Home Office – officially opened to public scrutiny for the first time in 1992 and 1993 respectively, but previously plundered by several enterprising authors – shed no new light on the mystery, much less unmask the culprit. Jack the Ripper, I believe, will always be the best known unknown murderer in the world, as another noted Ripperophile, Richard Whittington-Egan, has so perfectly described him.

In the absence of any definite proof to the contrary, however, it can be argued that Severin Klosowski, alias George Chapman, 'wife' killer, must remain a leading suspect. And that a censored gravestone in a Cheshire churchyard might just conceivably cover up a criminal connection of even more poisonous proportions.

12

Behind the Veil
(A Victorian Tragedy)

A great sensation was caused in Crewe and the neighbourhood on Sunday morning by reports of an extraordinary highway robbery and murder that had taken place on the outskirts of a little village known as the Hough during the darkness of Saturday night. At first the statements circulated were refused credence; but a Chronicle representative was despatched to the village only to find that the reports were too true, and that a most diabolical outrage had been committed...

Crewe Chronicle, 1 February 1890

THE NIGHT was wintery raw and, despite the hour, a fire still burned brightly in the big black-leaded range, casting a cheery glow around the kitchen of the modestly appointed farmhouse. On a table nearby, faintly illuminated in the pale yellow light of an oil-lamp, stood the remains of a late supper.

The room's occupants – Mary Davies and two of her sons, Richard, aged 18, and Arthur, six – had now sought the warming refuge of the hearth and were sat talking in subdued tones among the flickering shadows. In the background a clocked ticked away noisily, the minute hand already a quarter of the way into its final circuit of the day.

It was a familiar scene in the Davies household: an everyday story of Victorian country folk. But on this particular Saturday, 25 January 1890, the domestic routine of their rural middle-class existence was about to be shattered...for ever.

The first explosion came when into the kitchen burst another of the Davies children, 16-year-old George. He was the bearer of devastating news. In a breathless voice, he announced, 'Father's been stopped by two men in Crewe Lane.'

Then, responding to his mother's calming efforts, he explained how he and his father had been riding home in the family's pony and trap when, in pitch darkness in the little country lane, they were suddenly set upon by a pair of footpads. He had managed to escape but his father had been attacked by the men and, said the boy, he feared he might be dead.

When George subsequently led searchers to the spot where he said the incident had occurred, they found his suspicions to be correct. Like the *Crewe Chronicle* representative who was later sent to investigate, they discovered that a most diabolical outrage had, indeed, been committed. But if first reports of the extraordinary crime were refused credence, the facts eventually uncovered by the police were to prove even more incredible.

The body of Richard Davies Senior, 50-year-old tailor, draper, property-owner and, lately, part-time bookmaker, was lying in a pool of blood under a hedge about a quarter of a mile from the Davies home at (the) Hough, a tiny scattered community to the south of Crewe. The victim had been terribly battered about the head and there were further severe injuries to his hands, sustained seemingly in trying to ward off the murderous blows. A broken tree branch lay close by, also heavily bloodstained and with what appeared to be human hair clinging to it. The pony and trap stood unattended 50 or 60 yards away. But of the two mystery assailants there was no sign.

After George's panic-stricken homecoming, Mary Davies hurried to the home of her married son John, who lived nearby. Rousing a neighbour named Smith and grabbing a storm lantern, John had gone with his two younger brothers, George and Richard, to find out what had happened to their father; and, although it was Richard who first stumbled on the body in the blackness of the narrow winding lane, it was John who now took charge of the situation.

After first satisfying himself that there was nothing he could do for his father, he sent George to summon up some heavyweight help, in the shape of the village blacksmith, and Richard to fetch the police. Climbing into the blood-spattered trap, the latter headed for Shavington, about a mile and a half away; but finding no one at the police house there, he back-tracked and drove the three miles into Crewe where, at the station in Edleston Road, he found Inspector Alfred Oldham on duty. It was now almost 1 o'clock in the morning,

Richard told the officer, 'My father has been stopped in Crewe Lane.' And he repeated George's story about the two men who 'came out of the hedge' and waylaid his father and brother. After questioning the young man for a few minutes, the inspector went off to round up his sergeant and some lights, while Richard was allowed to continue on into the town centre.

At 85, Victoria Street, where he and his brother George worked in the family tailoring and drapery business their father had founded more than 20 years before, he stopped off to break the news of the night's terrible events to his sister Emily, who lived above the shop in what was the Davieses' second home.

Emily, the younger daughter among eight children, acted as shop assistant, housekeeper and general provider at the Victoria Street premises, sharing the living accommodation with another brother, Frederick, aged 10, and Mr Davies. His strict winter routine was to spend his weekdays in town and Saturday night and all day Sunday at Hough, before returning to the shop on Monday morning. Richard, George, Arthur and Tom (eight), all lived with Mrs Davies. An older daughter had left home four years previously when she married.

Victoria Street, Crewe, in the early years of the 20th century. Richard Davies, who was murdered in January 1890 by his two young sons, had his family tailoring and drapery business at No. 85, towards the far end of the street on the right of this photograph. Photograph courtesy of the Family History Society of Cheshire, Crewe Group.

Richard who, in his earlier conversation with the police inspector, had said he did not know whether Davies had been hurt or not, now told his sister unequivocally, 'Father is killed.'

It was the first in a series of inconsistencies that before too long would start to cast doubt on the theory that highway robbery lay behind the death of Richard Davies...though, at this time, the police were unaware of that particular discrepancy.

On his return from Victoria Street, Richard Junior overtook Insp. Oldham and the sergeant and he stopped to give them a lift in the trap. During the ride back to Crewe Lane, he became evasive when he was again questioned about the extent of his father's injuries. And the inspector also noted that, on such a bitterly cold night, young Richard was not wearing a top-coat.

When the three of them arrived at the murder spot, a group of about half a dozen people was gathered around the sprawling, stocky figure of the dead businessman, including John and George Davies. Moving them aside, and working by the light of their lamps, the two policemen began their survey of the scene.

The victim was on his back on the left-hand side of the lane, which at this point was flanked on either side by a low bank topped by a hedge. Although recently re-laid with stones, it was then in a muddy and rutted state owing to the previous day's rain. As well as the blood spread out under the body, there was a large pool of it towards the middle of the lane and some in both hedge cops. More puzzlingly, the inspector also noticed splashes on some twigs near a gap in the hedge on the opposite side of the lane. The seat that had been toppled, along with the deceased, from the trap during the attack was a few yards away. It, too, bore extensive traces of blood, as did the broken-off branch of a tree, which was also lying close to the body.

But if Insp. Oldham was tempted into thinking that the latter was the murder weapon, closer examination of the corpse was to quickly disabuse him of the notion. Richard Davies had plainly been hacked to death with a sharp-edged instrument, possibly a small axe. Though the dead man had been well-known in the Crewe area for many years, his chubby, heavily-bearded face was now battered almost beyond recognition. In addition, the thumb on the man's right hand was all but severed and there were three deep cuts on his left hand.

His initial site investigation completed, Insp. Oldham had the body conveyed to the Davies home at Hough and called in his 'governor', Superintendent Jesse Leah, head of the Nantwich Division of Cheshire Constabulary. The superintendent arrived at the house at about 4am to take charge of the investigation, and around mid-day the two senior officers were joined by the county's Chief Constable, Colonel J.H. Hamersley.

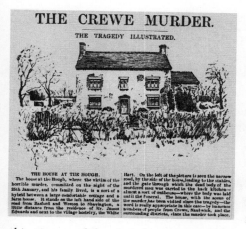

The Davies family's farmstead at the Hough, from an illustrated feature on the sensational killing in the *Warrington Guardian*, which described it as 'one of the most revolting and remarkable [crimes] of recent years'.

At the private conference that followed, the three men ran through the evidence so far to hand, ruminated on the strange tale of the vanishing villains recounted by George and Richard and came to the same conclusion: the story just did not add up. For one thing, if robbery had been the attackers' original objective – and the victim's empty pockets were an obvious pointer in that direction – why had they not taken Davies's valuable gold watch and chain, which were hanging out of his waistcoat pocket for all to see when the body was discovered? And why, after overpowering their man (remember the attack took place in total darkness, making identification difficult if not impossible), had they then proceeded to hack him to death? In fact, the savage and determined way in which Davies had been killed, and the vicious nature of the weapon employed, suggested strongly that other, more personal influences had been at work here. And that murder was more likely to have been the primary motivation.

Now, as the investigating officers considered the possibility for the first time, some sensational questions presented themselves: If George's story didn't ring true, had he himself committed the murder? Or were both he and Richard in on it? Could these two seemingly inoffensive young men be capable of hatching, and executing, a plot to kill their own father?

Before they had the answers, there was clearly a lot of work for the police to do. So later that same day, Sunday 26 January, while Insp. Oldham probed the brothers' family background for a possible motive, Supt. Leah quizzed them further about the late night incident on the road to Hough (its modern name is Back Lane, though it is still known to some older locals as 'Murder Lane').

The interviews took place in the late afternoon at the Davies farmstead (the property has long been demolished and the site, beside the A52, is now occupied by a modern double-fronted bungalow). The superintendent spoke to Richard first. The elder brother was, like his father, stoutly built, of average height and had a round face, dark eyes and dark brown hair. He sported a slight moustache.

Richard said he had left the shop in Victoria Street as usual at about 8pm and, after visiting a local skating rink, had walked home to Hough, arriving at about 10.15. He had his supper and then sat by the fireside with his mother and little brother Arthur. At about 11.15 George came running in, saying, 'Oh, mother, someone stopped father and me in Crewe Lane.' He told of going with John and George to look for his father, of finding the body and of later leading the police to the scene of the murder. But that was about all he knew.

Supt. Leah did not press the lad any further; he was more concerned at that moment with talking to George. The 51-year-old divisional commander, who had joined the police as a 19-year-old constable when the Cheshire force was formed in 1857, now brought his considerable experience to bear on the subject of the younger Davies brother and his account of the two shadowy figures and the ambush in Crewe Lane.

Without wishing at that stage to alert the boy to his half-formed suspicions, the superintendent questioned him patiently about the Saturday night trip home in the little yellow two-wheeled dogcart. George, similar in height and colouring to Richard but more slimly-built than his brother, was alleged to have said in his initial interview, 'Me and my father left the shop to drive home in the pony-trap. Nothing occurred until we got in Crewe Lane, when two men came out of the fence on each side of the road. One man went to the pony's head and stopped it, and the other went behind the trap. My father was driving, and I got up and hit the pony twice to try and make it go, but I could not. I saw the man was holding it. I then got down on the left side of the trap and got away round the trap, and ran home and told my mother.'

If the explanation was lacking in detail, the superintendent recognised that the youngster had been through a traumatic experience one way or another, so he was prepared to let matters rest there for the time being. Over the next 48 hours, however, he became more and more convinced he was on the right track. Shortly after noon on Tuesday 28 January, he called again at Hough to see George. And with an unmistakable note of caution in his voice, he urged the boy, 'Now then, I want you to tell me carefully all about it.'

George stuck to his story about the two men; though, under the police chief's questioning, he was now able to fill in some of the earlier gaps. He said that the man who had grabbed hold of the pony's head had twice lunged at him but he had run around the other side of the trap and got away. The man, said George, had pursued him for several hundred yards before giving up the chase.

As to descriptions of the attackers, he could recall only that one was large and the other small. The one who had chased him, he said, had worn dark clothes and a black felt hat. He did not speak. Of the other, George said, 'He did not appear to be doing anything. He was standing still.' His father meantime was 'sitting in the trap with the reins in his hand'.

Supt. Leah said, 'Did not your father say anything to the men when they stopped his horse?' George replied, 'No, he did not speak to them. He said nothing.' The men had not said anything to him, either.

Supt. Leah, 'Then I take it that neither of the two men who attacked you, nor you, nor your father spoke at all?' George, 'No, no one spoke until I was running away up the road, and then I called "Help!" twice.'

The superintendent remarked that he thought it strange that Mr Davies had not uttered a single word throughout the whole proceedings, whereupon George elaborated, 'He had a muffler [scarf] over his mouth and if he did speak I never heard him.'

Though he still did not betray his private thoughts, Leah was now satisfied that George Davies was lying. By this time, too, he knew that brother Richard had also been less than honest in his evidence about a particularly crucial area of the police investigation. The case was heading for an inevitable confrontation…and a shocking conclusion.

Richard Davies had made his fatal mistake earlier that day when Supt. Leah questioned him at the Victoria Street shop. Armed with the knowledge that the initial medical diagnosis was that Richard Davies Senior had been bludgeoned to death with some kind of a hatchet – the doctor's more detailed examination would later reveal no fewer than 10 separate head wounds – the superintendent decided to take a look around the premises before the 18-year-old arrived for work.

In the backyard he saw a pile of sticks which, judging by the splinters still lying about the floor, had obviously been chopped quite recently. At about 11am he interviewed Richard and asked him about the wood. Richard said it was his younger brother Freddy's job to chop sticks for the fire. The chopper he described as being 'a small axe like a butcher's cleaver without a handle'. But when he showed such an implement to the policeman, Leah saw that it was so highly rusted that it could not possibly have been used for some considerable time. So he asked whether there was another axe on the premises. Richard told him, 'No, we haven't any other. This is what we use here.'

That another hatchet was, indeed, more regularly used to chop firewood at the shop – and that it was now missing – the superintendent discovered when, soon afterwards, he interviewed Emily Davies and young Freddy. They confirmed that the axe had a distinctive handle, improvised out of a wooden roller bound with silesia, which Freddy himself had fitted when the original shaft had broken a month earlier. And Freddy admitted he had chopped sticks with it at about 5pm on the day his father was murdered.

The murder scene in Crewe Lane, from a sketch in the *Guardian* article. Key: 1. Body found here; 2, Large pool of blood near the middle of the lane; 3, Blood in both hedge cops; 4, Blood on twigs by a gap in the hedge (a short-cut to the Davieses' home).

It was an 'axe' like this, actually a roofer's lath hammer, that was the weapon with which tailor Richard Davies was battered to death. It had been used at his shop in Victoria Street to chop sticks.

After he had questioned George for the second time about the supposed attack in Crewe Lane, Leah also decided to give Richard another chance to come clean. About 7 o'clock that same Tuesday evening he saw him at Hough and told him, 'Now Richard, beyond a doubt there was another hatchet in the yard at Crewe, besides the one you showed me this morning, and it was used for chopping wood so recently as Saturday afternoon last. Can you tell me anything about it?'

Richard replied, 'No, I cannot. I do remember seeing one, but it is a long time since I saw it, and then I think it was without a handle.'

Emily Davies had also been able to tell the superintendent that when Richard left the shop on Saturday night to return home, he had been wearing grey trousers, leggings, lace-up boots, a 'hard hat' (bowler) and an overcoat. The latter garment – which, for some reason, he had chosen not to put on when he turned out later to go in search of his father – he was now asked to produce. Richard said the coat was at Victoria Street, claiming, 'I was not wearing it on Saturday night. I never wear it when I walk home.'

Leah did, however, examine the leggings Richard had been wearing that night and also some of George's clothing. On both, he would say on oath later, he observed 'some slight bloodstains'.

It was time for a showdown with the devious Davies brothers. For the first time Supt. Leah had the pair brought to him together. He told them, 'This is a very serious matter and I must go into it as fully as I can. The hatchet that I have before mentioned to you seems to be missing from your yard at Crewe. At least, I cannot find it there. I would like you two to come to Crewe and let us look together for it.'

They agreed and went with the superintendent to Victoria Street, again riding in the little dogcart, its re-fitted seat and interior now wiped clean of blood. They arrived at about 11pm and by the light of a couple of constables' lamps, the search for the missing axe began. But it was nowhere to be found.

In fact, the instrument which had despatched Richard Davies to an early appointment with his maker was at this time lying broken once more, its two parts buried separately only a few yards from where the killing took place. And, though the handle was uncovered a few days later, it would be almost two weeks before the axe-head resurfaced. For Supt. Jesse Leah, however, the absence of a murder weapon was not sufficient to deflect him from the course of action he now knew he had to take.

The Davies brothers were taken to Edleston Road police station and there, after conferring briefly with Insp. Oldham, Leah formally cautioned the two teenaged tailors, before charging them with the wilful murder of their father. According to the superintendent, they looked at each other 'very seriously' and then Richard said in a low voice, 'Oh, good heavens, I'm sure I'm innocent. Such a thought never entered my head.' George said, 'Yes, and I am.'

At midnight, George and Richard Davies were locked in separate cells at the station, continuing to claim they were innocent. But after 24 hours of almost continuous solitary confinement, broken only by a fleeting visit to the adjoining courthouse, they were ready to change their tune. And by late next morning, Thursday 30 January, they had made statements which left police in no doubt that they had, indeed, plotted to murder their father. The fact that they both accused each other of striking the fatal blows was a matter the lawyers could argue about later.

This is Crewe Lane today, close to where the murder took place. Its modern name is Back Lane, though it is still referred to by older locals as 'Murder Lane'.

The case had already been described by the *Warrington Guardian* as 'one of the most revolting and remarkable of recent years'; now, when news of this latest development got out, it caused 'the deepest horror throughout the length and breadth of the country', said the newspaper. The result was one of the most celebrated Cheshire trials of the 19th century...and the controversy did not end there. But first, there were some important, if routine, preliminaries to be disposed of.

After their brief Wednesday afternoon appearance before a local magistrate, the prisoners were remanded in custody for five days. The following day, Richard Davies Senior was buried in the graveyard of the Congregational Church at nearby Haslington; and even this sombre formality did not pass without incident. The deceased had been a big man and when his extra wide coffin was borne into the churchyard it would not fit into the grave. Consequently, the commital ceremony had to be held up while the hole was hastily enlarged.

The inquest into Richard Davies's death had been opened at the White Hart Inn, Hough, right next door to the Davies family's farmstead, on the Monday following the murder. But after the jury had viewed the body, the coroner, Dr Churton, announced he would not be taking any evidence at that stage and that he would adjourn the hearing. It was resumed on Friday 31 January.

It was then that mention was first made of the brothers' alleged confessions, though they do not appear to have been given fully in evidence, for they were not reproduced in the Press until after the following week's magisterial proceedings. The newspapers, unfettered by modern reporting restrictions, were having a field day, sparing no effort in bringing every minute detail of the case to the attention of their readers.

In its 1 February issue, in one of a series of articles recording the week's extraordinary events, the *Crewe Chronicle* said of the murder victim, 'From what we have been able to gather, he was a quiet, inoffensive man, and from his character and habits, one would think he could have had few, if any, enemies...He seemed always quietly and peaceably disposed.'

The paper also revealed the curious fact that Mr Davies had been attacked at almost the same spot three years before. On that occasion, his elder son John – who confirmed the details at the inquest – had been riding in the trap with him and beat off their assailants with a milk-stool.

At the resumed inquest there was speculation, too, about the apparent robbery aspect of the crime. The general consensus was that Mr Davies was not normally given to carrying large sums of money and that on the night he was killed probably had no more than £3 on him.

And there were attempts to draw out other possible motives for the murder. Davies's wife Mary, also around 50 years of age and a short, slim woman who, according to the *Warrington Guardian* reporter, 'looked ill and care-worn when she entered the room', was questioned at length on the subject of family relations.

A sympathetic figure dressed from head to foot in black, she held centre stage in the courtroom drama – and the unwavering attention of the on-lookers – for some time as she spoke loyally of her sons George ('a quiet, steady lad') and Richard ('fond of his father'); of how her husband was 'on good terms' with them both and how the whole family 'lived happily together'. And when the jury foreman asked whether she personally had had a happy relationship with the deceased, she replied that she had.

The young Davies brothers, George (left) and Richard Jnr. Both were sentenced to death for murdering their father, but George was reprieved on account of his youth.

John Davies admitted that 'a time ago' he had not been on the best of terms with his father, though for the past twelve months things had been all right between them. And sister Emily revealed that, although she had never known her father to punish either George or Richard, he did sometimes 'have words' with them when they did not do their work to his satisfaction. Otherwise, she too insisted, Davies had 'lived very happily' with his family.

Dr Frank Matthews, the Nantwich surgeon who carried out the post mortem examination, told the coroner that he had found 10 separate head wounds. The skull had been fractured in six places and three of the injuries were particularly severe; any one of them would have been sufficient to cause death, he said.

The inquest jury returned a verdict that Richard Davies had been murdered 'by some person or persons unknown'.

From Hough and the inquest the public spotlight next switched back to Crewe and the police court where, on Monday 3 February, the magistrates' hearing was resumed. Local interest had by then reached fever pitch; the previous day, though a week had passed since the murder, 'thousands of persons' had visited the scene of the crime and the victim's home, giving the usually quiet village 'an entirely unprecedented appearance', the *Warrington Guardian* reported on 5 February.

Outside Edleston Road police station, a crowd, believing the defendants were due to arrive at 11am, started to assemble at an early hour and was soon blocking the street. When the public was finally admitted at about 1pm, barriers erected by the police were broken down in the rush for seats in the tiny courtroom. The *Guardian* noted, 'In court a large table had to be placed in position for the accommodation of the reporters, who numbered at least forty.'

The court eventually came to order and the prisoners entered the dock for the second time in a week. The *Guardian's* correspondent observed, 'They appeared so cool and unconcerned that they might, for all emotion that was apparent, have been a pair of young scapegraces called up for admonition by the Bench prior to being "discharged with a caution"…their clothing was arranged as though they had just been despatched from home to some friendly gathering, rather than from a prison cell to answer a charge of wilful murder. Their perfect *sang froid* impressed everyone in court. Even when Inspector Oldham was describing the finding of the body of the murdered man, there was apparently no difference in the demeanour of the prisoners, except perhaps a slight heightening of colour in the case of the elder prisoner, Richard. The prisoner George was entirely apathetic, and gazed about him in a dull, unintelligent sort of way.'

Referring to Richard, the *Crewe Chronicle* reporter, watching more attentively perhaps, detected that when the inspector alleged there had been a 'diabolical plot' to murder Mr Davies, 'something like a smile passed over his features as the people in the court seemed trying to suppress their feelings of horror'.

The court heard of the conversations the prisoners had had with police after their arrest and of their subsequent 'confessions' (the police's version of this important sequence of events would come in for some hostile cross-examination at the trial); and, seemingly for the first time, complete transcripts of the alleged statements were read out. They were enthusiastically noted and comprehensively reported by a grateful Press corps who, for the second week running, were keeping close track of developments in the Cheshire railway town.

The evidence of the confessions will be given later in the more appropriate context of the trial; meanwhile, as the magistrates' court hearing entered its second day, police revealed that the broken-off handle of the hatchet missing from the Davies shop in Victoria Street had been recovered following a renewed search in Crewe Lane. It was about 20 yards from the bloodstained spot where Richard Davies had been slain, pushed into the soft earth of the field on the opposite side of the lane.

Of new interest, too, was evidence of the way the murdered man had treated his employee sons. According to Emily Davies, they were not paid wages; her father 'gave them sixpence sometimes', she said. That would have the buying power today of a little over £2. Last Christmas he had given Richard 10 shillings and George an extra sixpence.

There were further revelations at the committal proceedings on 13 February. Once again the courtroom was crowded with spectators, among whom, the *Guardian's* reporter noted disapprovingly, were 'a considerable number of the fair sex'.

First, the court was told that both parts of the murder weapon had now been recovered. It appears, in fact, to have been a roofer's lath hammer, having a chisel-shaped head, round and flat-nosed at one end and with a vertical axe-like cutting edge at the other. Using wooden rods to probe the ground, the police had finally turned up the business half of the weapon on the afternoon of Saturday 8 February. It was only a few yards further into the field in which the handle of the hatchet had been hidden; it had been forced into the soil and then, apparently, pressed down by the heel of a boot.

'When withdrawn from the earth', the *Crewe Chronicle* declared dramatically in its 15 February edition, 'it was found to be covered with blood, tufts of hair and brains.' Whoever had carried the hatchet into the field obviously left behind the clue of the bloodstained twigs that had puzzled Insp. Oldham when he first examined the murder site.

But what, with hindsight, can now be seen as the most telling moment at the committal, was the slight, but significant, shift in the evidence of Mrs Mary Davies. The first hint of the sensational disclosures to come was to be found in her revised opinion of homelife down on the Hough farm.

Mrs Davies – who, according to the *Chronicle*, 'appeared in widow's weeds with long black veil, with which she obscured her face during the whole of the proceedings' – was asked again how well her two accused sons had got on with their father. She answered, qualifying her previous statements, by saying that George was 'on good terms, *for anything I know*' and that Richard was 'on good terms *when he has been at home with me*' (author's italics).

More pointedly, in reply to further questioning by prosecution lawyer Mr Brooke, she admitted that the happy-family image she had projected to the inquest was false. The atmosphere in the house at Hough, she now acknowledged, was only 'middling'. Mrs Davies explained, 'We made ourselves comfortable. He [Davies] was not very comfortable with us.'

After entering pleas of 'Not guilty', George and Richard Davies were formally committed for trial, and that evening were taken by train to Knutsford Gaol to await the next county assizes.

With the lengthy lower court process conducted in a blaze of publicity, most of the circumstances surrounding the horrific murder were now common knowledge, and rumours about the rest were circulating widely, not to say wildly. But the whole truth behind the bitter domestic conflicts that turned two obedient sons into scheming parricides was to remain a largely private affair for another five weeks. Then, on Thursday 20 March 1890, the brothers' beleaguered family poured out its troubles to a jury at Chester Castle to try to save them from the scaffold.

Now, far from the 'quiet and inoffensive' man described in that early *Crewe Chronicle* article, Richard Davies Senior was portrayed as a quick-tempered and violent husband who often beat his wife in front of the children and on two occasions threatened to kill her; and as a tyrannical father who ruled the household with an iron hand and treated his sons almost like slaves. He was an extremely wealthy man but incredibly mean. At the time of his death he owned five shops in Crewe, including a block of four on a prime town centre site at the junction of Market Street and Heath Street, and at least two residential properties; yet his daughter Emily told the court that he allowed her only 13 shillings a week (worth about £55 now) to buy provisions for both family homes. And whereas her father, who always dined alone when he was at Victoria Street, ate meat every day of the week, for the rest of them it was a Sundays-only luxury. Also, Davies 'did not entrust his wife with money,' the court heard.

The Crewe murder victim Richard Davies Snr. His long-suffering wife Mary claimed he used to beat her regularly in front of the children and that he was especially violent after losing money at the races.

John, Davies's eldest son, now employed as a journeyman-tailor by a rival business in Crewe, said he had worked originally for his father but had left when he could no longer 'stand his ill-usage'.

But it was the testimony of Mrs Mary Davies that produced the biggest reaction in the crowded courtroom, and the boldest headlines in the newspapers later. Cast again as the doubly tragic, slightly mysterious lady-in-black – at once both sorrowing wife and despairing mother – she made her entrance to an expectant hum from the public benches, and was immediately engaged in a dialogue with defence counsel that might have come from the script of some fanciful Victorian melodrama.

Before giving her evidence this time, she was requested by the judge, Mr Justice Wills, to raise the heavy veil covering her face. This done, she proceeded to lift the lid on the painful secrets of her unhappy marriage.

Cross-examined by Mr Malcolm Douglas, defending George, Mrs Davies said she and her husband, a one-time foreman tailor with the Crewe Co-operative Society, had moved to Hough about 11 years ago. He had bought the farm, of between four and five acres, around the time he opened the shop at 85, Victoria Street. Davies had, in fact, first set up on his own at another address in Victoria Street more than 20 years before; a shrewd businessman, he subsequently 'put together a good round sum' (as the *Warrington Guardian* termed it) and then left the town to farm at Crewe Green. But not long afterwards he returned, running another successful tailoring enterprise on the corner of Heath Street for some years before moving back to Victoria Street.

Mr Douglas then turned to the couple's personal relationship; and, to gasps of astonishment from the back of the court, counsel led the witness through a series of startling disclosures.

Mr Douglas, Was your husband's conduct violent?

Mrs Davies, Yes – very, sometimes.

Q, Is it true, Mrs Davies, that he has pointed guns at you?

A, Yes.

Q, That he has threatened to shoot you?

A, Yes.

Q, And has searched about the house for cartridges to load his gun with?

A, Yes.

Q, Has he many times struck you in the presence of your children?

A, Yes, several times.

Q, Has he attempted to set fire to your bed?

A, Yes.

Q, Lighting newspapers underneath the bed for that purpose?

A, Yes.

By now there was something approaching pandemonium in the court. When the commotion eventually subsided, Mr Douglas next questioned Mrs Davies about her husband's most recent business gamble in the sport of kings...a venture from which he made rather less than a princely sum, it seems.

Q, Did your husband frequent race meetings as a bookmaker?

A, Yes, sir.

Q, And when he had lost money at race meetings was he particularly violent?

A, Yes, sir.

Q, Striking you and knocking you about without any cause?

A, Yes, sir.

Mrs Davies, who several times in her answers referred to her husband simply as 'Master', also revealed that he would never allow the older boys to go to church, insisting that they worked on the farm on Sundays. And when she had sent the little ones to chapel and Sunday school, Davies had 'threatened me many times for it', she said.

Cross-examined by Richard's counsel, Mr Glascodine, Mary Davies recalled a particularly violent incident which had occurred at the house only a few weeks before the murder. Richard, roused from his bed by her cries, had found his father once again thrashing his mother and he had stepped between them to save her from further punishment. He had intervened in this manner 'many times' before, she said.

Mr Glascodine, Richard has been a good son to you?

Mrs Davies, Yes, sir, he has.

Of her recollections of the night of the murder, Mrs Davies bore out her daughter Emily's assertion that Richard had been wearing an overcoat on the journey home from Victoria

Street. She said he had taken it off and laid it on the piano when he came in. She hung it up later but did not 'notice anything particular about it', she said.

The bloodstains observed by Supt. Leah on the coat were confirmed by the subsequent scientific examination carried out by the county analyst, Dr Joseph Carter Bell, who found traces on the front and back of the garment as well as the lining. There were 'large smears of blood and mud' on the leggings Richard had worn that night, too; and a pair of boots, also belonging to Richard, were marked 'as if someone had trodden in blood and mud', Dr Bell testified. George's top-coat, he said, was extensively bloodstained and muddied.

Superintendent Jesse Leah, head of the Nantwich Division of the Cheshire Constabulary who led the investigation into the murder of the Crewe tailor. He joined the police as a 19-year-old constable when the Cheshire force was formed in 1857.

The various articles of clothing had been gathered together and delivered to the analyst by another of Supt. Leah's senior colleagues at Crewe, Inspector Brittain. He also came up with two other surprise exhibits: a pistol and a revolver, both fully loaded, which he had discovered in a drawer in Richard's bedroom at Hough. According to Emily Davies, Richard had purchased the guns 'last Guy Fawkes Night'.

Emily also told the court that she had seen her two brothers talking together in the backyard of the shop on several occasions during the early evening of the 25th, the day of her father's murder.

It was, however, Insp. Oldham who was involved in the most controversial moments of the trial. He it was who gave the crucial evidence about the defendants' behaviour in the period between their arrest and the time they made their confessions.

His first contact with the prisoners, he said, took place around midnight on Wednesday 29 January, exactly 24 hours after they had been charged and locked up. He had received a message from one of his officers that George Davies wished to see him, so he went to the younger brother's cell. George said he wanted to talk to Richard and, after accepting that the meeting would have to be in the inspector's presence, the pair were brought together in Oldham's office.

Oldham cautioned them and George said to his brother, 'What are you going to say Dick?' Richard replied, 'I don't know what to say, I'm sure.' After a lengthy silence, Oldham said, 'Is that all?' And when neither appeared to have anything further to add, they were taken back to their cells.

Then, said the inspector, at about 10 o'clock the next morning there was another message from George, another meeting in his office and, after another caution, the following conversation took place,

George, Well Dick, what are you going to say?

Richard, I hardly know. What are you going to say? Are you going to tell?

G, Yes, I will.

R, So will I. [To the inspector] If you will give me a piece of paper, I will write it down.

They were each handed a pen and paper and returned to their cells. Shortly after noon they had completed their statements. At this point in his evidence, the inspector formally submitted the signed documents and, after Judge Wills had reminded the jury that neither brother's statement could be regarded as evidence against the other, they were then read out by the clerk of the court.

George stated,

Saturday, January 25th, Dick got ready to go home. He went the back way out, and when I got into the yard he said 'George, come here'. And I went to him and he said 'I want you to get me a box of pistol caps. I might not go that way...You need not let Emily know what I wanted you for.' When I got to the shop I stood looking through the window when someone knocked into me and I looked around and saw Dick standing there. He said 'Have you got those caps?' I said 'No'. He told me to get them at once. I went and got them and when I came out of the shop, I gave them to him and we walked up Victoria Street and went into John Street, where we stood against the trap. When we got there, he said 'I tell you what, I think I shall have a go at our old chap tonight.' I said 'Please yourself.' And he said 'I meant to have a go at him on Monday night but he fetched somebody up and gave them a ride.' He also said 'I shall get that little chopper out of the yard.' I said 'I should not because it might be missed.' And he said 'Not them miss it.' He said 'You will not see me before I have hit him. I shall go home and you must come running in about ten minutes after and say someone has stopped father in Crewe Lane.' Then Emily come and called me and we parted at that. I thought no more about it. I did not think he would do it. About half-past ten, me and my father started from the shop to drive home in the pony-and-trap...and we went on all right until we got to Crewe Lane. And when we got halfway down Dick hit father with something. And father said 'Oh dear, dear, what is that?' And then he said 'Whoa! Whoa!' And he hit him again and then he fell out of the back of the trap and the seat as well. The pony went on a bit and then I got out and went further down the lane and waited there and I did not know what to do. Then Dick came running down and said he thought somebody was coming, so he went across the fields and went home and I went round by the lane and got home about ten minutes after Dick. I went running into the house and said 'Father has got stopped up Crewe Lane.' And Dick got his shoes on and ran out of the house, and he went to Maddock's and told them father had got stopped. Then he ran up Crewe Lane to where father was and found him dead. And I think you know all the rest.

Richard's statement read,

I hereby confess that me and my brother George made it up to kill father on Saturday, January 25th. I left the shop at about eight o'clock to go home, and instead of going home I was to wait in Crewe Lane for father to come, and then I was to come out of the hedge and seize the pony's head while George, who was riding with him and was bringing the hatchet with him, should jump up and strike him, which we did do. After George had struck him two or three times I ran behind and caught hold of him behind and pulled him out of the trap and then George got out of the trap and I went home and left him there to wait until he was dead. Then he was to come running home saying that they had been stopped in Crewe Lane by two men. I arrived home about eleven o'clock and in about ten minutes or a quarter of an hour George came and told us. I ran and got to my father first and he was on the broad of his back on the opposite side to where I had left him and he was quite dead. I took his money out of his pocket and then Jack, my eldest brother, came up. The cause we had for it was because he was such a bad father, not to me exactly but to George and the rest, and a bad husband to mother. Mother and they have been very nearly starving sometimes, for he would neither buy them coal for the fire nor meat to eat when he was in a bad temper. But may God forgive us. We never thought what a crime we were committing, or the consequences of it, and I hope the law will deal mercifully with me and George. We do not deserve it, I know, but let it be for the sake of my mother and my little brothers and spare one of us to them.

Examined by Mr A.P. Roberts, leading for the Crown, Insp. Oldham said the two young men had another, more heated conversation after being given the opportunity to read through each other's statement. Richard declared his was the truth but, turning to George, he said, 'You know George, yours is not true. The first part is, but the last is lies. I wouldn't say that.'

George replied, 'What I have written there is quite true. Did you not come to me with the axe-head in one hand and the stale in the other and say "What shall we do now?" You took a pistol and said if I didn't finish him with the axe you would with the pistol. I never struck father at all and never handled the axe.'

Richard rounded angrily on his brother, shouting, 'You took the axe with you in the trap.' George said, 'No, I did not. You took it.' Richard, 'How could I take it when I was at the skating rink and other places before I went home? Oh, George, you know you did. How can you say that? I took hold of the pony's head and you struck him whilst he was in the trap.'

As tempers flared, Oldham prevented any further arguments by again sending the brothers back to the cells.

In a lengthy cross-examination of the inspector, Mr Douglas attempted to show that the statements attributed to the prisoners had been obtained incorrectly and that, in the case of his client George, 'an inducement' had been held out to him. Counsel put it to the witness that on the evening of the 29th, a few hours before he received the message that George wanted to talk to his brother, the officer had said to the younger Davies, 'We know you have done it, because of the blood on Dick's clothes and the axe-head being missing.'

He also suggested Oldham had told George, 'It is not right to put it on anybody else'; that he warned the prisoners that they had 'better tell the truth' and that he had then implied they should forget this conversation had ever taken place. The inspector strenuously denied talking to either prisoner before receiving the midnight call to George's cell.

Questioned by Mr Glascodine, Oldham said he had made a note of the Wednesday night's conversations with the prisoners at the time they took place. When they were brought together after making their written statements, he had again started taking down their comments, but they spoke so quickly he had to leave off. He said he had completed his notes after the brothers had returned to their cells and that they were confirmed as a correct record by PC Pickford, who had also been present.

In a blow-by-blow report of his post mortem findings, Dr Matthews said that of the 10 head wounds, seven were probably caused by the weapon's cutting edge and three by the blunt hammer end. It would have been necessary to use 'great violence' to inflict such injuries, he said.

The three severest wounds, either one of which would have been enough to kill, were all on the right side of the head: a clean-cut, vertical incision, two inches long, on the temple; an almost identical laceration slightly higher up, and – most serious of all – a peculiar star-shaped indentation below and to the side, which had five points, was about three inches in diameter and had exposed both bone and brain tissue. Only three of the wounds were on the left side of the head.

Some of the cuts were vertical, some horizontal, said Dr Matthews. But he told Mr Douglas that he had formed no opinion as to the position of the body when the blows were struck. He said the injuries might have been caused while the deceased was on the ground or upright.

Replying to Mr Glascodine, the doctor said that if the deceased had had a hat on it would have covered all the wounds except one on the left side of the head, between the eye and the ear, and part of the 'star' fracture.

The medical evidence completed, Mr Justice Wills closed the proceedings for the day. When the trial resumed the following morning, Mr Roberts put in the prisoners' statements before the magistrates. On that occasion, when the murder charge was put to them, Richard had replied, 'I have nothing to say. I am not guilty of the charge brought against me.' George had stated, 'I have got to say I am not guilty.'

In his closing speech for the prosecution, Mr Roberts first referred to the murdered man. He said he was willing to accept that Richard Davies's conduct was 'not what it ought to have been as a husband and father'. But, he told the jury, while that might provide the motive in this case, it was 'no possible excuse' for such a crime. There could be no suggestion, either, that the murder had been committed 'in hot blood'.

Turning to the evidence against George Davies alone, Mr Roberts said the younger man had made two statements about what happened in Crewe Lane and it would be for the jury to decide whether the story of the two mystery men was 'reasonable or probable'.

Against Richard, prosecuting counsel continued, there was the 'important piece of evidence' regarding his top-coat, which he had worn on his journey home from Crewe but had not put on again when he later went out in the bitter cold to look for his father. The coat was found to be bloodied and, said Mr Roberts, they had to ask themselves how the blood got on the coat.

Earlier, he had accepted that the blood on George's overcoat had probably got there when it was used by his brother John to support his father's head after they had found the body lying in the road. But Richard's coat, he said, had no opportunity to have become stained in this innocent manner, because he was not wearing it at that time.

Going through the prisoners' written statements, Mr Roberts pointed to passages which, he said, were entirely supported by the facts. There was proof that pistol caps were purchased; the two boys were seen talking together in the backyard of the shop prior to the murder. And as to the allegation that Richard had said he intended to 'have a go' at his father on the previous Monday night, counsel pointed out that, although Mr Davies normally stayed at the shop during the week, Mrs Davies had confirmed that her husband had come home to Hough that particular night in order to attend a local livestock sale the following day.

Then there was Richard's remark about taking the little chopper out of the shop yard. The hatchet was in the yard at 5 o'clock that day, said Mr Roberts, and both defendants, who went in and out of the yard several times later, had the opportunity to take it. The court also knew that the implement was found close to the scene of the murder.

Furthermore, the arrangement, whereby George was to run home and break the news of the attack, had been carried out. And, Mr Roberts continued, Richard had stated he had taken money from his father's body. When he was arrested, Richard, who was never paid wages and whose mother was never allowed to handle money, had just over £1 on him.

Mr Roberts said Richard's statement, if it was to be believed, was 'practically a confession'. He had admitted he was present and assisted his brother and, therefore, was 'no doubt guilty of the crime'. The two statements together seemed to him to be 'clear evidence of a conspiracy to murder their father'. And, he submitted, if the jury believed the two acted in concert, they were both guilty of murder.

Mr Douglas, addressing the jurors on behalf of George Davies, described the case as 'difficult and painful'. Of the purchase of the pistol caps, which the prosecution had alleged was proof of a plot between the two boys, he said the evidence of the shop-keeper who supplied the items was that the lads had frequently made similar purchases, 'probably for the purpose of shooting birds or something of that sort'. And, he argued, if the prisoners intended shooting their father, Richard's loaded pistol and revolver afforded 'ample opportunity without making these purchases'.

He said he did not dispute that the crime must have been committed by one of the prisoners. But which one? Arguing his client deserved sympathy on account of his extreme youth, Mr Roberts reminded the jurymen that they must eliminate from their minds anything that Richard had said about George in his alleged statement. And he insisted that in his own statement, George had made 'no admission of any participation in the crime'.

After so much ill-treatment by their father, it was, perhaps, no wonder the boys had discussed retaliation, Mr Roberts added. But he claimed it had been 'mere wild talk'; there was never any intention to carry it out.

When Mr Roberts sat down, there was a ripple of applause from the public seats.

For Richard, Mr Glascodine said he could not pretend his client had not been a participator in the crime, and a participator to such an extent 'as to place his life in jeopardy at this moment'. But it would be wrong, he said, for him to allow it to be considered that Richard was also a coward who had attempted to throw the blame on his younger brother. In his alleged statement, Richard had admitted 'only too clearly and precisely' his part in the crime. But, said Mr Glascodine, he had not admitted he struck his father.

So, asked counsel, what were the probabilities? Which of the brothers was more likely to have carried the axe? Richard's immediate reaction, he pointed out, was to say 'How could I take it, when I went to the skating rink and other places?' His was the more likely tale of the two, Mr Glascodine contended.

He then asked the jury to consider the positions of Mr Davies's injuries which, he submitted, showed conclusively whether they were caused by someone in the trap or out of it. He drew attention to the deep wound on the left-hand side of the deceased's head, running between the corner of the eye and the top of the ear, and suggested it could only have come from 'a blow dealt by a person in the position in which George was' – i.e. sitting on the victim's left. Moreover, it was the only one which would not have been fully covered by the hat Richard Davies had worn that night and which was later found undamaged some 60 yards from the scene of the attack.

He asked the jury to say that that was the wound which 'must have been the first one' and that Richard was 'not the one to give that blow'. The trap, he said, was four-feet high; Mr Davies had been a big man and his head would have been at least 7ft from the ground. Richard, on the other hand, was a small-made man and would have had to strike a blow with the axe held above his head. From such a position, said counsel, the resulting wound would 'tend in a downward direction' rather than a lateral one.

Mr Glascodine also reflected on the character of the dead man and his treatment of his wife and children. Mrs Davies, he said, had been 'inured by years of suffering to submit to blows and starvation at his hands' and had had to rely on her sons to save her from the consequences of her husband's violent actions. It was no excuse to say their father was bad; but it was something that must have a bearing on the verdict, he contended.

He went on, 'The first idea that would occur to anyone would be to do as John had done, and leave home. But these boys had one weak spot in their hearts, and that was their mother. They could not leave her to the tender mercies of that man, and they stayed by her and stuck to her to save her from his villainies. At last, moved by persecution dire for years, they did that which none of us could say was otherwise than wicked and wrong. To save their mother from him, which was really at the bottom of this fearful crime, [and] in the immaturity of their minds, they committed a serious crime.'

Appealing for justice and mercy, Mr Glascodine pleaded that such provocation was grounds for a manslaughter verdict.

Mr Justice Wills began his summing up by remarking that it was a sad thing to 'have the veil lifted from such a household'. The head of the household, he said, appeared hard, very selfish and 'not sparing either words or blows' to his family. But if the father was brutal, the circumstances of his death outlined during the trial could not possibly reduce the crime from murder to manslaughter, he ruled.

Reviewing the evidence against the elder prisoner, his Lordship maintained that, even without his alleged statement, the case against Richard was 'formidable'. He pointed to the discovery of cash in Richard's pocket after the murder – reminding the jury of Mr Davies's reputation as a 'near-fisted' father – and to the 'great significance' of the bloodstains on his overcoat. He said it would be 'difficult to suppose' he had come by them innocently.

The judge also put a different interpretation on the victim's wounds, the point Richard's defence counsel had earlier cited in his client's favour. The deceased's right thumb was almost cut through, he pointed out; and most of the head wounds were on the right side. Mr Davies must have received one or two blows before losing consciousness, said Mr Justice Wills, who went on, 'After the first blow was struck, deceased would naturally put up his hand. The blows were given on the right side and he naturally put up his right hand. The blows being on the right hand side of the head it was impossible that a boy sitting on the left side of his father could have given them.' Also, he said, the blows were heavy, suggesting they were given by the stronger of the two.

The evidence against George, said the judge, required 'more anxious thought'. The real question for the jury to answer, he suggested, was whether George was 'an accidental assenting party' to the murder or whether he 'helped his brother, standing by him and encouraging him'. If the crime was committed by Richard alone, George could not be guilty simply by doing nothing to prevent it. And if he made false statements afterwards merely to 'screen his brother', that made him an accessory after the fact, not a murderer.

However, his Lordship continued, 'It makes no difference whose hand struck the blow if there was a common mind operating with the arm that gave it. If there was a common mind that their father should cease to live, then both are guilty.'

He accepted that, in the case of George, there were no bloodstains which could be relied upon and no confession as such. But he added, 'The jury will have to ask themselves whether it was not a very difficult thing to suppose that the murder, carried out by means of 10 tremendous blows, could have been inflicted by one with the trap going along and with nothing but the acquiescence of the other.'

What, the judge also wondered, was the meaning of the words 'have a go at the old chap' which George, in his alleged statement to police, claimed Richard had spoken. Was Richard expressing an intention to murder? If so, Mr Justice Wills commented, the manner in which George subsequently acted showed 'a terrible callousness and a terrible want of moral sense' and indicated that 'it would not need much to turn him into an active participator'.

He also commented on George's apparent advice to Richard not to use the hatchet from the shop–offered, not because it was in itself a wicked thing to do, but out of fear that its absence would be noticed.

Though he said he did not believe there was anything in the police's conduct which gave rise to 'legitimate adverse criticism', the judge did finally warn the jury that they should not place too much reliance on the notes of the conversations at the police station.

It was 2.53pm precisely when the jury went out; forty-five minutes later they filed back into the courtroom and the foreman pronounced both brothers guilty of murder, with a strong recommendation to mercy because of their youth.

His words set off another noisy reaction in the public gallery. When it had subsided, Mr Justice Wills turned to the two distraught figures in the dock and told them, 'You have been convicted, on evidence which must bring satisfactorily home to every mind that the jury have arrived at the right conclusion, of the terrible crime of the wilful and deliberate murder of your own father. I will not seek to find words in which to characterise such an act, nor do I desire to prolong the painful ordeal which you must be going through. I will address you in no other words except the words of solemn exhortation. Make the best of your remaining days to try and prepare for the great change which you have so disastrously brought upon yourselves at so early a day of your lives.'

His duty was plain: for such a crime the law knew but one sentence. 'It is my duty,' said the judge as the black cap materialised menacingly at his side, 'to pronounce the doom which you have brought on your own heads.'

It was the unanimous conclusion of both jury and judge, then, that there had been a prior agreement between George and Richard Davies to murder their father and that they carried out the plan in cold-blooded complicity. The debate over which brother actually wielded the axe, however, was far from over. And the arguments, though academic in the context of both the court's decision and the dictates of the law, were to be given a particularly keen significance less than two weeks later when the Home Secretary, Henry Matthews, responded to the massive campaign which had been speedily launched to back the formal appeals to the minister for clemency for the two condemned young men.

His decision, which provoked a national outcry and angry scenes in Parliament, was that, because of his age, the death sentence imposed on George would be commuted to penal servitude for life…but that there could be no reprieve for Richard, who had reached his 19th birthday on 17 February while in Knutsford Gaol awaiting trial.

The Press, apparently echoing the sentiments of the public at large, greeted the announcement with astonishment and indignation. The *Warrington Guardian* of 5 April published an interview with one of the trial jurors. He expressed surprise that both brothers had not been treated alike. 'He says the decision is unjust,' the report stated, 'as the jury had no doubt that, of the two, George was the more guilty, and furthermore, that his hand struck the first and fatal blow.'

After the court judgment, the only opinion that mattered, however, was that of the Home Secretary. And he had no doubt where the main burden of guilt lay…as he was to make clear during a stormy House of Commons debate on Tuesday 12 August 1890. Mr Matthews had refused once already to give a detailed explanation of his decision to reprieve only the younger of the two convicted murderers, to the anger of MPs.

Mr Walter McLaren, in whose Crewe constituency the murder took place, said the Home Secretary's decision had come as 'a serious shock'. The public of Cheshire, if not the whole country, was of the strong opinion that both brothers should have been shown mercy, he insisted. He argued that the boys had committed the murder in defence of their mother and that their father's conduct towards her had 'aroused them to a terrible pitch of exasperation'. Of the two, though, there were 'strong circumstances' that suggested that George was the more guilty and had struck the fatal blow, he alleged.

Well used to criminal controversy – he had been one of the major public figures attacked over the authorities' handling of the Jack the Ripper case in 1888 – Mr Matthews would have none of it, however. Berating Mr McLaren for seeking to make political capital out of the case – the Crewe MP had apparently made a speech on the subject at a recent rally in the town – and for arriving at a 'hasty and crude conclusion', the Home Secretary explained that his decision had been based on a voluminous amount of evidence, not only from the trial papers but also contained in private communications from the judge and the police, and on information which 'could not come before any other tribunal'. This extensive dossier could not be laid before the House but, he said, members could be assured that no one knew more about the case than him.

The nature of the murdered man's wounds, he said, was 'most significant' and to his mind 'proved conclusively' that they must have been inflicted by the elder and stronger of the two youths. The conclusion on which he had advised Her Majesty to act was that 'the youth that was hanged struck the blows and suggested and contrived the murder'.

He had sifted all the available information and arrived at what might be termed a 'popular judgment', though whether that decision met with public approval he neither knew nor cared. And the Home Secretary added, 'I trust the day will never come when a minister exercises the prerogative of Her Majesty at the bidding of some popular outcry.'

The clamour to save both Davies brothers from the gallows was certainly popular. Numerous petitions, reportedly containing well over 50,000 signatures, were sent to the Home Secretary, including one from members of London County Council. Leading churchmen, as well as MPs and the Press, both local and national, also joined in the campaign.

Pulling no punches, the *Warrington Guardian* declared on 9 April, 'This decision was received with mixed feelings, some being of opinion that if both were not reprieved both should die, whilst others thought that if leniency should be extended to any it ought to be to Richard, who was not considered to have actually committed the murder. Others, again, feel that it must have been easier for George to have ended his life on the scaffold than to undergo, probably, many years of life with the weight, not only of his father's death, but also that of his brother resting upon him.'

Right to the end, however, the two brothers continued to claim that the other was the murderer. Thus, Richard Davies died on the scaffold, alone, on Tuesday 8 April 1890. The day dawned cold and showery but the weather could not keep the crowds away.

The *Guardian* described the scene outside Knutsford Gaol in its following day's issue, 'At 7.40 some half-a-dozen reporters were admitted to be eye-witnesses of a final scene of a ghastly tragedy. The wicket door closed again and was securely fastened. Then there was a period of deadly silence, broken at length by the mournful tolling of the prison bell. All eyes were now turned to the flagstaff above the side entrance. At three minutes past eight there was a quivering of the halyards, and the next moment a thrill of horror passed through the spectators as the black flag was swiftly run up to the masthead to proclaim to the outer world the grim fact that Richard Davies, a self-accused principal in one of the most dreadful and sensational tragedies of modern times, had undergone his allotted punishment and had expiated his crime on the scaffold.'

Public reaction to the hanging had expressed itself the previous evening in a hostile demonstration directed at the executioner, James Berry of Bradford. He was met at Knutsford railway station by a large and noisy crowd who hooted and harangued him as he walked the few hundred yards from the train to the gaol. On his departure the following morning, he was accompanied by a police constable but this time, although a few dozen people gathered around him on the platform, there was no trouble.

A former shoe-salesman and one-time policeman, Berry apparently believed that the ritual of judicial hanging was depressing enough without him adding to the morbid atmosphere, and he eschewed funeral clothes on these occasions. He was reported to have worn a fez at Richard Davies's execution.

According to his biographer, Justin Atholl, however, the event had a deep and lasting effect on him. In his book *The Reluctant Hangman* (John Long, 1956), Atholl claimed Berry had no doubt that he was hanging an innocent man; that he had to be helped from the gallows by a warder and that, later, 'the ghost of the frail boy...came back to haunt him'.

In Berry's autobiography *My Experience as an Executioner*, first published in 1892, there had been no such unbosoming, the author contenting himself with a short factual account of the murder and the furore caused by the Home Secretary's decision, together with a brief description of the execution.

Of the latter, he wrote, 'When I entered his cell he was pale, but calm. After pinioning him, his face seemed still paler and his mouth worked convulsively as he strove to keep back his emotion. Along the corridor he walked firmly, with bent head, but when we reached the yard, where a fresh breeze was blowing and the blue sky was visible, he raised his head and eyes for a last look at the world and the sky. He died firmly, with a brief prayer on his lips.'

Berry, who by 1892 had become a staunch campaigner for the abolition of the death penalty, did agree, however, that the Davies case was 'one of the strongest possible arguments' for a change in the law.

Hangman James Berry, who performed the execution of Richard Davies. Berry later become a staunch campaigner for the abolition of the death penalty and cited the Davies case as 'one of the strongest possible arguments' for a change in the law.

A similar claim had been made when MPs added their voices to the controversy in that heated House of Commons debate in August 1890; while another view forcibly expressed on that occasion was that the case highlighted the need for the establishment of a court of criminal appeal. The latter legal machinery, with its ultimate recourse to the House of Lords, was eventually created in this country in 1907; but the depressing ritual of state execution did not finally come to an end until 1964.

The following year, Parliament abolished the death penalty for murder. Since then several attempts to re-introduce capital punishment for certain types of homicide have all failed – though, officially, it is still the penalty for treason.

Final word on the Crewe murder goes to the *Chester Chronicle*. In a paragraph buried among the late news items in its edition of Saturday 1 April 1905, it was reported that one George Davies, convicted of murdering his father at Crewe in January 1890, had been released from Parkhurst Prison after serving 15 years of a 20-year sentence. At the age of 32 he had paid his debt to society and was heading off, apparently, into a life of obscurity.

13

The Ballad of Knutsford Gaol

> The convict walked with firm and unfaltering steps across the yard and took his place on the platform. As the clock struck the hour of eight, the bolt was drawn, and the culprit's body fell with a sickening thud into the yawning abyss which opened beneath him...the signal was given...and the dread messenger of death was run up to announce to the outside world that the extreme penalty of the law had been carried out...After gazing upon the flag for a few minutes, the crowd separated and shortly afterwards there was nothing left to show anything unusual had happened...

Warrington Guardian, 24 February 1886

i. 'The Town Where Executions Take Place'

THE SLOW, relentless toll of Owen McGill's death knell punctuated the early morning quiet for 15 minutes. But its mournful echoes were to disturb the tranquillity of a sleepy little community for almost 30 years. For the doleful chime of the church bell, as it counted off the final anguished moments in the life of the convicted wife murderer, rang in a new dark age in the history of Knutsford.

When the treacherous trapdoor slammed open to snatch the world out from under the prisoner's feet the small Cheshire town, whose atmosphere of unhurried elegance was the inspiration for Elizabeth Gaskell's Cranford, was plunged into the improbable role – as unwelcome as it was incongruous – of the county's official place of execution.

The date was Monday 22 February 1886. The location: Knutsford Gaol, a sprawling brick-built monstrosity perched uncomfortably on the back of the colonnaded, classically designed Sessions House. Originally a House of Correction, it had been an unwanted presence – and an ill-matched neighbour to the splendid Parish Church opposite – since 1817. Fifty years later, when transportation had ended and the English penal system as we know it today had its beginnings, the re-styled 'prison' was forced to change both its character and size, subsequently expanding into a massive four-storey edifice, shaped like a huge capital 'K' and sustaining up to 700 men and women at a time on a typically Victorian diet of discipline, hard work and religion.

Now, following the military take-over of Cheshire's long established Castle Gaol in Chester, the city in which executions had been carried out since mediaeval times, its 40ft high walls cast a dreadful new shadow over the life of the town. Up to 1915, when it finally closed as a civil prison, there were in all only eight executions carried out there. But its doubtful status as the county's death house hovered over it like a black cloud: a constant threat on the horizon… and, in some small measure, the consciences of the townspeople.

Though it made an appreciable contribution to the local economy, and its senior officials were prominent in the social life of the town, it may not be without significance that, apart from the newspaper reports of the executions (which recorded every painful detail, down to the origin of the rope and the length of the 'drop'), little has been written about Knutsford Gaol over the years. Like the imposing sandstone Sessions House, which projected outwards from the east wing of the prison itself, the local population at least seems to have turned its back on the distasteful part the town once played in the judicial process.

Knutsford Gaol photographed early in the 20th century from the tower of the Parish Church. Demolition of the prison buildings was completed in 1934, by which time the bodies of the eight men hanged there had been removed and reinterred at Strangeways Prison in Manchester.

That attitude of reluctant acceptance was briefly acknowledged in an article on the first execution at the gaol, published in the *Warrington Guardian* of 24 February 1886 – though in the course of the column or so of closely printed type the reporter took full advantage of the descriptive opportunity afforded by the dramatic new subject matter.

It began, 'By the turning of Chester Castle into a military prison, the pleasant and picturesque little town of Knutsford has attained the unenviable position of possessing the only gaol in the county, and as a necessary consequence has become the town where executions take place.' The report went on,

A few months ago the scaffold was brought from Chester Castle and has been erected as a permanent structure within the walls of Knutsford Gaol. A detached building known as the "Execution House" contains the scaffold. In the middle of the floor a pit 10 feet deep, by six or seven feet square, has been dug and faced with brick. It is covered on the one half by a trap which conceals a flight of steps by which the executioner may get to the bottom. The other half is covered by double trapdoors which, upon moving a lever, fall down against the sides of the pit. Over this half the cross-beam…is erected. The arrangements…having been submitted to the most rigorous test, have been found highly satisfactory.

The "Execution House" is situate a few yards to the left of the entrance lodge… about 50 yards from the door leading to the condemned cell. A convict coming out of the cell crosses the open yard, enters this building and goes on to the scaffold, which is level with the floor. This plan has been found to answer much better than the old-fashioned and often very trying one, of having to mount steps to get on to the platform.'

A typical Victorian gallows of the kind that was used at Knutsford Gaol. It was constructed originally for the county gaol at Chester Castle, where four private executions were carried out between 1877 and 1883.

Owen McGill, the first of the eight members of the murderous brotherhood to 'suffer the extreme penalty of the law' at Knutsford, was a 39-year-old farm labourer. He had been convicted of killing his wife in 'circumstances of a peculiarly brutal and revolting character', according to the trial flashback included in the *Guardian's* report of the execution and of the inquest formalities that followed.

McGill, who came from County Louth in Ireland, worked for a Mr Zeigler in the village of Landican, about four miles from Birkenhead on the Wirral peninsula, and he and his wife Mary lived in a tied cottage close to the farm. McGill had been working for Mr Zeigler for three months when, on Saturday 31 October 1885, he took a cart-load of corn into Birkenhead, accompanied by his wife. Some time during the journey they stopped for a drink but, when they arrived back at the farm in mid-afternoon, they both appeared sober.

At tea time, as she went to the farm for milk, Mrs McGill heard a disturbance in the stable, involving her husband and some of the other hands. McGill was an ill-tempered man at the best of times and she 'entreated him not to fight'. He calmed down and the couple went home together. But shortly afterwards a violent quarrel began which, several witnesses confirmed, continued well into the night. At one point, a young man living in the adjoining cottage saw Mrs McGill run from the house 'screaming murder', pursued by her husband.

At about 8.30pm the witness and another neighbour were passing the house and, looking over the front garden fence, they saw the woman lying on the ground moaning, with McGill standing over her yelling at her to get up. An hour or so later, a cry of 'Murder! Murder! Owen, for God's sake don't kill me!' was heard through the thin dividing wall in the cottage next door.

But, as the *Guardian* reported, the witnesses explained that it was dark and 'as they were afraid someone might come out of the house, they did not like to interfere'.

A baker, who called at the house around 8pm, said he could hear Mrs McGill's screams a quarter of a mile away. At the doorway, he said, he heard McGill calling to his wife, followed by sounds 'as if it were the beating of a carpet' and a woman's voice crying 'Don't! Don't!' But when no one answered his knock, the baker, too, decided he did not want to get involved and quickly went on his way.

The following day, Sunday 1 November, McGill visited a cousin, Alice McNamee, in Back Pitt Street, Birkenhead, and told her, 'Alice, you must come quickly. My wife is very ill and wishes to see you. If you don't come quick she will be dead.' Yet, emergency or not, McGill insisted on stopping for a drink on the way back to Landican.

At the cottage, Mrs McNamee found Mary McGill in the bedroom lying on a mattress covered with sacks. Her partially visible face was 'very black' and when she did not respond to her call, Mrs McNamee said she touched the other woman's cheek and found it 'quite cold'.

Told his wife was dead, McGill appeared shocked at the news and said that while returning from Birkenhead the previous day she had 'fallen off the cart while drunk and hurt her leg', a claim he repeated later to the police.

He said in a statement that after his wife had 'sauced' him in front of the other farm workers, she had sworn at him when he prevented her from going to the pub 'for beer'. He had punched her in the eye but not hard enough to knock her down. He had then gone for sixpennyworth of rum, which they drank between them. In the morning, he said, his wife had felt unwell and asked him to go and fetch his cousin. When he got back she was 'just breathing her last'.

When charged with his wife's murder, McGill said, 'I can't help it, sir. I shan't say a word more than I have said. It's the truth, and if Marwood was here with the rope round my neck, I would not say more.'

He was referring to the late William Marwood (1820–1883), the Lincolnshire cobbler-turned-public-executioner who in 1871 devised the 'long drop' method of hanging designed to ensure that death was instantaneous. The required length of drop was calculated according to the weight and build of each condemned person, who thus died from dislocation of the vertebrae rather than being choked to death, as was usually the case before. That, at least, was the theory. However, as McGill's executioner, Yorkshireman James Berry, had discovered in 1885, the Marwood formula still required some refinement. In an horrific incident at Norwich Castle Gaol the victim had ended up being decapitated. But more of Berry later.

Examination of Mrs McGill's body revealed multiple bruising which, a doctor testified, had been caused by 'kicking and blows from the fist'. She had also received a broken nose, a black eye and lacerations to the back of the head. Death was said to have been due to 'shock or exhaustion consequent upon her injuries'.

At the trial at Chester Assizes on 3 February 1886, the defence made much of the fact that McGill had not attempted to conceal his wife's death. And, in his summing up, Lord

Chief Justice Coleridge remarked upon the 'unmanliness' of the two neighbours and the baker who had heard 'screams of murder' but had not gone to the poor woman's aid.

It took the jury less than half an hour, however, to find the Irishman guilty. And before donning the traditional black cap to pronounce sentence of death, the judge described the murder as one of the most cruel – 'I almost said ferocious' – he had heard of in his long experience.

McGill was reported to have made a full confession to a Roman Catholic priest visiting him in Knutsford Gaol shortly before his execution. In it he, too, complained about the cowardice of his neighbours, claiming that had they intervened, both his life and that of his wife would have been spared.

He said that, generally, he and his wife had lived on the best of terms, apart from the occasional quarrels caused, according to the *Guardian's* report, by his 'ebullitions of temper'. During that last fatal row he 'had not the remotest idea' of hurting her. But, as the newspaper report stated, 'maddened by drink, which he had consumed in enormous quantity, his passion got the master of him'.

McGill's final hours in the condemned cell – located at the intersection of the prison's three corridors – passed uneventfully, if fitfully, and the only slight hitch in the execution preliminaries came as he was being fitted with the customary restraints.

The *Guardian's* man-on-the-spot who, along with the County High Sheriff, the gaol's Governor, surgeon and senior warders, was among the official observers at the proceedings, reported, 'The convict was very submissive during the process of pinioning, [but] the straps being a little too tight, he drew the executioner's attention to them, and asked him not to hurt him.'

Then, headed by the deputy Governor and the prison chaplain reciting the prescribed prayers, the solemn procession lined up, the cell door swung open and Owen McGill strode purposefully out to a swift death...and lasting notoriety.

ii. Ordeal in a House of Death

Eighteen months later, Thomas Henry Bevan also exited from the world wearing the white death hood, and became the second man to enter Knutsford's black hall of fame. Bevan, a 20-year-old apprentice living in the famous Cheshire railway town of Crewe, killed his sick and elderly aunt for the 17s 6½d contents of her purse (about £75 today), then attacked his 11-year-old half-sister and left her for dead, after she had returned unexpectedly to the murder house.

Bevan, described by the *Crewe Chronicle* as 'one of the most callous, hard-hearted and cold-blooded wretches it is possible to conceive of', was said by the newspaper to have confided to a fellow inmate, while in Knutsford prison awaiting trial, that he hoped the girl, Mary Jones, would not live long enough to give the evidence which would 'fasten upon him the hideous crime'. Indeed, as the *Warrington Guardian* recalled in reporting

Bevan's execution in its edition of 17 August 1887, she had been 'so shockingly beaten that the very faintest hopes were entertained of her ultimate recovery'.

But recover Mary Jones did. And at Chester Assizes on 28 July 1887, the little girl – a frail, pathetic figure, her head still swathed in bandages – stood shyly beside the judge, Mr Justice Denman, and whispered the dramatic testimony that gave Bevan a one-way ticket back to Knutsford and the scaffold. Most of the time her voice was so faint the judge had to repeat her answers to the jury.

The crime, said the *Guardian*, was 'memorable for its cruelty, and for the cool effrontery of the murder, as well as the meagre provocation that caused it'.

It happened on 26 March 1887, in a small newly-built cottage in what is now Henry Street, Crewe, then an unfinished roadway in the adjoining township of Church Coppenhall. At No. 37, one of a pair of houses tacked on to the Primitive Methodist Chapel, lived Mrs Sarah Griffiths, aged 59, her husband Henry, 63, and Mary Jones, their adopted niece.

At 5.30am Mr Griffiths left home to go to his labouring job at Crewe Railway Works, where Bevan was also employed. His wife, a short, stout woman, was at that time in bed; she was suffering from some sort of chest complaint, apparently. This being a Saturday, Griffiths worked until noon and returned home at 12.30pm to find his wife dead on the living room floor, with his niece cowering beneath the old woman's voluminous skirts.

On recognising the man, the child jumped up shouting 'Uncle, Uncle!' and collapsed unconscious on to the blood-soaked floor. Nearby, also coated in blood, was the pair of heavy metal fire tongs used to bludgeon the girl. They had been bent out of shape by the force of the blows. The old woman had been attacked with a wooden dolly-peg, which was lying broken in two on the back kitchen floor.

As well as a serious head injury, all Mrs Griffiths's ribs had been fractured on the left side and one of the shattered bones had punctured a lung. Dr Moody diagnosed death as resulting from 'concussion of the brain and loss of blood consequent to the injury to the left lung'. The body wounds, he stated to police later, were consistent with 'some forcible pressure, such as the weight of a person's body or their knees, or being jumped upon'.

Mary Jones had also been beaten with considerable ferocity; Dr Moody's examination revealed 17 separate head wounds 'extending down to the bone' and at least four skull fractures. When the doctor first arrived at the house, the girl was 'pulseless and almost lifeless', he said. He administered artificial respiration to revive her, however, and she was taken to Chester Royal Infirmary where to the delight of everyone but Bevan, she made a complete recovery. The child's abnormally thick skull had saved her life.

Because of her condition, it was several hours before police could interview Mary about the murder. 'But shortly after 4 o'clock the same evening,' the *Guardian* reported, 'an arrest was made that caused considerable sensation'. Thomas Bevan was charged with both murder and attempted murder after the little girl had at last been able to give police a full account of her terrible ordeal. It was the final riveting detail of a story that had by now pushed the day's other main item of local news – Crewe Alexandra's appearance in the final of the Cheshire Football Challenge Cup – firmly into the background.

When Superintendent Jesse Leah visited Bevan at No. 2, Orchard Street, Crewe, where he lived with another uncle and aunt, Mr and Mrs Clutton, he was having his tea, 'apparently little concerned about the crime'. The apprentice iron-moulder said that, as his shop was on three-quarter time, he had not been to work that morning but had spent it 'walking around Crewe Park'.

Various witnesses were later to contradict that statement, claiming they had seen him in the vicinity of Henry Street around the time of the murder. And tell-tale bloodstains were found on his trouser legs and boots.

But it was the faltering story told by little Mary Jones that most impressed the jury at Thomas Bevan's trial. She said her half-brother had appeared at the Griffiths house at breakfast time, as he usually did on Saturdays. Twice during the morning, Mary was sent by her Aunt Sarah to the Co-operative store just around the corner in Market Street for groceries.

When she returned home the second time, at about 11.30am, she said, Bevan pounced on her as she entered the kitchen door, knocking the shopping bag from her hand. Grabbing her around the neck with one arm, he began beating her about the head with the fire-tongs. The child managed to break free of her assailant, however, and ran into the living room. There she stumbled over the body of her aunt stretched out on the floor and crawled under the old woman's clothing to shield herself from further blows.

Mercifully for her, Bevan appears to have believed she, too, was now dead and left the house; but not before taking a purse from the oak chest in which he had seen his aunt lock it after paying the milkman earlier in the morning.

Thomas Bevan of Crewe, who was convicted in 1887 of murdering and robbing his elderly aunt. The 20-year-old apprentice, described in one newspaper as 'one of the most callous, hard-hearted and cold-blooded wretches it is possible to conceive of', also attempted to murder his 11-year-old half-sister.

Bevan sat impassively through the girl's evidence, his face, according to the *Crewe Chronicle*'s reporter, a mask of 'hardness and brutality'. It was a description borne out by the sketched portrait of the prisoner accompanying the newspaper article.

Defence counsel, the Hon. R.C. Grosvenor, argued that because of her serious head injuries, Mary Jones's recollection of events that morning had to be considered untrustworthy. He claimed she could not have seen her attacker as he had struck from behind; but that, as Bevan had been in the house earlier, she had 'naturally thought' it was him.

Mary insisted she had no doubt who her would-be killer was, however…and neither had the jury. They were out only 10 minutes deciding Bevan was guilty on both counts.

In Knutsford Gaol later, Bevan was reported to have made a written confession in which he said he had first tried to strangle his aunt then finished her off by 'jumping upon her body many times'. He admitted murdering her for her money but said he had subsequently thrown it over a hedge into a nearby field.

When the prison's Deputy Governor, accompanied by the chaplain, went to the spot they found the stolen purse with the missing money still inside. It was the remains of Henry Griffiths's 18s weekly wage which he had handed over to his wife the night before her murder.

Bevan, it transpired, had stolen money from relatives and friends on several occasions before, but each time they had declined to press charges. His five years at reformatory school had clearly had no effect on his criminal inclinations or his character which, in general, was said to be 'very dangerous and vindictive'.

He was hanged by James Berry on Tuesday 16 August 1887, displaying the same chilling lack of emotion with which he seems to have viewed the devastating events that brought his short and wretched life to an end.

iii. Bloody Revenge of a Scorned Seaman

In Knutsford prison's bloody calendar, 1890 was unique: there were two executions that year. The first, in April, was that of Richard Davies, one of the two Crewe brothers convicted of parricide whose controversial story and its far-ranging reverberations are detailed in Chapter 12. Then, in August, seaman Felix Spicer joined the homicidal crew.

Spicer, a 60-year-old rigger on a sailing ship, was executed after being found guilty of murdering two of his illegitimate children, William, aged 14, and Henry (four) at their home in New Brighton, and of attempting to murder his common-law wife, Mary Ann Palin, 32.

The couple lived together for 18 years, sharing an apparently volatile relationship; though, in between his voyages, they managed to produce seven children, the youngest of whom was still a baby. The woman seems to have harboured a deep-seated sense of resentment, stemming from Spicer's scoffing refusal to marry her when she was expecting their first child. Then, early in 1890, a major rift developed which brought this recurring source of friction to the surface once more…with terrifying consequences.

When he was not at sea, Spicer, a thickset man with a sandy-grey beard and wispy white hair who had also worked as a ship's cook, helped run the couple's two businesses, both of which were connected with the popular-resort-town status New Brighton then enjoyed. They rented a 'refreshment room' at No. 3 Bickley Parade, Victoria Road – close to the promenade, the pier and New Brighton's famous ferry – and kept a lodging-house at 18 Richmond Street, where the five children then still at home also lived: three girls, the eldest aged eight, and the two boys.

The development of this new holiday town at the north-east corner of the Wirral peninsula had begun more than 50 years earlier. But by 1889, according to local historian Philip Sulley, the golden vision of the town as a fashionable and elegant watering-place had become well tarnished by the appearance of ugly lodging-houses and tawdry side-shows and its unwanted reputation as 'the favourite resort of the Liverpool and Lancashire trippers and roughs'. Sulley complained, too, about the eating-house and refreshment room keepers 'whose constant solicitations to dine early and often are such a nuisance'.

The major domestic nuisance caused by the Spicers' refreshment room at this time concerned the lease of the premises. It was originally in Spicer's name, but in 1888 he got into financial difficulties and it was transferred to Mary Palin. The humiliation niggled away at Spicer and at Easter, 1890, he created such a rumpus over it that police had to be called in to calm things down.

A week later Spicer went to the café, a lock-up, but Mary was out; and while he was there he took some money out of the till. When she later challenged him about it, there was a furious row. She told him he had no business being there and kicked him out.

Spicer, now angrier than ever at his indignity, retaliated by writing to the property's letting agent, informing him that Mary was not, as she had all along maintained, a married woman. At this juncture, Mary left the couple's Richmond Street home, and began sleeping in, on a put-up bed, at the café. The split had become irrevocable.

Spicer wrote several times in contrite, not to say melodramatic, terms pleading for forgiveness. 'In the name of Heaven, have mercy and pity on me,' he implored in one letter. In another, he said, 'I humbly beg your pardon for this strife…Do consider my broken-down heart.' And, 'Let your wrath go down with this day's sun.'

Mary, it seems, had left home several times before following assaults, but had been persuaded to return by promises of marriage; and once, when she had relented and gone back to him, Spicer tried to strangle her, she claimed. She now decided she had had enough of him. When she answered his letters she did not mince her words.

She called him 'a mean contemptible scrawl' for having 'disgraced and betrayed' her and reminded him of the derisive way he had reacted when she asked him to marry her 'out of her shame' all those years before. She wrote, 'I hated you ever since the day you laughed at me…I prefer the gallows before one night under the same roof as you.'

On Saturday night, 24 May, Spicer made one last attempt to patch things up, offering to help out in the café during the busy Whitsuntide holiday week ahead. But, once again, Mary told him emphatically she wanted nothing more to do with him.

After brooding over this latest rebuff, Felix Spicer finally snapped. At about three the following morning, Whit Sunday, he took a newly sharpened knife and, creeping into the bedroom they shared, he cut the throats of his two young sons, almost hacking off their heads in his madness. Then, with a length of wood in his hand and more thoughts of murder in his heart, he left Richmond Street and hurried the quarter of a mile or so to Bickley Parade.

Reaching the café, the powerfully-built Spicer went berserk again, smashing in the windows of the room in which his estranged 'wife' lay. Mary tried to escape by jumping through one of the broken windows, but Spicer knocked her to the ground and, straddling her body, pulled out of his pocket the bloodstained knife with which he had just murdered the children.

The woman fought frantically, however; and, though receiving a badly gashed hand fending off the knife thrusts and cuts to her face, she eventually managed to wrest the weapon from his grip and break free. As she ran to a neighbour's house for help, Spicer took off back to Richmond Street, pursued by two patrolling policemen alerted by the sound of breaking glass.

When they reached the lodging-house, the officers found Spicer covered from head to foot in blood. His seaman's jacket was saturated in it and was still wet. And there were stains on his waistcoat, trousers, socks and shoes.

After discovering the two murdered boys upstairs – a scene one of the lodgers later likened to 'a slaughter-house' – the police confronted Spicer. He protested, 'I have not murdered my children. I know nothing about it.'

There were smears of blood, however, on his upper arms, which had clearly got there before he put on his coat to go to Victoria Road. Also, a pattern of bloodstains on one of his trouser legs matched perfectly a patch on the children's bed, indicating where he had knelt to murder them. And the murder weapon, a knife Spicer had brought back from a recent voyage, was recovered from its hiding place in a chimney flue in a subsequent search of the kitchen.

This is how the *Liverpool Mercury* of 27 May 1890 illustrated its story of the tragic double murder in New Brighton. Seaman Felix Spicer, who killed two of his children and then attacked his common-law wife Mary Ann Palin, was hanged at Knutsford on 22 August. Courtesy of www.historyofwallasey.co.uk.

At the trial, at Chester Assizes on 31 July 1890, defence counsel Mr E. Burke Wood described the prosecution evidence as 'faulty and undependable'. But, in case the members of the jury were inclined to believe it, he suggested an alternative explanation less damaging to his client that might convince them that a manslaughter verdict was more appropriate.

He said that Spicer, intent on attacking, possibly even killing, the mother but knowing he would be unable to escape detection, had gone into the boys' room for a last look at the children – of whom, it had been generally agreed, he 'appeared so very fond'.

Mr Burke Wood went on, 'The man's mind might have been clouded over with anxiety and trouble, consequent upon his suffering following the useless and repeated appeals he made to his wife for forgiveness, and he might have had his faculties obliterated for a moment, during which time he cut the throats of the children.'

In a trial in which the murder allegations were based entirely on circumstantial evidence, the one witness who was most likely to sway the jury was Mary Palin. It was a situation about which the judge (Mr Justice Stephen) made a highly pertinent observation. In his summing up, he pointed out that, had Spicer made Mary his wife, she would not have been able to testify against him. The fact that he did not think it proper to marry her, said his Lordship, had been 'strangely avenged' and he (Spicer) was 'here on trial for his life because he did not do justice to that woman, which he certainly ought to have done'.

In little more than five minutes the jury decided there had been premeditation, and pronounced Spicer guilty of both charges. A petition for his reprieve on the grounds that he was 'of unsound mind' at the time of the murders was subsequently turned down by the Home Secretary.

He was hanged on the morning of Friday 22 August. A crowd of about 300 assembled outside the Knutsford prison in the pouring rain to see the black flag hoisted.

Berry was again the executioner. He had a reputation for pressurising condemned prisoners into making a last-minute confession and declaration of repentance; Spicer, on the other hand, consistently claimed he had no recollection of killing his sons. And, stated the *Warrington Guardian* on 23 August, his last words on the scaffold, before begging divine absolution, were 'I was mad if I perpetrated the murder of my poor dear children.' The rope, the newspaper diligently reported, was a new one from Holloway.

Victoria Road, New Brighton, c.1905. The refreshment room Felix Spicer and Mary Palin ran in Bickley Parade was just out of shot next to the large corner building on the right of the photograph.

It was James Berry's fourth and final official visit to Knutsford. He resigned as the country's 'Number One' public executioner two years later, following another unfortunate incident, this time at Kirkdale Gaol in Liverpool. Under pressure from the prison medical officer, he revised his calculations for the length of the drop and all but had a second decapitation on his record.

Almost immediately after his retirement at the age of 40, Berry, a thickset, muscular man with sandy hair and a full beard whose ruddy features had been given a slightly sinister appearance by two large scars received during his previous career as a policeman, undertook an extensive tour of the music halls billed as 'The Late Hangman – The Man Who Will Entertain You With Exciting Episodes'.

During the nine years he had the job (1884–92), he carried out more than 130 executions, having his own special business cards printed with the legend 'James Berry: Executioner' and keeping framed portraits of some of his more famous victims on display in the sitting room of his terrace home in Bradford.

He was a freelance operator and earned £10 plus expenses for each grim assignment (£5 if there was a last-minute reprieve). It was a situation which, both from a professional and financial point of view, he came to feel was unsatisfactory. He expressed his opinion in February 1887, when he tried (unsuccessfully) to persuade the Government to make him a full-time public official with an annual salary of £350. At that time there were about 25 executions a year.

In a letter to Lord Aberdare, President of the Parliamentary Committee on Capital Punishment, Berry wrote, 'I am to a great extent alone in the world, as a certain social ostracisation is attendant upon such office, and extends, not to myself alone, but also includes members of my family.'

In 1894, following his conversion to the belief that capital punishment was wrong, he became an Evangelist preacher and continued to campaign for its abolition until his death in October 1913.

iv. Booked to Stay at 'Nelson's Hotel'

In 1899 a new Governor was appointed at Knutsford Gaol. Major James Osmonde Nelson was an ex-Army man, formerly in the 20th Regiment, Lancashire Fusiliers, and an experienced prison officer who had previously served at Wormwood Scrubs, Pentonville, Newcastle and Reading. It was during his spell as Governor at the latter that Oscar Wilde served time there and was inspired to write *The Ballad of Reading Gaol*.

Nelson's was a strict but humane approach to prison discipline and he pioneered many reforms, including cells without bars and the introduction of hand-loom weaving. And, throughout his career, his treatment of prisoners was 'uniformly kind', said the *Knutsford Guardian* in a report of 16 February 1912, announcing his imminent departure to become first-class Governor of Strangeways in Manchester.

It was a regime by which, the major said, he was convinced 'many a man has been reformed' – though, for possibly different reasons, the prison was at this time known among the old lags as 'Nelson's Hotel'. The nickname stuck after one departing inmate expressed his feelings in the following verse,

The fine air of Knutsford, the truth I must tell,
It causes me some pain to give up my cell;
The good I have derived makes me feel right well,
And everyone is welcomed, at Nelson's Hotel.

The brief eulogy was discovered in the prisoner's cell on the day he was released. For some, however, there was no checking out of 'Nelson's Hotel'.

After 1868, when the shameful spectacle of public hanging was finally ended by Act of Parliament – Cheshire's last public execution was that of murderer Samuel Griffiths at Chester in 1866 (see *Cheshire's Execution Files* by this author) – the bodies of executed murderers were buried within the precincts of the prison in which the death penalty was carried out. In this manner, four of his 'guests' were booked permanent accommodation at Knutsford Gaol in the 13 years Major Nelson was Governor.

Like their four predecessors, they were interred in a patch of unconsecrated ground close to one of the perimeter walls, a discreet stone tablet, inscribed simply with the prisoner's initials and number, marking each new plot in this exclusive cemetery.

The first of the quartet was William Alfred Hancocks, sentenced to death in 1905 for the senseless slaying of his teenaged daughter at their home in Birkenhead. There had not been an execution at Knutsford for 15 years and, although the event attracted the usual amount of Press attention, it does not seem to have aroused a great deal of public interest. A crowd described as 'moderate' (both in size and behaviour, by all accounts) was outside the gaol when the tolling of the Parish Church bell signified that the sentence had been put into effect. There was no black flag this time, though; the practice had ceased in 1902.

Describing the scene outside the prison, the *Chester Chronicle* reported on 12 August, 'The majority [of the crowd] waited hard by that portion of the outer wall nearest to the gallows, and averred that they could distinctly hear the gruesome thud of the trapdoors of the gallows as the fatal bolt was drawn.'

The executioner was John Billington, assisted by Henry Pierrepoint. The latter, the first of three members of the famous Yorkshire family to hold the office of public hangman, improvised a special pinioning strap for use on Hancocks, who only had one arm. He had lost the other limb after surviving a terrible, if mysterious, accident while working on the railway.

Shrewsbury-born Hancocks, 35, latterly a general labourer employed by the Sheriff of Birkenhead, lived with his wife and family in rented rooms at No. 7, Old Priory. On 23 March 1905 Mary Elizabeth Hancocks, aged 15 and then living away as a domestic servant, visited her parents' home.

In the evening, Mrs Hancocks went out, leaving her husband, who had been drinking, and her daughter in the house together. Cries were later heard coming from an upstairs bedroom and when neighbours rushed in to see what was wrong, they found the girl stretched out on the bed with her father lying with his head on her arm.

At that moment Mrs Hancocks returned and Mary told her that her father had tried to throttle her. The two of them took refuge in a friend's house a few doors away but Hancocks, in a drunken rage, stormed after them and ordered his daughter back home to look after the couple's two younger children.

Hancocks followed and minutes later the girl was again heard screaming. When neighbours investigated a second time, Hancocks brushed past them on the stairs and ran into the street. Mary then came staggering out of the bedroom and collapsed on the landing, bleeding badly from a stab wound in the temple. She died in hospital a week later. Hancocks's penknife, covered in blood, was found in the bedroom.

There was a dramatic sequel to the knife attack when the fleeing Hancocks, realising the full horror of what he had done, attempted to commit suicide by leaping into the River Mersey at nearby Woodside Ferry. But he was rescued by workmen and ended up being taken to hospital in the same ambulance as his dying daughter.

Later, on his way to Walton Gaol across the estuary in Liverpool, he told police officers, 'I must have been mad when I did it. I thought such a lot of her.' And he claimed, 'The wife was the cause of it all. She was always harping at me for money, and caused me to break teetotal.'

At the Chester Summer Assizes on Tuesday 17 July 1905, Hancocks pleaded not guilty to murder. His defence counsel, Mr Montgomery, tried to show that the girl's death had been a tragic accident. Mary, he submitted, had lain down to rest and Hancocks, standing near the bed, had suddenly turned round to speak to her. And 'being rather more drunk than had been suggested', the prisoner, with his one arm, had stumbled with the knife in his hand and fallen heavily on top of his daughter.

Mr Montgomery pointed out that Hancocks had always maintained he had no recollection of the incident. And, said counsel, it was not the first time his client had suffered from loss of memory.

He then related the strange story of the defendant's railway accident. It seems the first anyone knew about it was when Hancocks was seen wandering beside the track in a daze, clutching the severed limb in his remaining hand. He was never able to say what had happened.

In his summing-up, however, the judge, Mr Justice Channell, said he could see nothing in the evidence to justify a verdict of manslaughter rather than murder. The jury, after retiring for 35 minutes, concurred, but made a strong recommendation to mercy. However, the resulting petition, appealing for a reprieve on the grounds that the accused's judgment had been impaired by drink, was rejected by the Home Secretary.

So, after twice being spared a sudden and premature death, William Alfred Hancocks (who was also exposed at the trial as a bigamist) finally had his life wrung from him on Wednesday 9 August 1905. He made no last-minute confession but left a letter for each of his two 'wives', the first of whom he had abandoned after a brief teenage marriage while living in Bristol.

v. Violent Victims of the 'Cheshire Malaise'

When charging the Grand Jury at the start of the 1905 summer sessions, Judge Channell had commented on the number of violent crimes on the court calendar in which 'the direct cause' was drunkenness. Drink, his Lordship said, affected people in different ways; he had even observed that its effects varied from county to county.

'Here [in Cheshire],' he declared, 'it seems to cause violence and unrestrained anger and assaults of all sorts and kinds.' And he made particular reference to the Birkenhead murder to illustrate his point.

But the booze factor was an even more significant feature in the case of Edward Hartigan, the next man to be executed at Knutsford. The additional explosive ingredient in this sorry affair was that the murder victim also suffered from what Mr Justice Channell implied was the Cheshire malaise.

Hartigan, a 58-year-old building labourer, and his wife Catherine had been alcoholics for years and their drunken quarrels were a routine aspect of family life at No. 11, Peter Street, Stockport. That their stormy relationship should erupt periodically into violence surprised no one who knew the couple. But few could have imagined it would have such a shocking ending.

Catherine Hartigan was battered to death on 7 August 1906. Almost immediately afterwards, her husband surrendered to police and confessed, 'I have bashed her brains out.'

He was not exaggerating. For in a savage and sustained onslaught, father-of-four Hartigan had rained a score of blows down on his wife's head with a coal hammer as she lay in a drunken stupor on her bed upstairs. At one point, he was interrupted by a neighbour, alerted by the woman's screams. But Hartigan threw him out, threatened the crowd which had by then gathered outside his house that he would shoot anyone else who tried to interfere…then went back inside and resumed the murderous attack on his wife. She died in hospital three hours later.

The couple's final row had flared in the early evening after Hartigan had consumed a gill of beer which he had sent his eldest child, a girl of 17, to fetch from a nearby public house. He had also been drinking heavily at lunch-time and had already had one argument with his wife that day, apparently over her refusal to cook his breakfast.

When he discovered her 'sleeping it off' he 'seemed to get into a violent passion' and laid into her with the coal hammer, said the *Knutsford Guardian* in its edition of 1 December, in which it reported Hartigan's execution.

At the murder trial, at Chester Assizes on 6 November, it was claimed that Hartigan was afraid of his wife because she had such a violent temper. During one set-to 10 years before, she had thrown a lighted lamp at him and put him in hospital for six months. Since that incident, said defence counsel Mr T.E. Morris, Hartigan had 'not been right in his head'.

Mrs Hartigan had also been locked up once for assaulting a policeman. And, on the night in question, Mr Morris submitted, the defendant 'laboured under such great provocation, and was so mad with drink, that he did not know what he was doing'.

The jury found him guilty, however, and Mr Justice Walton passed the inevitable sentence of death.

Hartigan was hanged on Tuesday 27 November, by Henry Pierrepoint. Public curiosity was continuing its decline and, according to the *Guardian* report, only a small crowd, consisting mainly of young people, waited outside Knutsford Gaol for the official notice of execution to be posted.

vi. When 'the Lamp of Reason was Extinguished'

There was no lack of interest in the case of James Phipps two years later, however. The murder of little Eliza Warburton in the Mid-Cheshire salt-mining town of Winsford caused widespread revulsion. An angry crowd besieged the police station the night Phipps was arrested. And local feeling – a mixture of horror and outrage – ran high throughout his unusually speedy progress from magistrates' court to assizes and right up to the day of his execution.

This apparently motiveless crime occurred on 12 October 1908. Phipps, 21, an unemployed painter living with his parents in New Road, Winsford, enticed the 10-year-old girl into a field and, after knocking her into a ditch, he held her head under water, forcing her face into the mud beneath.

There was some evidence (disputed at the trial) of sexual assault; a piece of string, puzzlingly, was found tied loosely around the child's neck. And, clearly, the killer had first made an attempt at manual strangulation. But Eliza Warburton died, a month away from her 11th birthday, from suffocation after being drowned in eight inches of stagnant water.

All because she was good-natured enough to run an errand for a complete stranger.

She had been among a group of children playing in the street outside their homes in Station Road – then part of the main eastern route into the town – when Phipps approached them and said he would give twopence to anyone who would go and buy him some cigarettes. Eliza, one of the twin daughters of a local salt-boiler, volunteered and, on returning from the shop, was asked by Phipps to direct him to the house of a lamplighter named Hulse in Gilbert Street.

The pair were going in that direction when they turned the corner into Coronation Road and disappeared from view. But they were last seen together a quarter of a mile away in School Road, Wharton, heading for an area of land, then undeveloped and known as Middlewich Fields, through which ran an isolated track formerly used as a footpath by salt-workers travelling to and from the neighbouring town.

The time was then about 7.30pm and Phipps was wearing a distinctive white handkerchief tied around his head to cover the empty socket of the eye he had lost in a schoolyard stone-throwing accident when he was seven. When next seen, just over an hour later, however, the bandage was missing…and he was alone.

Walter Warburton, the murdered girl's father, who had led the hunt for his daughter after being told she had gone off with a strange-looking man, met him on the field path and challenged him about the child's disappearance. Phipps, presently, made some vague reply then, as a posse of about 20 other searchers converged on the scene, he bolted. He was eventually collared halfway down Wharton Hill by a police constable who had given chase on his bicycle.

Safely locked up in Wharton police station, out of reach of the hostile crowd outside, Phipps was said to have told the officer, PC Jones, 'Some little girls have been throwing stones at me. I caught one and wrung her neck and threw her into a ditch along the footpath by Wharton Church.'

Fifteen minutes later, the body of Eliza Warburton was found at the spot he had indicated.

At his trial, at Chester Assizes on 19 October – remarkably, just seven days after the event – James Phipps pleaded not guilty to murder by reason of insanity.

Defence counsel, Mr Walter Yates, told the jury that the allegation about the little girls throwing stones was all part of a private delusion, one of several classic symptoms of insanity which the defendant had exhibited lately, he claimed.

The cruel loss of his eye, said Mr Yates, had 'preyed on his mind' off and on for 14 years and had proved a particular handicap during his recent despairing attempts to find work. Depression set in, counsel went on, and three times Phipps attempted suicide: twice by jumping into the River Weaver at Winsford Dockyard and once by cutting his throat.

He had also suffered 'concussion of the brain' in a bicycle accident; while at home relations between Phipps, one of 11 children, and his father had got progressively worse. They had come to blows on several occasions.

Bit by bit Phipps's self-control gave way until, said Mr Yates, 'the lamp of reason was extinguished'. When he saw the children playing, it brought on the old delusion associated with his unfortunate accident at school and 'owing to his weak intellect and depression, he had not the self-control to resist it when the critical moment arrived'. He had attacked the girl 'in an act of uncontrollable impulse'.

In the dock, with his mop of unruly hair and the fixed sightless stare of his now installed glass eye, Phipps certainly had a wild look about him. But the members of the jury were not convinced he was a madman. After a trial lasting six hours, they took just seven minutes to reach a guilty verdict, the foreman announcing their decision 'amid breathless silence', according to the *Knutsford Guardian* on 24 October.

There was no recommendation to mercy and the judge (Mr Justice Lawrence) told the convicted man he held out no hope of a reprieve. 'You have been found guilty of the most brutal murder of this little girl and I have heard of no facts throughout this case which throw any extenuation or excuse upon your crime,' his Lordship declared.

Responding to the subsequent petition, submitted on Phipps's behalf, Home Secretary Herbert Gladstone, as expected, said he could find no reason to interfere with the sentence of the court.

The execution was carried out by Henry Pierrepoint, assisted by his brother Thomas, on Thursday 12 November 1908. In keeping with the uncommon haste with which the whole affair had been conducted, the final process was completed in record time…just 47 seconds elapsing between the prisoner's departure from the condemned cell and his fatal plunge from the scaffold. And that included a brief hiatus when Phipps collapsed as he was placed on the trap and had to be helped to his feet.

vii. Last Call for the Hangman

The execution that took place at Knutsford Gaol on 19 March 1912, was swifter still: according to the *Knutsford Guardian*, John Ellis and his assistant Lumb took just 35 seconds to perform their deadly duty on this occasion.

But the event's real significance only became apparent later. For it was to reserve a place in history for Welshman John Williams as the last man to be hanged in Cheshire.

Three years later, as the prison population declined, the gaol was handed over to the military authorities for use as a detention barracks (World War One was by then into its second year) and the remaining inmates were transferred to either Strangeways or Walton. No more would Cheshire play host to the hangman; Knutsford's shadow of death had been lifted at last.

Williams, aged 38 and born in Llangefni, Anglesey, murdered his wife Hilda for reasons that are not compellingly clear from the trial reports. The couple had only been married for three years and Williams was said to have been 'passionately fond' of his wife. Yet late one Sunday night, in a back alley in Birkenhead, he left her lying in a pool of blood after slashing her throat with a razor.

The alcoholic Williams, a printer by trade, had lived in Birkenhead for 12 years and latterly he and his wife were in lodgings at No. 7, Brighton Street, Seacombe. On 10 December 1911, Mrs Williams, live-in servant to a family residing at 9, Victoria Mount, Birkenhead, had a day off and spent the afternoon with her husband at Brighton Street, apparently on affectionate terms. In the early evening they went out drinking for an hour or so while their landlady prepared a meal for them.

At 9.30pm they left the lodging-house, Williams indicating he was escorting his wife back to her place of employment. They rode on an open-topped omnibus from Seacombe Ferry to Charing Cross and were last seen together shortly after 10 o'clock alighting from the bus and heading in the general direction of Victoria Mount.

Twenty minutes later, however, the body of Hilda Williams was found, with a 6½in gash in her throat, in a nearby passageway called Price's Lane as, half a mile away in Oxton Road, a policeman came upon Williams weaving drunkenly down the street. In between swigs from the noggin bottle of whiskey he was carrying, he was shouting, 'I have done my wife…I have committed murder…I have murdered my wife!'

At the police station, a razor, still wet with blood and with human hair adhering to it, was found in his overcoat pocket. At this time Williams was unfit to be charged, so he was locked in a cell to sober up. He spent the next hour alternately wailing to God for forgiveness and singing hymns, before being moved to the town's main bridewell.

On his way there he told a constable, 'Me and my wife was all right until the third party came between us. All the bother has been the difference between our religions, my wife being a Roman Catholic and me a Protestant. I will say nothing this morning. I have been on the booze for about three weeks and when my head clears I will make a clean breast of it.'

The 'third party' in this case seems to have been Mrs Williams's brother. Williams was said to have told Thomas Beecroft, a joiner friend, in a pub on the Tuesday before the murder, 'My wife loves me. It is the brother-in-law that has caused all the trouble between me and my wife.'

And, brandishing an open razor he had apparently stolen from his landlord's living quarters, he said, 'I will do either the one or the other of them down. Mark my word, Tom, I will do it before Christmas!'

This oblique reference to family conflict, which may have provided some small clue as to the motive for the killing, does not appear to have been pursued, however. At Williams's trial at Chester Assizes on 24 February 1912, the arguments centred on a more fundamental examination of the prisoner's mental state and the defence's contention that he was insane at the time of the murder.

Medical opinion differed widely. For the defence, Dr Lyburn, of the Victoria Central Hospital, Liscard, said he had been treating Williams after he had three times attempted suicide, most recently by taking hydrochloric acid. And the defendant had once visited his surgery under the delusion that he had a hollow in his throat large enough to insert his hand into. The doctor said he believed Williams had committed the murder 'in a paroxysm'.

Other witnesses described the accused as 'simple-minded' and 'half-silly' and revealed that he had a sister who had been confined in an asylum.

Crown prosecutor Mr T. Artemus Jones argued, however, that the theory of a paroxysm or 'irresistible impulse' was not consistent with the prisoner's 'arming himself' with his landlord's razor – which would have required a search to obtain, he said – and with his conversation with Beecroft.

And Dr Fennell, the prison surgeon at Knutsford, said he had had Williams under observation for several months and he had not betrayed 'the slightest trace' of insanity.

Defence counsel, Mr T.H. Parry, stressing the apparent lack of motive, invited the jury to accept that Williams's mind was so sodden with drink he did not know what he was doing and that, at the same time, he was also suffering from 'homicidal mania'.

It was a submission that the judge, Lord Coleridge, in his summing-up, considered 'somewhat embarrassing'. Counsel was saying the prisoner was not responsible for his actions because he was drunk and, alternatively, because he was mad. They were two different defences, his Lordship pointed out.

As to the former, the suggestion of drink was valueless if the jury connected the taking of the razor with the deed of murder. And of the plea of insanity, Lord Coleridge said 'irresistible impulse' was a dangerous expression. Anger was one of the strongest impulses, said the judge; but it was nonsense to say a man could escape the consequences of his acts simply by pleading that he was in a towering, ungovernable rage and could not resist the impulse.

Offered two grounds for acquittal, the jury resisted both and returned with a guilty verdict after a 15-minute absence. When efforts for a reprieve failed, Williams, a former Army regular who bought himself out of the Royal Welsh Fusiliers, was left with one final resolve: to go to this death 'like a soldier and a man'.

He was as good as his word. At the appointed hour of 8am, he marched with strict military bearing to take his place on the scaffold...and that roll of dishonour anonymously recorded in stone on the Knutsford prison wall.

The rough memorial tablets have now disappeared, carted off with the rest of the rubble when the gaol was being demolished in the early 1930s. The remains of the eight murderers still lie in unhallowed plots, though nowadays their unmarked graves are to be found more than a dozen miles from Knutsford.

After a variety of uses, including a school for trainee parsons and makeshift council housing, the prison buildings were finally closed about 1925. And, when an application for re-interment in the parish cemetery was turned down by the local authority, the bodies were exhumed and re-buried in the grounds of Strangeways.

The demolition of Knutsford Gaol was completed in 1934, though the Sessions House (built originally to accommodate the Quarter Sessions but these days functioning as a fully fledged Crown Court), together with the former Governor's house and what were the married officers' homes still remain. A large superstore and the town's bus station now stand on the prison site.

Archive and documentary sources

The National Archives
Chester Assize Court Gaol Files (CHES 24/ series), Plea Rolls (CHES 29/ series) and Crown Books (CHES 21/ series): CHES 24/171/3 (Thorley case); CHES 24/190/1 (Clarke, Brooks, Boon and Sumner cases); CHES 24/189/6 (Brierley); CHES 24/188/3 and CHES 24/189/3 (Mealey); CHES 24/188/7 (Walker); CHES 24/174/1 (Steer); CHES 24/184/3 (Done); CHES 24/130/2, /131/4, /133/2, /134/3 and /134/4, CHES 29/410, /445, /450, /457, /462, /676, /708 and /789, CHES 21/3, /4 and /5 (witchcraft chapter).
Home Office files: HO 11/5 (Brierley), HO 47/64 (Clarke, Brooks, Boon and Sumner).
Lancaster Assize documents (Miles, Fleming cases): Assize Rolls PL 25/187, /190 and /191; Indictments PL 26/50 and /102; Depositions PL 27/7 and /10, and Miscellanea PL 28/3.
Worcester and Gloucester Assizes (Higgins's court appearances): Crown Book ASSI 2/21 and Indictments ASSI 5/72, /74, /83 and /87.
Crown copyright material is reproduced with the permission of the Controller of HMSO.

Cheshire Record Office
Clarke, Brooks, Boon and Sumner cases: Mf/96/2, 3/ and /4.
Witchcraft chapter: Consistory Court files EDC 5/1662, No. 63 and EDC 5/1667, No. 50 and various Parish Registers and Bishop's Transcripts (all by permission of the Lord Bishop of Chester and Chester Diocesan Record Office); Quarter Sessions records QJF 89/3 f175, 89/4 f112 and 90/1 (No. 104).
Records held by the Cheshire Archives and Local Studies Service are reproduced with the permission of Cheshire East Council and Cheshire West and Chester Council and the owner/ depositor to whom copyright is reserved.

Warrington Library
The Trial of William Lewin (P1156).
An Accurate Statement of The Trial of James Price and Thomas Brown (P1170 and P1171).
An Account of the Trial and Execution of William Hill (P1383).
Sermon, preached in the Parish Church of Warrington by the Hon. and Rev. Horace Powys, Rector, April 22nd, 1838, the day after the execution of William Hill (P1378).
A Full and Correct Report of the Trial of John Davies and Others (P1298).
Reproduced by permission of Warrington Borough Council – Libraries, Culture and Heritage.

John Rylands Library, Manchester
The Trial of John Eaton (Press Mark R62527.26).

Post Office Archives
Trial of Edward Miles: Prosecution Brief (Post 74/239); Postmaster General's Minute (Post 40/113C/1793).
Reproduced by courtesy of the Postmaster General.

Liverpool Central Reference Library
The Hope Street Cellar of Horror, *Liverpool Colonnade*, No. 33 (1955).